Escape from Al-Ould

To Tom my brother
and all my family

Escape from Al-Ould

Ian Fraser

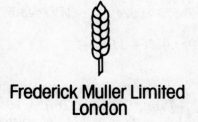

Frederick Muller Limited
London

First published in Great Britain in 1983 by
Frederick Muller Limited, Dataday House,
Alexandra Road, London SW19 7JZ

Copyright © 1983 by Ian Fraser

British Library Cataloguing in Publication Data

Fraser, Ian
  Escape from Al-Ould.
  1. Prisons—Saudi Arabia   2. Escapes
  I. Title
  365'.953'80924   HV8448.6

  ISBN 0–584–11063–4

Phototypeset by Input Typesetting Ltd, London SW19 8DR
Printed in Great Britain by
Billing & Sons Ltd, Worcester

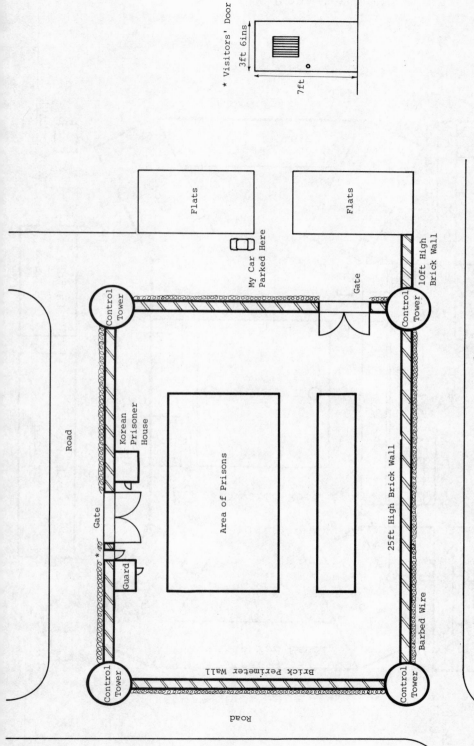

LAYOUT PLAN OF AREA SURROUNDED BY 25FT HIGH BRICK WALL

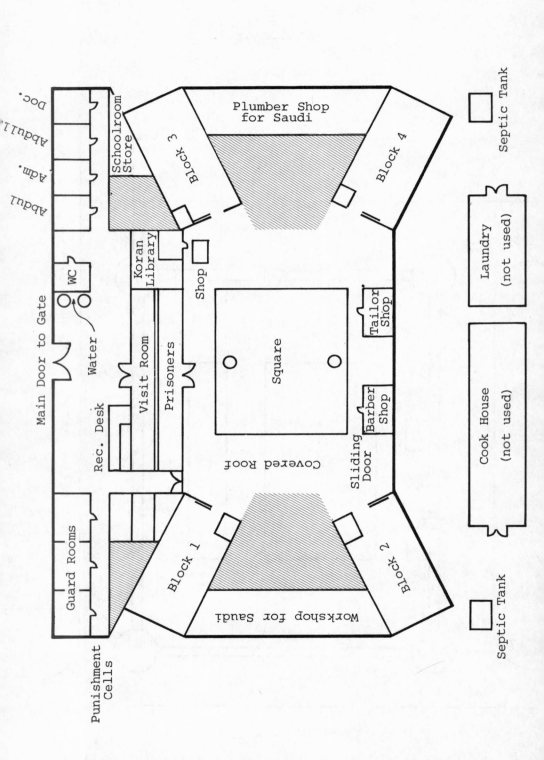

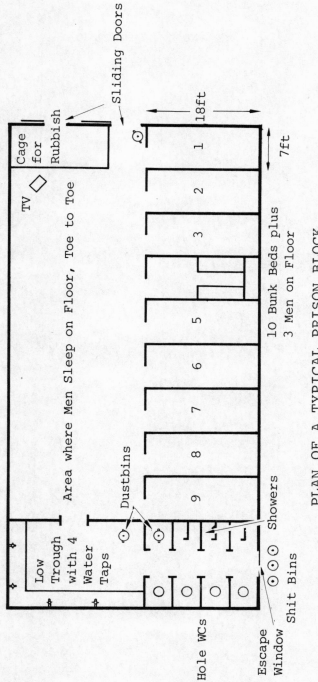

PLAN OF A TYPICAL PRISON BLOCK
(approx. 200 prisoners per block)

ONE

I lay on my bed reading the *Arab News,* one of the two English-language newspapers printed in Saudi Arabia. In my opinion it wasn't much of a newspaper for its news was nearly always the same. Every night the big story was that 'the King did this or that' or 'the so-and-so Prince opened this or that' or that the Kingdom was giving more money to build more mosques (as it was, they already had them on every street corner). There was little but 'political' news which I found difficult to work up any interest in, for it seemed to me to be no more than princely propaganda. When you can't get hold of a proper newspaper, however, you'll read anything.

It was about ten o'clock in the evening on 6 May 1980. Back in England the press that day had been full of Saudi protests about an ITV television programme called *Death of a Princess* which had alleged that the Kingdom's ideas of justice were, to put it mildly, pretty mediaeval. As I lay there, there was a sudden bang on the door which at once flew open (it wasn't locked) and I found a posse of police pouring into my room, along with Harry Hall, my steelfixing foreman. Anxiously, Harry tried to explain, 'They asked for you, Ian – they made me bring them up to you.'

'That's OK, Harry,' I reassured him, although by now I was more than a bit worried myself as there were no fewer than ten policemen in the room, all waving guns. I jumped out of bed, grabbed my underpants and trousers and pulled them on. I had no sooner done this than I found myself standing there with my hands handcuffed behind my back. I was ordered to stand still while a thorough search was made of my room.

Not that there was all that much to search in my room. The

place was a reasonable size – some six metres square – but I had only a bed, a bedside cabinet, a small wardrobe, a chest of drawers, a coffee table and two chairs, so it wasn't quite a suite at the Ritz although I wasn't complaining. But the Saudis were all very excited and intent on business and kept waving their guns in the air which started me worrying about the whisky. Indeed, within seconds of their arrival, all I could think about was whisky – and it wasn't as though I were thirsty or in need of a pick-up. The fact was that I had six boxes of Scotch hidden in my wardrobe and in Saudi Arabia whisky spells sin with a capital S. I decided that this raid must be part of a purge, part of the Saudi reaction to what they saw as a travesty of their monarchy and their society in the television programme which had told the story of how a royal princess had been beheaded with her lover for allegedly committing adultery.

The sergeant in charge of the squad quickly got round to my wardrobe where, when he opened its doors, he discovered six boxes wrapped up in plain brown paper. He grabbed at the nearest and tearing off the paper, triumphantly pulled out a bottle of whisky.

'A whisky,' he announced and I've rarely seen anybody look more happy or more fulfilled. Meantime his gang were turning out all my drawers and tossing my bed upside down and, in general, searching every nook and cranny.

Eventually they unearthed my private correspondence and as I watched the precious bits of paper from home being subjected to an 'inspection', I felt the first surges of indignation. However, normally I am able to keep my temper well under control and on this occasion I knew that there was little point in trying to prove I could win the VC. Instead, I began to think of some way of inducing this gang to make do with what they had got and to take me away, which was like hoping for ice cream in hell. They not only hauled me from my room but dragged me in and out of several other bedrooms, each of which they entered without the courtesy of a knock. I still recall the startled faces of my mates as the gang, pulling me along in their wake like some sacrificial Aztec victim, burst in waving their guns in the air like assassins. This lack of the ordinary courtesies clearly reflected the anger of the Royal family and showed how determined the police were, acting on orders no doubt, to make things difficult.

By this stage, my worries had begun to zone in on our roof;

for the one thing I didn't want this mob to do was to go anywhere near our roof. Unfortunately, our block of flats was just three and a bit storeys high and as the Saudis had started off on the third floor, where I had my room, it was inevitable, I suppose, that they should get around to the roof. In fact, once they had finished going through the other bedrooms – and luckily for the occupants, finding nothing – they dragged me up the final flight of stairs and out into the night air. 'Fraser, now your goose is cooked,' I told myself, for although I might argue that the whisky found in my room was for personal use, what could I say about the stuff they could find on the roof?

The roof, in fact, was where we company employees had our club, the Steering Wheel, named after that well-known haunt of the car-racing fraternity in the West End of London frequented by the likes of Stirling Moss and James Hunt. The firm which held the tenancy of the block just before us had built an annexe of four rooms up there and when we moved in we converted these rooms into a drinking club. To give the place the right atmosphere, we had stuck up posters of racing cars on the walls and pinned two steering wheels just over the bar.

As soon as the police spotted the annexe, they made straight for its door but finding it locked, the sergeant signalled that I should produce a key. I shook my head and then on a mad impulse said, 'Madam,' hoping to kid them that there was a woman in there for, according to their faith, as I understood the Islamic creed, that would prevent them going in. The remark certainly produced the desired effect; there was some brief confusion followed by a great deal of indecision among them before they hauled me downstairs again and ordered me to finish dressing. I tried to get my shirt on but couldn't because of the handcuffs, so they kindly took these off. When I finished dressing, I casually picked up my wallet, passport and bunch of keys, among them the key to the club.

Then they hauled me out of the room again. Harry Hall was standing outside and anxiously asked if I were all right.

'I'm OK,' I replied and indicated to the sergeant that I wanted Harry to have my wallet and other things. The sergeant agreed, so I handed over my stuff although when I spotted a look of anxiety in Harry's eyes, I cursed myself for an idiot realising that by giving him the key I might perhaps be putting him on the spot also. But Harry was a good mate, he took everything without protest and walked off towards his own room. I waited there as he disappeared, my heart in my mouth, wondering just how long it would be before the sergeant twigged about the key.

The next thing I knew I was being hauled down to the second floor where the posse began doing what it had already done on the third. When we got to the room occupied by my younger brother Tom, he was still fast asleep. He woke up at once, as startled as everybody else by the sight of armed police in his room. I started to walk towards him, intending to turn my back and show him the bracelets on my wrists but two guards, convinced I was up to no good, suddenly jumped me. They flung me down on the floor where I yelled, 'Brother, brother!' hoping to make them understand. The guards in their turn began shouting back excitedly before they finally got the drift of the matter and allowed me to get to my feet again. I had scarcely time to explain to Tom about the whisky when the sergeant reappeared and said I was to be taken outside again. Once more I found myself being dragged up to the roof but this time they seemed to know exactly where to go and I wondered who they had been talking to in the meantime. They made straight for the door of the Steering Wheel and began kicking and battering on it, trying to knock it down. They must have spent a good twenty minutes kicking and hammering away before one bright spark had the highly original idea of breaking a window and gaining access that way.

I was dragged straight through the hallway and into the bar and main clubroom where the gang almost went bananas at the sight of so many goodies. They had suddenly found themselves a fully stocked bar, a brewing room and a general stockroom and they began pointing excitedly to the bottled beer, fruit juices and mineral water saying, 'A whisky!' I kept telling them that none of this was whisky. Then the sergeant asked, 'Where is the still?'

'What still?' I replied. 'There's no still.'

So they pulled me into the brewing room and pointed to two large plastic dustbins on a table which contained beer freshly brewed the night before.

'*Siddeeky!*' accused the sergeant – *siddeeky* being Arabic for 'my friend' which is how all expatriates describe 100 per cent-proof alcohol. I shook my head, 'No *siddeeky.*' I might as well have been talking to pickled mushrooms; this lot of Keystone Cops were too busy running about shouting at each other and telling themselves in Arabic what a fantastic find they had made. The sergeant finally found what he had obviously been hoping to find – four sealed cardboard boxes which should have contained twelve bottles of mineral water. I must explain that, with some cunning I had placed these four boxes, which *did* contain *siddeeky*, among eight others of real mineral water. Heart in boots now, I decided to bluff. When the sergeant held a bottle up for close inspection, I pointed to the label, printed in Arabic and English (and which I had personally stuck on) which stated clearly, 'Sohat Mineral Water'.

'Water,' I told him.

He broke the seal and took a sniff. Then his face broke into a radiant smile. 'No,' he contradicted, *'siddeeky.'*

I shrugged. There was clearly no point in arguing any more. I had figured out by now that I had been stabbed in the back, that there was a traitor in our camp; I even thought I knew who he was for there was only one other bloke who knew there was *siddeeky* in those four boxes – and that was the guy who had supplied them. Everything added up because only a few days earlier I'd had a run in with him over another job he did for us and I had threatened that he would be sacked. I now vowed to myself that as soon as I laid hands on him I'd break his neck.

I was ordered to sit down at a table while the search continued. It was obvious that none of the gang had ever seen a bar before because they were as curious as children about the measuring optics on the upturned spirit bottles and about our darts equipment as well as about the banknotes which members had collected from all over the world which we had pinned up on the wall at the back of the bar. Finally, they came across a selection of nuts which I kept under the bar and they began scoffing these in handfuls. Watching them, I decided, that if those guys could eat, then I could smoke. So I indicated to the sergeant that I would like some cigarettes from off the shelves. 'No,' he told me in Arabic, 'you cannot smoke. You are a gangster!'

A *gangster!* – clearly this was a much more serious charge than I had imagined. In a country where men regularly have their hands chopped off for offences which might earn them only a six-month suspended sentence in Britain, being a gangster spelt trouble. I pretended I couldn't understand what had been said but I began to feel wonky. I looked at my watch – it had just gone 11.30 p.m. Almost an hour and a half had passed since these thugs had broken into my room and now matters were beginning to look decidedly uncomfortable. Sitting there, I suddenly found myself ruefully reflecting on how I had got myself into this awful predicament in the first place.

I had already been working in Riyadh, capital of Saudi Arabia and burgeoning city of a million and a quarter inhabitants, for over two years when, at the beginning of January 1979, I signed a contract to work as site manager on a big construction project to build three schools for the children of members of the Saudi armed forces. My employers were a local company under British management now in liquidation under royal decree.

At that time there were only two of us actually out in Riyadh – myself and Mike White, the deputy project manager, but as more and more people joined us from Britain, the company decided to rent a block of flats to accommodate everyone and Mike and I formally took possession of these on 9 February 1979; we christened the block Humming Bird House after the company's logo. We had almost no furniture in the beginning, each man having a bed and one single hardbacked chair only, but more furniture, of course, was due out from England.

One of the first things we found we needed to decide was the kind of facilities necessary to occupy our off-duty leisure time which, otherwise, threatened to be very boring. John Smith, company director, Ken Smith, chief quantity surveyor, Mike White and myself got together and decided we needed a TV room (with video), a reading room, a sitting room, a pool and darts room and, of course, a 'tea bar'. The previous tenants had had their 'tea bar' in one of the rooms on the roof but although they had gutted the place when they went, they had left the false ceiling which had stretched over their bar. I suggested we should start with the false ceiling and build up our own bar underneath it and this was quickly agreed upon. Eventually the company informed us that they would provide us with bar stools and tables and any other equipment we needed and also engage sub-contractors to build the club for us. On top of that they were also starting us off with 5000 riyals (about £800) to buy stock.

It was intended that we should have a properly constituted

committee when more people arrived from Britain but in the interim it was decided that Ken Smith should act as treasurer, Mike White run the bar and I, who was supposed to know my way among the Saudis by virtue of my two years' residence, would be responsible for buying drink. Fired with enthusiasm, I started the job the very next day by visiting a club run by Saudi Tarmac (all subsidiaries of European and US companies of course run 'tea bars'). Saudi Arabia is officially 'dry' and the faithful are expected to follow the teachings of the Qur'an but foreigners are normally favoured with a blind eye. The trade, of course, has to be carried on discreetly and every effort made to see that Muslims are not corrupted. When I went to see the Tarmac steward, therefore, I was merely following long-accepted practice.

A few nights later, two men turned up at my flat. They told me that they ran a brewery operated by employees of the British Aircraft Corporation inside the compound at the international airport. Beer, they said, would cost me two riyals a bottle (about 30p), so I placed an initial order for twelve dozen crates of beer, each crate to contain a dozen bottles. I asked them about spirits and was told that I would be put in touch with suppliers who would be able to let me have imported stuff as well as the local *siddeeky*. So far as imported stuff was concerned, I could have as much as I wanted, provided I was prepared to pay for it. Two nights later the '*sidd*-man' made his appearance. He told me he could sell me five US gallons of the stuff at a time but that it would cost me 350 riyals a gallon. I was about to protest that this was sheer extortion when he explained that I had to dilute the *siddeeky* – two parts of water to one of *siddeeky* – before drinking it; so my five gallons really amounted to fifteen gallons of drinkable booze. As imported stuff cost 180 riyals a pint, I didn't have to be an Einstein to realise which was the better bargain – so I ordered five gallons of *siddeeky*.

Next I visited a local supermarket where I purchased drink mixes as well as every kind of glass I needed – pint pots, whisky glasses, brandy glasses, sherry glasses. I remember asking myself how it happened that all these glasses were available if Saudis didn't drink.

Having done everything I had promised to do, I now sat back and waited for the 'tea bar' to begin operations. Regrettably Mike, who had promised to do the organising job, found himself far 'too busy' so like a chump I told him that if he liked I would take over instead. He jumped at the chance so I went ahead on my own and had the bar built. One of our sub-contractors, a British plumber, fitted a footrail to the bar; our chief engineer trotted off to the local car dealers and came back with an armful of car posters as well as two steering wheels so that, as a result, by Thursday 18 March our 'tea bar' was all set to open. We drew up a set of preliminary rules which were as follows:

Only British citizens (and those working for Bovis) to become members.

One guest per person per evening only to be permitted.

No Arabs to be admitted.

Thursday night opening only – to begin with.

The opening night turned out to be a roaring success. To start the ball rolling I declared all drinks on the house. I had also brought along a tape-recorder and we were able to play a lot of popular songs which gave us a chance to indulge in the sort of knees-up we were used to at home. Opening 'night' in fact, extended itself until six o'clock on Friday morning.

By July our site team had risen to more than 40 bodies, so it was decided that the bar should, from then on, open every night. I continued to act as bar manager, mainly because nobody else wanted the job. It was hard work for the only assistance I ever had was the occasional help of two senior members of staff and my young brother Tom who had joined the firm as general foreman. Then I was lucky enough to find just the sort of help I needed – and an asset that gave the Steering Wheel an edge over every other 'tea bar' in Saudi Arabia. Eva was a genuine Swedish blonde who didn't wear a bra and who had a bust rivalling that of the younger Sophia Loren. She was married to a BAC employee and proved a sensation. Bar takings soared overnight – and stayed soared.

So successful did the whole enterprise become that the membership eventually decided to stage their own show on the club premises. A wooden stage was built, complete with proper sliding curtains. Rehearsals were held over three weeks. As both Eva and I would have to work behind the bar during the performance, we were not given roles. On several occasions I tried to find out what was going on behind the curtain but each time I approached, I was politely requested by the producers to clear off as they did not want the contents of the programme leaked.

Once the performance had got under way I soon discovered why.

When the curtains opened, there sitting at a desk counting money was a 'Busy site manager'. On his desk was my ashtray, my penholder and even the calendar from off the wall of my office; on top of that the fellow playing the role was wearing my boots and shorts! Any further doubts as to who the character might be were quickly removed when he bawled out (in typical Fraser fashion, I was told) 'Noor-*shy*!' and on tripped Barry, our fitter, his face blackened with cork, playing Noor, my teaboy, and carrying a cuppa. The sketch continued with our site clerk, Bill Hunter, joining 'me', carrying a bundle of telex messages and playing the part of my immediate boss, Alan Hills. This led to more shouts from 'me' of 'Noor-*shy*!', followed by an order to Muhammad, my driver, to go the 'beer *souk*' and bring back twelve cases of beer. The sketch was hilarious, and all the funnier because it so accurately reflected the atmosphere of the site and of its characters.

So successful was the show that at the next committee meeting which was chaired by Ian Wylie, our general manager, it was suggested that we should stage further shows. This idea was well received but some of the more recent arrivals from Britain queried the existence of the bar, pointing out that it appeared to be illegal. They were assured – though not by me – that there was nothing to worry about. So long as the bar was open to British personnel only and nobody left the building drunk, there was no need to worry, and the whole project, after all, was under the protection of Prince Khalid.

For some reason I grabbed this opportunity to ask the general manager what my position would be if the club were raided? Neither of us, of course, regarded the question as anything but hypothetical. But I still thought it wiser to get the situation cleared up. Wylie told me that even if I were arrested, my salary would continue to be paid although I would have to do my best to keep the company out of it. I said that this seemed fair enough and on this understanding I agreed to carry on dispensing the goodies.

As the weeks passed and there were never any incidents at the club, my ambitions for it began to expand. I arranged a number of disco dances – our guests were the nurses from the nearby military hospital. I then set up a second bar out on the roof itself which could be used during the disco nights and on any other special occasions. I organised barbecue nights and put on a variety of competitions with big prizes as a special attraction. I grew immensely proud of the whole set-up which, as I saw it, could not have been run better even by professionals. Soon indeed, so far as we expatriates were concerned, the Steering Wheel club became the only thing that made life in Saudi Arabia even half-tolerable.

And now, suddenly, here I was, sitting in this very same club, my arms handcuffed behind my back, wondering anxiously what was going to happen to me and learning the hard way what it was like to feel absolutely scared.

TWO

A captain of police entered the club, marched straight up to me and demanded my name. I gave it readily enough and then he asked me where I came from and I replied 'Edinburgh, Scotland.'

'Oh, Edinburgh!' he said. 'I was there last year. What a beautiful city.'

Even in such dire straits, I couldn't help trying to make a joke – I had to keep up my spirits somehow.

'So what bars did you drink in when you were there?' I asked.

He favoured me a very sour look, indeed. 'I do not drink,' he replied stiffly, 'I am a good Muslim.' I took a closer look at him, trying to make up my mind about him. He was extremely well dressed and spoke English fluently, if with a slight American accent.

'Where is the still?' he suddenly shot at me.

'There's no still,' I replied almost as quickly. And then, determined to go over to the offensive, I said, 'Anyway, anything that's kept on these premises is intended only for company staff and for people living in these flats. And I'd like to remind you also that at last Ramadan, the Governor of Riyadh publicly declared that what westerners did in their own houses in Saudi Arabia was their own business and that they had no need to fear any police interference.'

He handled this inswinger with ease. 'Oh, that order only applied if they were not running a still.' This was news to me – there had been no mention in the Governor's speech of stills.

'Look,' I said, 'your men have already searched the place and they have found no still. Go ahead yourself and see, if you like.'

'Come with me,' he said briskly.

I followed him into the brewing room.

'This is a still,' he said, pointing to the big dustbins we used for beer.

'That is not a still,' I declared angrily. 'You've been to Scotland, so you must know what a still looks like. You have to use heat and the alcohol comes out of a copper tube in the form of steam.'

He interrupted me impatiently, 'No, no – this is a still.' Then he moved away and picked up some of the bottles on the shelves. 'Whisky,' he said. 'Whisky. Whisky. Whisky'. There was no whisky of course – they were merely bottles containing apple juice, tomato juice, dry ginger, bitter lemon and soda water.

We went back to the bar where he began looking over the optics on the whisky and gin bottles. 'What are these?' he eventually enquired.

'Are you kidding me?' I asked. 'You mean to tell me you've been to Edinburgh and yet you don't know what these are?'

'I *don't* know,' he said, speaking very severely. 'How do they work?'

I made a rattling sound with my handcuffs. 'If you will be kind enough to take these off, I'll show you,' I said.

He signalled his sergeant who quickly released me.

I went behind the bar and taking down a glass from the shelf, poured myself out a measure, using the optics.

'Show me how you do that again,' the captain demanded.

'A pleasure,' I said and poured myself out a second measure. Then I turned to the captain. 'Will you join me?' I asked 'It's a shame to waste this opportunity.'

'I do not drink,' he repeated almost angrily. 'But please – do drink yourself.'

I am not a whisky drinker; indeed I hate the stuff and usually never touch it. However, that glass of whisky turned out to be possibly the most beautiful drink I have ever tasted. When I had finished, I pointed to the shelf where there was a good stock of cigarettes. The captain nodded and said, 'Yes.' So I took down one packet.

'Oh, no,' said my captor pleasantly. 'Do take a few – take some more.'

Even as I took down four packets of king-size cigarettes, I guessed what this ready agreement meant: it would be a long time before I slept in my own bed again.

Meantime, his men had been carrying every bottle and case

they could find downstairs to the ground floor where they began stacking them up prior, I assumed, to removing them to head-quarters. I had begun to recover my nerve a bit when two police-men arrived escorting Muhammad, one of our Pakistani waiters in Humming Bird House. Muhammad, I must hastily explain, had absolutely nothing to do with the club; he worked in the ground-floor dining room where everybody who lived in the block ate their meals. His appearance at this particular point seemed to me a sinister development.

'This man works in the bar here,' said the captain accusingly, 'and he is a Muslim.'

'That's a lie!' I shouted angrily, 'and a damned lie at that! Only British staff are allowed up on to this roof – the company knows only too well that there'd be trouble if they allowed Saudis into our club.' This, indeed, was as near the truth as makes no differ-ence; the fact was that some Saudis *had* visited the club on *two* occasions but they had been brought in by one of our most senior staff and then they had been admitted only because they were personal advisors to His Highness, Prince Faisal.

I noticed that Muhammad had begun to tremble although he was not handcuffed nor, so far as I could judge, otherwise under threat from the police. Then I realised that he was trembling through fear *of me*. I didn't have time to worry about this little point, however, before the captain announced that it was time for us to leave. He led the way out on to the roof where he stopped immediately when he spotted our roof bar. He wanted to know what it was and I told him about our disco nights and its part in them. This did not appear to please him and he gave me a disapproving glance; then I remembered that Saudis consider it wrong for males and females to dance together. Two men, yes; a man and a woman, no.

'We only serve soft drinks here,' I explained

He shook his head. 'No – you sell whisky here.' I didn't bother to reply for there was no whisky in that little bar now.

I was taken downstairs and then led outside to a big, American-built police car which had a metal screen to separate driver and passengers as well as doors that could only be opened from the front seat. As I climbed in, I noticed a gleaming Cadillac drawn up just behind the motorcade of six cars in which the original posse of cops had arrived. I was taken aback when I noticed that the car registration number had only three numerals, for in Saudi

Arabia, the number of numerals indicates a man's rank. A car with one numeral belongs to the King. One with two means that the owner is part of the immediate royal family and one with three shows the car belongs to royalty further down the line (Saudi Arabia has at least 5000 princes). Four numerals indicates a mere sheikh while everybody else in the country has to carry six. My captain, therefore, was clearly royalty, if not a member of the monarch's intimate family.

Muhammad was roughly shoved into the back seat beside me. He still looked absolutely terrified and began to protest to me that he had been 'made to do it'.

'Mr Ian – he *made* me do it!' He repeated this umpteen times within the first few seconds.

'Who made you?' I eventually asked him. And then I mentioned the name of my supplier.

'Yes. But, Mr Ian – he made me do it. He told me to telephone the police and tell them that you had a still in your room.'

'And what else did you tell them?'

'I told them that you had several bottles of *siddeeky* – that you put it into bottles marked Sohat Mineral Water and that you had sealed them.'

'OK, Muhammad, you can stop shaking now. I'm not going to hit you, you poor ignorant bastard!' There was no way I could have hit him anyhow even if I had wanted to.

Then the captain reappeared at the car window which was open a couple of inches and shoved a bundle of notes amounting to 700 riyals through the gap and told Muhammad to take them and put them in my pocket adding, 'He will need them.' I knew, of course, that he had found the money in the cash box which was kept in the bar. At this point my brother Tom came to the window and asked the captain's permission to speak to me and the latter agreed.

'Are you all right, old fellow?' asked Tom, peering in anxiously at me.

'Yes,' I said rather impatiently, 'but I do want you to do something urgently for me. Go to our office staff villa and tell them what has happened to me and tell them to get rid of their drink. Then go to the general manager's office – he's on leave in England at the moment – and get rid of any stuff of his you find there. When you've done that, go and see Paul Nathan (project manager of the site) and tell him I'll take all the blame for the club and tell the police that the company knew nothing about it – that way they'll not arrest anybody else.'

'You know you're daft, of course, Ian!' protested Tom.

'Ours is a good company,' I told him. 'They'll do everything they can to help me.' I asked him to make sure nobody told my wife Anne back in England; I hoped I'd soon be out so there was no need to worry her.

'Certainly I'll do it, Ian,' Tom assured me, 'but I still think you're being daft, that you're wrong. You ought to tell the police the whole truth. The Saudis, after all, aren't going to jail the company bosses. Prince Khalid is sponsoring the company and he wouldn't stand for that!'

Even as we were talking I could see the bottles that had been found in the club and in my room being stacked up in a nearby pick-up truck. I nodded towards the truck and remarked to Tom, 'I'm afraid the fellows are going to have a bad thirst for a while.' We grinned miserably at each other.

Two policemen jumped smartly into the front seat of our car, one taking over the wheel. Tom asked them where they were taking me but they refused to answer. The captain then came along and told me he would follow along in the car behind. Tom tried to find out where I was being taken and went back with the captain to his car, but before he could get back to me with the information, our car had shot off with Muhammad still cowering away from me in the other corner of the back seat, apparently frightened out of his life.

We drove down Airport Street. I still felt absolutely convinced that I would be released very quickly. Every company operating in Saudi Arabia has its 'fixer' and I was sure that my employers would immediately start pulling strings on my behalf. Only a few months earlier our general manager had been arrested following an absurd allegation that our company owed a local businessman half a million pounds sterling and he was out within ten hours after our 'fixer' had intervened with Prince Khalid.

The car eventually drew up outside the main police station in Riyadh and we got out. We expats had christened this place '99' because all police cars operating from it – and there were never fewer than 50 cars parked at any one time in its car park – have the numberals '99' painted on their backs both in English and Arabic. There are, incidentally, three types of police in Saudi Arabia – traffic police (who carry no guns), patrol police (guns but no bullets) and '99' police (guns with bullets). I realised I must be in the big league.

I was led through the main door and brought inside where the first thing I saw was a glass showcase full of bottles of spirits, plus a sealed bottle of Sohat Mineral Water, a display which had obviously been put there so that the police could recognise alcohol when they saw it. I was taken upstairs to an office adjoining the radio control room. Staring through a large glass window into this room I saw an enormous street map of Riyadh on the wall. Inside the office itself a police captain was sitting at a desk and when he had finished kissing my guards, he spoke to me.

'English?' he enquired politely enough.

'No, Scottish,' I replied.

'No, English,' he corrected me.

Now I am as proud to call myself British as anybody and I have children who were born in England but as for myself, I was born in Scotland and I am Scottish-British, not English-British. So OK, I told myself, I am arrested and I am being humble but I am not going down on my belly for anybody. If this guy is going to insist I'm English, then –

'All right,' I told him, 'I'm English. But in that case, you're Yemeni.' The Yemenis, of course, are the Saudi Arabian work-horses and Saudis, who like to think of themselves as the Chosen of Allah, regard any suggestion that they are anything else as a profound insult. As I had hoped, this allegation flung the captain into a rage. He shouted at his policemen who rapidly surrounded me. Now you're in trouble, Fraser, I told myself, these guys are going to beat hell out of you.

I picked out the biggest policeman and made up my mind to go for him. Then bawling, 'Scotlander! Scotlander!' I flung myself at him. My intention was to butt him with my head but several hands grabbed me before I could reach him and there was a right old mêlée before a shout from the door put a stop to our activities. In the doorway stood the VIP captain and once the policemen saw him they desisted immediately as did I.

'What is the trouble?' demanded the VIP captain sternly. I told him that I had been insulted by the duty captain. The Saudi said I had insulted him back.

'You must apologise to each other – and then forget the whole thing,' advised the VIP. As this seemed a fair enough suggestion to me, I apologised and in return received an equally gracious apology from the duty captain.

The VIP captain then invited me to take a seat in one of the office armchairs. All Saudi offices are furnished with leather armchairs and settees for Saudis like to use their offices the way we British use coffee bars. The captain then ordered a sergeant to remove my handcuffs and indicated that I was to be allowed a smoke. He then left us. Afraid that once we were alone I was going to attack him, Muhammad warned me that it would be bad 'for both of us' if I made more trouble. I merely spat at him and told him, 'I don't know why I haven't beaten your head in yet – but I'm telling you now, don't say another word to me.'

While we sat there, policemen continually came in and out about their duties, kissing each other and then taking a quick look at the Scotlander. One or two even came over to me and said 'whisky'. Every time anyone said this, I simply shook my head and refused to speak. 'Whisky no good,' they told me but I still stubbornly refused to say anything.

After about twenty minutes of this pantomime a police lieutenant entered the office. He was an extremely well dressed and natty looking bloke but although he seemed to me to be of lower rank than the duty captain, the latter immediately got up to give him his chair. The newcomer sat down and politely asked my name – which I gave – and then asked me where I came from.

'From Scotland,' I replied and then waited for more of this Saudi nonsense about my being English. The lieutenant, however, had apparently been warned.

'Ah, the home of Scotch whisky,' he observed. He then asked me where 'the rest of the still' was and I told him that there was no still; the whisky found in my own room was for my own use.

He then turned to the waiter Muhammad. Where was the still? he asked. Muhammad said he did not know; all he did was to serve food to the British in the dining room downstairs.

'No. You served in the bar, you told a policeman that.'

Muhammad was, by this time, trembling like a leaf, so I chipped in at once and said, 'No, he never worked upstairs – he never worked in the bar. I never allowed any staff upstairs. This man is a Muslim and the Governor of Riyadh has warned British people in the English-language *Saudi Gazette* not to corrupt Muslims. So we don't allow it.'

We were interrupted by the entry of two Britons. The first was

Mike, supervisor of our catering company, and the other my
siddeeky supplier – the man who had betrayed me. The moment
I saw this man I had the greatest difficulty keeping my temper.
I quickly explained to Mike that this was the man who had
started the whole trouble by telling Muhammad to tell the police
a pack of lies. Face flushed as a beetroot, the supplier tried to
reason with me.

'You shut up, you!' I bawled at him. 'You'd better get out of
this country quick – or else I'll see you go to jail with me.' I
don't, in fact, know why I kept my mouth shut about this rogue;
all I had to do was tell the police that he had supplied me with
the *siddeeky* and he would have been behind bars immediately.
Instead, my instinct was to keep everything as low-key as
possible, to keep everybody else out of the mess.

Anyhow, the traitor left the room and Mike said he could not
believe that the man had betrayed me.

'Then ask Muhammad,' I said.

Mike asked Muhammad but the latter's only reply was to stare
silently at his own feet.

The upshot of Mike's intervention and his assurance that I was
telling the truth when I said that Muhammad had never been
allowed into the bar, was that Muhammad was given permission
to leave the police station.

'Make sure, however, that this man does not leave Riyadh,'
the lieutenant warned Mike. 'In the meantime, I shall want both
your passports.' All foreigners in Saudi Arabia, of course, are
required to carry passports just as Saudis themselves must carry
identity cards.

Before he went, Muhammad came across to me and said,
'Thank you, Mr Ian. I am so very sorry about all this.'

'Look, Muhammad, you just fuck off before I change my mind
and belt you one.'

Later I found myself sitting alone so I lit another cigarette. Oh,
well, I consoled myself, I suppose they'll deport me – I do hope
Tom packs all my belongings. Anne, of course, would be
surprised when I turned up at home but she and my two children, Paula and David, had spent a month in Riyadh the previous
year and she thought then that it was a terrible place to live, so
she would be glad I had finished with it.

My reverie was interrupted by the return of the lieutenant who said I was being moved to jail – and so I would have to have my handcuffs on again.

'That's OK by me,' I told him and so two policemen snapped the bracelets back on before leading me down the stairs and out into the police car. We then drove off towards the city centre, passing through 'Chop Square'. I have never found out what the real name of this square is, for everybody simply refers to it as 'Chop Square'. It is where, after noon prayers every Friday, the Saudis chop off a few hands and heads, just outside the Governor's palace. On such days people come from all over the city to see the sight – men, women and kids together. The Saudi women enjoy it because seeing people having bits of their anatomy sliced off is one of the few activities in Saudi Arabia in which both men and women are allowed to participate together in public. The only people who don't enjoy the show, it always seemed to me, are the poor guys who are there for the chop.

We stopped at another police station near the square and I was again taken out of the car. In front of us I could see several policemen lying asleep on a large carpet. People sleeping in the street is a normal sight in Riyadh; everywhere you go you see carpets outside buildings and people asleep on them. We walked round the side of the building and there on the main steps, I saw more police sleeping on more carpeting and a guard standing up against the wall, also fast asleep (all government offices, banks and other important buildings in Riyadh are guarded by at least one man armed with a machine gun). The guard woke up with a start when he heard us coming, then relaxed again when he realised that I was merely a prisoner.

I was led into a room which I later came to know as the chain room. Here a series of chains hung down from the walls and at first I thought I must be in a torture room. In fact, it was the room where prisoners are searched. Chains are put on your legs and wrists and if you are a particularly bad boy, a neck chain is also hung on you.

I was ordered to stand in the middle of the room while the two policemen who had delivered me asked for a signature from my new captors. Within seconds both parties were bawling and shouting at each other while I stood there, ignored. My escorts insisted upon a signature for me and the station police insisted on refusing to give it to them.

'We must get back to our station,' bawled my escorts by way of explanation.

'All right, go then. Bring him back in the morning.'

'But we can't bring him back in the morning. Our orders are to leave him here.'

'Bring him back in the morning. Then you can have a signature.'

At any other time and in any other circumstances, I might well have found the exchange hilarious. However, it was early in the morning and I was dog-tired and worried out of my skin; I had been dragged round like a sack of coals for long enough.

'For God's sake, why don't you sort it out!' I shouted. They turned and looked at me in amazement; they had completely forgotten my presence.

In the end, one of the sleeping guards was wakened and told to take me and my escorts to see the duty officer. We climbed slowly to the fifth floor and entered an office. At the far end of this room I saw a double bed in which two figures appeared to be sleeping wrapped together in a close embrace. The moment I saw the couple, of course, I knew that they could not be a man and a woman for the Saudis insist on keeping their women wrapped in black from head to toe and hidden behind thick walls. On our entrance the two figures woke up and the duty officer, a major, climbed out of bed, leaving his companion, an ordinary constable, to continue with his 'rest'. The major pulled on trousers over very large, baggy underpants and then sat down at his desk. Addressing me in English, he invited me to take a seat in the usual office leather settee and, grateful for the courtesy, I collapsed into it, flaked out.

The major took a letter from one of my escorts and read it. When he had finished, he nodded, wrote out a delivery receipt for me and handed it back before curtly dismissing the men. Then he asked me my name, where I came from, what kind of work I did and whether I was married. I answered all these questions as politely as I could. Then came the question, 'Where is your still?'

'Look,' I answered, almost in despair, 'there is no still.' I was so fed up by now with this stupid question that I made up my mind that the next time anybody asked it, I was going to say I'd lost it.

The major half-smiled, then told me he would speak to me

again in the morning. In the meantime, he said, I would be taken downstairs.

Escorted by two guards, I was led down stairs and into the basement where I was hit by a strong stench of sewerage. The smell was so overpowering that I felt sure I was going to be sick. My guards, however, refused to allow me to register any disapproval but led me straight to a double steel door where they stopped. One guard then kicked the door sharply and, a minute or two later, a small hatch was opened. A face peered out at us, then the door was opened and I was taken inside while a guard quickly locked the door behind us. Along one side I saw a line of cell doors, five in all and wondered which was mine. My handcuffs were taken off and I was led to cell number four. The guard had some difficulty opening the door for someone was lying asleep on the floor inside. However, he was quickly wakened up and made to move over and the guard finally shoved the door open. I was pushed inside and the door was shut behind me.

There was a light on in the cell and so I had a chance to study my lodging for the night. The cell itself was some twelve feet long by six feet wide and already held eight other prisoners who by now were lying half-asleep on the floor. It was all pure sardines-in-a-tin stuff for I was totally unable to move. There was considerable grumbling as one reclining body pushed against another in order to squeeze up to make room for me. Finally Abdul, the one who had been asleep with his back to the door, moved back into his original position and signalled to me that I should lie down beside him.

I was so tired and exhausted that, unsavoury though this prospect seemed, I had no hesitation in stretching out on the cold, concrete floor. Then, with my feet pressed up against the wall at one end and my head up against the other, I closed my eyes, hoping that sleep would arrive quickly to blank out my thoughts and allow me a respite, if only temporary, from thinking and worrying about my predicament.

THREE

I fished a cigarette from my pocket and lit it. Abdul said I must not smoke; it was forbidden.

'Not for me, it isn't,' I told him, speaking in Arabic, and took a few puffs. I offered a pull to some of my other cell-mates, including Abdul, and some accepted. Abdul, however, warned me not to give the others a pull although it was all right to offer him a cigarette.

'Why is that?' I asked him.

'Because I'm special,' he replied but he didn't bother to explain why. And, for that matter, I didn't bother to ask.

I shut my eyes again, hoping for sleep. I was obviously in big trouble, but what was the use of worrying about it now? There would be plenty of time to worry tomorrow. Still sleep refused to come, so I asked Abdul the time. He said it was 3.30 a.m. and I had an odd feeling that time had stopped.

Suddenly there was a noise outside the door and the key turned in the lock. At once everybody began pushing and shoving again to allow the door to open and eventually a guard stuck his head around and ordered me to get up. I rose wearily and shuffled out and was led upstairs again to the chain room. Once again I was handcuffed but this time my arms were put in front of me. How nice, how kind, I thought. Nobody was being kind, however, for as well as handcuffs, they suddenly put chains on my ankles. I knew then I must be a real desperado. At the same time I was wondering what the hell was going to happen to me now.

I was taken out, hobbling along as best I could, and shoved into a police car in the company of a driver and three guards.

Five minutes later we pulled up outside a police station just off Sitteen Street about three miles from Chop Square. Oh, God, I thought, not another bloody police station! Not another load of questions about imaginary whisky stills.

The driver got out and went into the police station and then returned within a few minutes with *eight* other policemen. They at once piled into two other cars and then the driver turned to me and asked me for directions as to where I lived. My heart lifted at once (I still believed in fairies and Father Christmas at this time) and I named our block of flats, 'Humming Bird House'. I knew that an early-morning flight to London left Riyadh at 6.30 a.m. and I was now sure that we were off to collect my belongings before they put me on a flight home.

I directed the driver to Humming Bird House and eventually our motorcade pulled up outside it and everybody got out. Still hobbling, I was led, escorted by twelve policemen, to the front door where one policeman, going ahead, pushed through into the entrance hall. I saw him wake a policeman who was asleep just inside and speak to him. There was a brief exchange between them before we all turned back again and got into the cars again which immediately took us all back to where we had started from – the police station near Chop Square! Seconds later I was once again standing in the chain room, trying to figure out what the hell was happening to me. Why all this rigmarole? Why the journey out to Sitteen Street and why the trip to Humming Bird House? All I could think of was that some of these guys had been hoping for a drink on the side and had been surprised to find a policeman on guard at Humming Bird House. Maybe there was some other explanation, but if there were I never found it.

I was still standing in the chain room, still pinioned at wrists and ankles, when I heard a truck pull up outside the station. A policeman released my ankle chains, and led me to the front door where I saw the pick-up truck I had last seen parked outside Humming Bird House and into which the bottles found in my flat and in the club had been dumped.

'You will unload the truck, please,' said the guard.

I raised my hands and showed him the cuffs. 'Take these off, then,' I told him. I didn't consider this an unreasonable request and was taken aback when the guard shouted 'No!' and then shoved me violently towards the truck. Staggering, I turned and roared at him.

Saudis do not like to be sworn at. Every Arab, whether he can speak English or not, always knows when you swear at him. This guy proved to be no exception and he looked as though he were about to boil over. Exploding with rage he pushed me back into the chain room and peremptorily ordered me to empty my pockets. I still had three packets of cigarettes as well as a silver cigarette lighter which had been a birthday present from my colleagues. The guard snatched the packets away, then crushed them in his hands and scattered the broken remnants over the floor. Next he tried to take away the lighter which I still held in my hands. I told him to 'fuck off!' Eyes popping with anger now, he made a grab for the lighter which proved a bad move on his part. I jumped forward and using my head gave him what I insist on describing as a gentle tap in the face. Others might describe it as a violent butt in the mug. Whatever it was, the guy reeled back, blood cascading from his nose like a waterfall clattering down Ben Nevis.

At once policemen were coming at me from all directions, including the guard with the machine gun – and the way he pointed it at me rapidly led me to the view that I had finally and definitely cooked my goose. He did not open fire, however, and none of the other coppers came close enough for me to favour them with a second butt. Instead, they gathered round in a respectful circle and stared warily at me. The impasse ended only when the major strode angrily into the room and demanded to know why I had hit the policeman.

I pointed to the crumpled cigarette packets on the floor and the broken fags scattered about. I told him that his bloke had also tried to take away my cigarette lighter. I finished by saying, 'And if anybody else tries it, he'll get the same.'

The major turned and said something sharply to the injured policeman. The latter answered that I was mad, a lunatic.

'All right!' declared the major sternly turning back to me, 'you will be taken down to your cell at once. And I must warn you that nobody is allowed to smoke in jail.'

'*You're* wrong, mate,' I told him. 'I'm going to smoke wherever I want to. And what's more, I need fresh cigarettes for that cunt has just gone and crushed mine!'

'Don't use bad words to me,' rebuked the major. 'You know only too well that Saudis do not like bad words.'

'You needn't use them, then, need you. But as for me – *fuck you!'*

The major glowered angrily at me but said nothing. Instead, he walked out of the room but was back shortly with another packet of cigarettes which he handed to me.

'Return to your cell, now,' he instructed. 'You yourself can smoke – but you must not give a smoke to anyone else. Is that understood?'

'Yes, I understand,' I replied. 'That's OK by me.'

The major then turned to the nearest policeman. 'Take off his handcuffs.' I was immediately released and led back to my cell in the basement.

Abdul asked where I had been and I told him.

'You'll be set free all right,' he reassured me, 'you're a foreigner.'

'I hope you're right,' I replied, although I had my doubts.

I decided to have another go at trying to get off to sleep but no sooner had I closed my eyes than the key was turned in the door and we all had to shove up again so that a policeman could put his head round and call out my name. I could scarcely credit it. More weary than ever, I stumbled out of the cell and was taken back to the chain room where I noticed it was now 4.45 a.m. Once again my arms were pinioned in front of me and cuffs put on my wrists and ankle chains also fixed. Feeling like a trussed turkey, I was led hobbling outside again and back into the police car with guards piling in all over the place on either side of me. We shot away, going, so far as I could judge, in the direction away from Humming Bird House. This time I did not even try to kid myself that we were making for the airport.

Eventually we arrived at what I took to be a government building where we were halted, par for the course, by a guard with a machine gun who, having 'checked' us, then lazily waved us on. We drove round to the other side of the building and drew up before what was clearly the main entrance. There were ten marble steps leading up to the front door and I was made to hobble up these as best I could. The steps had recently been hosed down, however, and were therefore extremely slippery. With ankles chained, I found the footing unsteady and I fell down twice. Fortunately, I did not hurt myself but I could have done with a helping hand. None, I regret to say, was forthcoming. Once inside I was led along a corridor through a door and then, suddenly, out into the open air again, this time into large gardens. We walked through these gardens and entered another wing of the building where we began walking down another long corridor. Suddenly I spotted a notice saying 'Medical Department' and I realised we were in a hospital. What on earth was I doing in a hospital?

I was led into a small room whose use I could not even guess at. It was simply the dirtiest and most overcrowded room I have ever seen in my life. On a table was a collection of glass tubes, bottles, slides and dirty bandages. Other materials overflowed from what was obviously supposed to be a waste bin but one which looked as though it had never been emptied since it had been bought. Lying on the floor I saw a man clad in what I took to be a black-and-white coat. It was only when I looked more closely that I realised that the *whole* coat was supposed to be white. One of my escorts prodded the fellow awake and said something to him, as a result of which the man got up, walked to the table and, after poking about in the rubbish for a moment or so, unearthed a ledger.

He then turned to me and asked me my name, my age and my country of origin. I gave him all the answers and then asked him, 'Why am I here?'

'You drink whisky,' he replied curtly.

That bastard of a captain! I thought. The fellow had not only allowed me to drink that double whisky in the club but had actually encouraged me to do so, knowing that I was going to have a blood sample taken. My anger, however, was rapidly replaced by genuine anxiety – surely I would die of blood-poisoning if they attempted to take a blood sample in this dump!

I was led across to one of the walls of the room where a curtain about two feet square had been hung over what I took to be a hatch. The attendant pressed a bell and we waited until eventually I heard a voice speaking in low tones emerge from the room next door. The attendant at once ordered me to stick my arms through the curtain.

'Open it then,' I told him, anxious to check what lay on the other side.

'Push your arms in curtain,' he repeated.

This instruction made me very angry indeed; why in hell couldn't I see what was going on?

'Look,' I said quietly to the guy, 'fuck off, baldie.'

The man at once began bawling to the guards. I have never yet seen a posse of policemen look less interested in what was supposed to be happening to their prisoner. My view is that they had still only too clear a recollection of what had happened to their colleague – he of the bleeding nose. Faced with their massive indifference the attendant calmed down.

'Madam in curtain,' he consented to explain to me. 'She take blood but you no see her because she is a Muslim.'

'You must be kidding pal,' I told him. 'What difference does that make?'

'What is kidding?' he asked, mystified.

'You must be joking,' I told him.

'Oh, no. No joking.'

I had had quite enough of this by now, however. So before the guy could stop me, I simply pushed the curtain aside and there, from the other side, I was confronted by the startled face of a female.

'Oh, hello there,' I said and, without further ado, stuck my arms through the small hole in the wall. Unfortunately the gap was no more than twelve inches or so square, so the moment I pushed my arms through, I lost sight of the woman. Next thing I knew – and it happened without any preliminary antiseptic rub or anything like that – she had plunged the needle deep into my arm. It was anything but a gentle little prick – a really painful sting. I got my reward, however, when she withdrew the needle because she then began to feel my hands, rubbing her fingers most suggestively in the palm of my right hand. Just as I was really getting to like this treatment, however, the attendant wised up to what was going on and pulled me away. I decided that madam was either very sorry for me or that she was a very frustrated lady – many Saudi women are.

I was taken back to the car where we discovered our driver slumped over the wheel, sound asleep. A policeman quickly prodded him awake and off we shot again, back towards Chop Square. Back again in the chain room I was divested of my chains and taken down into what I had come to think of by now as the smell-hole.

This time, however, as I stretched down beside him, Abdul did not even bother to enquire where I had been and my head had no sooner touched the cold concrete floor than, totally exhausted, I at last fell asleep.

I had scarcely closed my eyes when I was again wakened up. It turned out to be 8 a.m. and breakfast had arrived. When the cell door was opened, a tray was pushed in along the floor. Breakfast for me and my eight other cell-mates consisted of some dreadful-looking type of gruel along with nine boiled eggs, still in their shells. These eggs were placed on top of the gruel at regular intervals around the large tray and then nine pieces of Arab bread, each flat, thin and rounded, had been carefully placed one piece on top of each egg. Having shoved the tray into the middle of the cell, Abdul invited me to join in but I thanked him and said I wasn't hungry – which was true.

What I was actually dying to do now was pass water. I asked Abdul to tell me where the toilets were and he pointed to a hole in the floor at the upper end of the cell. I had failed to notice this convenience before because of the number of people in the cell but now that I had seen it, it began to preoccupy my attention like a sore thumb. The facility, indeed, proved to be so off-putting that the need to pass water rapidly disappeared. I found myself worrying about what I would do if I needed a shit.

While I was still ruminating on these problems, my cell-mates got on with their breakfast and as soon as the tray had been passed out again, two plastic Sohat water bottles, half-filled with red-hot tea, were handed in. Abdul placed them on the floor, then blew on his hands to cool them. He offered me one of these bottles but I again shook my head. Instead, I lay down and closed my eyes and once again fell asleep. I must have been asleep for only a moment or so for the next thing I knew I was being awakened again by the door being pushed against me and Abdul telling me that I was to go out. I was again led upstairs where this time, on reaching the ground floor, I saw several boxes of my home-made beer stacked up. I saw no sign, however, of any whisky or *siddeeky* bottles.

On entering the major's office, I saw Roger Lilly, the company's personnel manager along with one of our office drivers sitting on the big leather settee. Roger rose and shook me by the hand and asked me anxiously if I were OK. The major invited me to sit down and Roger asked if it were all right for me to smoke. The major nodded and Roger gave me one of his.

He then turned to the major and asked him what was going to happen to me.

'When he has given me a confession, then he will be taken before the sheikh,' explained the major shortly.

'Can I be there when he gives you this confession?' asked Roger.

'Yes, of course,' replied the major graciously, 'but you will not be able to understand it, I'm afraid. The conversation will be in Arabic.'

'I'm afraid neither Mr Fraser nor I speak very good Arabic,' objected Roger. 'Could not the proceedings be held in English?'

'I regret,' replied the major. 'I'm afraid everything must be in Arabic. I can only advise that you bring a translator with you when you come tomorrow. And he must be a Muslim.'

The position made clear, the major rose, gave a little bow and quit the room, leaving two policemen to guard us. I glanced across at the bed the major had been using but saw no sign of his male companion of the previous night, although the bed had not even been made.

Roger wanted to know what I intended to say in my confession. I told him I didn't want to see anybody else go to jail, so I intended to say the bar was mine, that all the drink found was mine and that as I was the senior person living in Humming Bird House, I was responsible for everything. In return, all I asked Roger to ensure was that my salary was sent home every month to my wife. 'No doubt I'll get three years at least,' I told him. 'For that's what other British and Americans I've heard of who've been sent to prison here have got.'

'You'll never get that!' declared Roger flatly. 'You're not like them – you haven't committed any crime. And our company is big; they'll get you out.'

'Let's hope you're right, Roger but I hae me doobts. Anyway, tell the top brass and the company not to worry, I'm not going to involve them. But if you don't get that bloody man who betrayed me out of Saudi Arabia right away – then I'm going to split on *him*.'

'Why, what has he done?' asked Roger, astonished.

I told him.

'I'm amazed,' he said when I had finished. I told him he could believe what he liked.

He then asked me if there was anything else I needed and I

told him I needed a change of clothing, a blanket, a small mattress and some cigarettes. I also asked him to get a supply of headache tablets from our company doctor. At this point the major returned and told Roger he must leave. The latter asked if it were all right to bring in the articles I had specified and the major said it was. All that is, except the mattress.

'I must have a mattress!' I interrupted. 'Damned if I'm going to sleep on a concrete slab!' I thought the major was going to say no again but to my surprise he said, 'All right, so be it.'

Roger asked him about the food and the major assured him that all food was supplied, adding that it was 'first class'.

'Listen, Roger – if you believe that, you'll believe anything,' I interrupted. 'Anyway, I'm not hungry.'

I was taken from the room and led back down to my cell where I once more flung myself on the floor and again fell asleep. Any hopes I had of enjoying a solid eight-hour kip, however, were soon dashed. That damned cell door was once again pushed open and once again Abdul told me to go outside. Back in the chain room, I was handcuffed once more but this time spared the ankle chain. Then I was led out into yet another police car.

Escorted by a driver and three policemen, I was driven towards Airport Street but before I could get round to any fancy ideas of flights home or any of that nonsense, the driver turned off and we stopped outside Humming Bird House. On entering the house I found it was just 2 p.m. I could hear the sound of a pin-ball game in progress upstairs and thought it odd that I should be in such trouble while everybody else connected with the site should still be living normally, although I wondered why they were not *at* the site. We climbed to the second floor where I saw four of my staff playing a game of table tennis. They stopped playing for a moment when they saw me and I said a cheery, 'hello' to them but all I got by way of reply was a sort of cautious mumble. I was taken on up on to the roof and into the club where I found the major with four more policemen in attendance. The major said I could sit down but I asked if I could first use the bar toilet. A policeman was told to check up on the toilet and having apparently assured himself that I could not escape through a window or some other mouse-hole, I was permitted to relieve myself.

I hesitate to linger on the details of the natural functions except to say that under certain circumstances, they pose a problem which is apt to loom much larger in the consciousness than is normal. I had never found the experience of passing water more pleasurable than in this case. I returned to the bar feeling like a new man and ready to take a much greater interest in what was happening. The police at this time were busy poking and searching everywhere but with no perceptible results. One policeman tried to work the optic on a whisky bottle but was utterly unable to fathom the mechanism. I was still sitting at the table, enjoying the whole pantomime when in walked Harry Hall to whom I had given my belongings the night before. We briefly exchanged greetings and then Harry asked the major if he could bring me tea. The major gave a nod of indifference, so Harry went outside and returned within seconds with a tray on which there was a pot of tea and a plate of excellent sandwiches.

'Why aren't all the lads at work?' I asked. 'Most of them still seem to be here in the house?'

'Everybody's under house arrest I'm afraid,' explained Harry.

'Really,' I said, surprised. 'Well tell them not to worry. Tell them I'm going to take all the blame, so no one else should be involved.'

'The lads will be glad to hear that,' said Harry. 'Oh, they'll also be sorry for you, of course – but they'll be glad for themselves. But they're still not sure they won't be arrested as we're all involved.'

We were allowed to sit there for about an hour while the police continued with their work. Neither Harry nor I could understand what they were up to for there were no drawers or cupboards anywhere nor any secret hole in the wall. Harry tried to get me to eat up the sandwiches but I told him about the awful hole in the cell and explained that if I ate anything, I'd have to use that hole and I simply didn't intend to use it. I would be forced to piss in it all right for the heat in the cell was at least 100 degrees and if I didn't drink water I would dehydrate. But I would not eat.

After some two hours or so the major told me that it was now time to go. I was allowed to take 40 cigarettes from the bar – later I found out that the police shared out the rest between them. Before we reached the door, however, the major halted.

'Before you go,' he said, 'what is this – hashish?'

He was holding a bag of Irish Moss which I used in making beer. I had, in fact, bought this particular bag at Boots on my last visit to the UK. Like an idiot I said, 'Yes, hashish.' When his eyes lit up, I realised I had said the wrong thing and tried to correct my error. I said I had been joking and went on to explain to him what Irish Moss was and what I had used it for. He ignored this explanation and turning to one of his men said, 'This is hashish. This man has been telling me lies and he'll pay for it.'

We left Humming Bird House without seeing any of my colleagues. When I returned to my cell, my fellow prisoners asked me where I had been and I told them. I had decided not to get into a long conversation with them, however, and to stay aloof as far as possible. After all, I was British and was certain I would soon be sent home.

FOUR

I had my first experience of *salha* in the cell that night. At about 7 p.m. one of the prisoners, who looked like a *matela*, spoke to the other prisoners and said '*Salha*'. At once they began shuffling to a tap in the wall beside that awful hole in the floor and began splashing water over their hands, feet and face. They then pulled on Arab robes over the pyjama-type underwear which we expats called 'nightshirts'. They then turned and stood facing Mecca.

Abdul asked me if I would be kind enough to stand in a corner while they prayed. Prepared to respect their customs, I agreed and waited while they went through their ritual of prayer. They then took off their robes, rolled them up and gathered round the *matela* who began reading from the Qur'an. After he had finished, he answered questions on the text and other theological points. Incredibly, all this lasted for four hours, until about 11 p.m. By the end of it all, I felt that my head was about to explode and I groaned with relief when the whole performance was over and everybody lay down to get some kip.

The next thing I knew the *matela* was again saying '*Salha, salha*' and looking at my watch I saw that it was 3.30 a.m. I attempted to shut my eyes again but the ever-active Abdul began shaking me, telling me that I must again stand in the corner. This time I felt in no mood to be charming and said, 'Fuck off!' Everybody understood this all right and left me alone while they got on with *salha*. The ritual didn't seem to last so long this time and eventually all was quiet.

Breakfast arrived on the dot, once again wakening me up. It was exactly the same as before. I felt sick just looking at the stuff and refused to eat it. Abdul tried to make me change my mind, urging me to keep up my strength but I told him he could have my portion which he ate with obvious relish. At 10 a.m., the door was opened and Abdul said I had to go out.

Two policemen were waiting in the corridor to escort me upstairs. This time they handcuffed me immediately and I decided they must be taking me out of the station again but they merely led me back to the major's office. Passing the ground floor on the way up, I noticed my boxes of home-made beer still standing at the door where they had been stacked up the previous day and I grinned when I thought of what would happen once the Saudis started to shift them again. The fact is that home-made beer will explode in the bottle if it is moved before it is ready and I had glorious visions of a startled gendarmerie being bombarded by exploding beer when they came to touch the stuff.

Roger Lilly was waiting for me in the major's office, along with Hassan, the company's interpreter, an Egyptian. The major told me to sit down but before I did so, I held out my hands and asked him to remove the cuffs.

'No, no,' he shook his head. 'You bad. They must stay on.'

I thought I had behaved rather well since my arrest, taking everything into consideration. So, without further ado, I said, 'Good-bye, Roger, good-bye, Hassan,' and turning on my heel, I walked straight out of the office and then down the stairs. The policemen who were guarding me were so taken aback that they made no attempt to follow me. I had reached the ground floor before Roger came running after me and told me not to be 'silly'.

'I am not going to be questioned wearing handcuffs,' I told him and carried on down the stairs before knocking on the door to the cells. The hatch opened and the guard peered out. He seemed amazed at the sight of me all by myself without an escort but opened the door and I went in. My two escorts came running after me yelling out that I was trying to escape. They burst in after me, each grabbing me by an arm and started to pull me back towards the door. I refused to go and struggled with them, quickly breaking free.

'No!' I yelled at them and walking to the door of my cell, ordered them to open it for me.

Clearly they had never met a prisoner before who refused to obey orders. The situation was that I was telling them what to do and they suddenly found themselves obeying *me*. As though hypnotised they quietly unlocked the cell door, took off my handcuffs and allowed me to walk back into the cell. Abdul asked them what all the trouble was about and they said, 'He's crazy. He has just tried to escape.' I laughed and sat down on the floor.

The door was opened again almost at once and in came the major, a handkerchief held to his nose.

'All right,' he said brusquely, 'no handcuffs.'

'OK, then,' I replied. 'In that case, I'm happy to answer all questions.'

Roger, white-faced, was still waiting upstairs. Later he told me he had decided we would both be shot. 'That was an idea that had crossed my own mind,' I admitted.

The major began by asking me why I had refused to eat since I had been arrested. I told him I didn't like the food or the toilets but he insisted the food was 'good' and the toilets 'good enough' for prisoners. He would withdraw the food ration as a punishment if I did not eat.

'How do you punish me by not giving me food if I won't eat?' I asked him, but he did not seem to appreciate the joke.

Roger interrupted to urge me to eat but I told him he was unable to imagine what it was like down below.

The major reached down to the floor and brought up a Sohat bottle and two small bottles of dry ginger.

'Where did you get these?' he asked me.

'In the supermarket,' I answered. The Sohat bottle may have contained *siddeeky* but the dry ginger could be bought anywhere.

'I do not believe you,' replied the major but both Roger and Hassan broke in to assure him that what I said was true. I knew he knew it was true for in Saudi Arabia men normally shop for food in order to protect their women from other evilly disposed men. Realising that this whole line of questioning was a farce, I debated with myself whether or not to go back to my cell again. The major interrupted to say that Hasssan must now translate all his questions as the proceedings had to be in Arabic.

'Well, that's damned silly,' I said. 'You speak English as well as I do.' The major insisted, however, that according to law, the proceedings had to be conducted in Arabic.

'Who ran the Steering Wheel?' he asked. 'Who built it? Who built the roof bar?' I answered that I did.

'Where did you get the timber?' he enquired.

'From our building site.'

'So you stole it?'

'No, I didn't steal it. As site manager I am allowed to take any materials I need to make alterations or improvements in Humming Bird House.'

'Then your company knew you had a still in the house?'

'We had no still. And the company did not know of any.' And then I told a lie. 'Indeed, my company did not even know we had a bar.'

He then tried another tack. 'You sold drink?' he accused me.

'No, I didn't. Drinks were subscribed for by members of the staff, my friends. I was aware it was a crime to sell alcohol, but the drink was not on sale in that sense.'

'Where did you buy the *siddeeky*?'

'I got it from a man called Mickey.'

'Mickey who?' he demanded.

I was going to say Mickey Mouse but decided that would be stretching my luck a bit. At one stage I thought of involving the chef but decided to stick to my intention of not incriminating anybody else.

The interrogation lasted a full two hours with the major returning again and again to the same questions, only to receive the same answers. He then announced that questioning would be resumed the following day. In the meantime, he would allow me five minutes' conversation with Mr Lilly.

Roger said that our boss, Ian Wylie who was then in England, had sent him a message to say that everything must be done to secure my release. As a result, he Roger, hoped to see the deputy Governor of Riyadh who could certainly get me out. In the meantime, did I want my wife Anne to be told of my arrest? I told Roger not to worry her but I would like him to arrange to have a bunch of red roses sent to her for her birthday. Roger said he would do that and as the major returned, he handed me a bag containing the change of clothing I had requested. The guards at once insisted on searching this. I said good-bye to Roger and was then led back to my cell where the guards again insisted on searching my bag, this time, emptying the contents on the floor. Roger had brought me a towel, two pairs of underpants, two sheets and two pairs of socks – so what they were looking for I could not imagine.

As the cell door closed on me again, I found I had interrupted yet another session of Qur'an readings which was followed by a further long session of questions and answers. 'Oh, God!' I moaned loudly, 'surely not again!' But on and on they went and they were still at it at 2 p.m. when I was once again called from my cell.

Handcuffs were once more put on me in the chain room. Even as they clicked home there was a series of terrific bangs from the direction of the front door. In the chain room they sounded like shots and my guards suddenly panicked, presuming they were under attack. I could hardly stop laughing. I allowed them to run around like a bunch of scared rabbits for a few moments before yelling at them, 'It's only the beer bottles.' As they knew nothing of the mysteries of brewing – and home-brewing at that – they obviously did not understand and it was not until a sergeant came running up from below and yelled at me, 'Fraser no good!' that they began to connect the explosions with me personally. The episode was so funny and the sergeant's remark so incongruous that I roared with laughter. The policemen looked at me in amazement and the thought occurred to me then that the only way to avoid going insane, and even to extract a bit of fun while I was at it, was to do exactly the opposite of what my guards expected.

I was taken back to Humming Bird House again where I looked forward to another cup of Harry Hall's tea as I had not drunk or eaten anything in 24 hours. When we entered the place, however, I decided to go my own way and went into the dining room instead of going upstairs to the club as the guards wanted me to do. They shouted at me but I paid no attention to them. Some of my staff were sitting at tables drinking tea so I said 'hello' to them, then walked across to the refrigerator, opened it and took out a one-and-a-half-litre carton of milk. I drank the contents in a single gulp. I put down the empty carton, said 'cheerio' to the lads and went upstairs to the club while the guards followed me like poodles. I sat down at the table I had occupied the day before and almost at once Harry walked in with his tray of tea and sandwiches.

He told me that my young brother Tom and Bill Hunter had managed to sneak out of the house the previous morning while their guards were enjoying breakfast; they were still at large and not yet under house arrest. He had no idea where they were nor did anybody else (in fact, they were still working openly on the site but sleeping at nights in a villa belonging to one of our sub-

contractors). While we talked, the police began stacking glasses
and other items of my home-brewing equipment in the middle
of the floor. When they brought out the plastic dustbin, the
sergeant said to me, 'That is the still.'

'You have no brains,' I told him, 'you are a silly man.'

'That is the still,' he insisted angrily.

I laughed and he turned and walked away. Later I found out
that I was supposed to show I was terrified at this revelation and
my reaction had succeeded only in confusing them. God only
knows why my presence was needed anyway for a little while
later I was once again led away and taken back to my cell.

I arrived just in time for more *salha*. Muslims pray five times
a day; usually at 4 a.m., twelve noon, 2 p.m., 5 p.m. and 7 p.m.
although times change depending on the season. 'Oh, to hell
with you all,' I muttered and lay down on the floor while they
got on with it, I was soon fast asleep. I woke up shivering and
sweating but my fellow prisoners helped by covering me with
their own robes and nightshirts. They could not have been kinder
or more compassionate and I was deeply touched. I lay there
shivering with the cold and although Abdul called the guard, he
was told nothing could be done that night and I would have to
wait until morning to see a doctor. It was a terrible night and on
several occasions I felt certain I was going to die but somehow I
survived and next morning when the door was opened to slide
in the breakfast tray, I had fully recovered. I still have no idea
what was wrong with me but it was a frightening experience.

Once more I was taken out for further questioning by the
major. Roger had brought along a packet of cornflakes as well as
a plate and a carton of milk. I told him I would drink the milk
but would not touch the cornflakes. As I began drinking I found
everyone gazing at me as though I were an exhibit in a zoo. So
I shouted at Roger, 'Look, I'm not an animal in the zoo at feeding
time,' and promptly stopped drinking.

'All right, you drink, we wait,' said the major.

'This isn't a zoo!' I told him, 'although there are animals here.'
He missed the point but it gave me some satisfaction to say it
anyway.

Roger then asked if he could give me the paracetamol headache
tablets which the company doctor had prescribed for me.

'Later. After questions,' said the major.

He began again by asking, 'Where is the still?' and I gave him my usual answer. Then he asked, 'Where did you get the four boxes of whisky?'

'Hold on, there,' I interrupted him. 'There were six boxes in my wardrobe plus two boxes in the bar. If I'm going to be charged with having whisky, then I think all the boxes should be declared.'

'You had only four boxes of whisky and four of *siddeeky* – and that makes eight,' said the major.

'OK,' I said hurriedly, 'OK! But I hope they catch you with the other four!' He did not reply but went on to ask the same questions he had already put to me, only to get exactly the same answers.

It proved to be a long, pointless process with each question put in Arabic and then translated into English by Hassan and my answers in English then translated back into Arabic. After two hours of this the major indicated that he had finished questioning me until Saturday. As this was only Wednesday, I wondered how I was going to survive in my noisome cell until then. Roger intervened to ask if he could visit me on Thursday and Friday and the major said, 'Yes, but we must now go and see the general.'

Accompanied by two guards, we walked down to the next floor where the major first knocked on an office door and then went in. The rest of us waited outside for at least five minutes before the major reappeared and called us in. The general was sitting with his feet up on his desk engaged in the number one Saudi sport of picking his nose. Two other officers were also in the room, all three wearing red collar tabs indicating that they were staff officers. The major having saluted smartly left with my guards. The general invited us to sit down so Roger, Hassan and I sank into the inevitable leather settee. 'What was the problem?' inquired the general.

Roger explained that I suffered from very severe headaches due to the fact that I had a plastic plate in the top of my head. Twenty years earlier, a fifteen-pound weight had fallen sixty-five feet and crushed the top of my skull. The top of my head is now covered by a plastic plate some five by three inches. The company doctor had written a letter in Arabic to accompany the tablets and Roger handed this over along with the bottle. The general spoke to his two officers and showed them the letter and the tablets but I heard the word hashish mentioned and wondered why in hell they were talking about hashish as the bottle only contained paracetamol.

'I am sorry,' said the general, 'he cannot have these. He uses hashish. Some was found in his bar.' I suddenly regretted my earlier remark to the major. As flippancy was obviously unwise with a general who could have me shot, I launched into a serious explanation of the way in which I used Irish Moss.

The general seemed puzzled and turned to the other officers. One of them nodded and the general said, 'All right. You may have them. Now go.' I thanked him and left, wondering what the other officer knew about moss; did he brew beer himself, I wondered?

Even so the guard on the prison door insisted on trying to take away my bottle of tablets despite a warning from my escort that I was allowed to have it. There was some argument before the man gave way and in exasperation he shoved me towards my cell and then, when the door to this had been unlocked, tried to push me in. I put up my fists and shouted, 'Try that again!' he jumped back like an electrified rabbit before turning to my escorts and appealing for help. They, however, merely shook their heads and walked away.

That afternoon I was again called from my cell and told I was being taken back to Humming Bird House. I was very glad of this because I hadn't passed water since the previous day during my last visit there. As usual I was handcuffed but when I got into the police car I found that the cuff on my right wrist had somehow come undone. My instinct was to say nothing and keep my hands out of sight until I got a chance to escape. Once on the loose, I thought, I could keep the cuffs out of sight by keeping my hands in my pockets. Then I remembered an old Saudi custom; if a man escapes from prison, they arrest a member of his family or a close friend instead. The chances were that they would pick up Tom or other colleagues of mine and jail them in my place. So I informed the guard that the cuff was loose and he tried to fix it. The thing wouldn't lock properly, however, because my wrist was too large. So he alerted the other escorts and when I got out of the car at Humming Bird House, it was with the muzzles of several revolvers pointing at me. I went quietly and gave no trouble. Soon I was back in the bar again, cheerily chatting to Harry Hall and drinking the inevitable cup of tea which he had ready for me.

'Somehow, I don't think I'll be back here after tomorrow,' I said. 'I don't think so either,' agreed Harry. 'We've been told that house arrest will end tomorrow but that none of us is to leave the country.'

I had my piss (very important), and then my tea (and another piss) and then I asked the sergeant if I could walk out on the roof. He said yes, so I stretched my legs for a while in the company of Harry and one of my escorts. We were still lounging about near the stair-landing when Mike, our catering supervisor, came up and said he had a car outside.

'If you want to make a break for it, I promise I'll get you to Dammam and then out of the country,' he said. Dammam is a Gulf port.

'Thanks, Mike,' I said, 'but there's no point trying it – they'd only arrest others instead. I'm grateful for the offer though.'

'Remember, if there's anything I can do to help . . .' said Mike.

While we were talking I saw the guards coming out of the club and decided to give them trouble. I knew they were without a key to my handcuffs so I chained myself to the rail.

'We go now,' said the sergeant when he reached me.

'Sorry, mate,' I told him, 'I'm afraid I've handcuffed myself accidentally.' He looked at the cuff, which I had locked to the rail and then he exploded. He shouted that my behaviour was disgraceful but I pointed out that the whole thing was an accident which could happen to anyone. In the end he was forced to order one of his men to take a taxi and return to the station to pick up the key. Mike kindly brought up a chair for me and I sat down with some of my colleagues and had a chat. A few were still so afraid of becoming involved that they refused to talk to me. Harry Hall, however, had no qualms; friendship, so far as he was concerned, was all that mattered – and I shall never forget him for it. I sat there for an hour, which meant one hour less in the hellhole. Finally, the policeman returned with the key and I was unhooked.

Next day, on the Thursday, I was again called from my cell. This time it was around two o'clock in the afternoon when I was led up to the second floor and taken into a room opposite the general's office. A colonel dressed in full Arab robes was sitting at a desk and opposite him, Roger Lilly and Tom. I am far from being a sentimental man but Tom and I were so overcome with emotion that we were in danger of shedding tears. We quickly managed to regain our composure and the colonel asked me if I wanted tea. I said I did, so the colonel sent for tea which, when it came, was placed on a coffee table. Tom sat down beside me and he and I had tea. Roger, meantime, had continued to sit opposite the colonel and now he leaned forward and attempted to say something. The colonel brusquely interrupted him and, holding up his hand for silence, smiled and then said confidentially, 'You know, I like to drink a little myself sometimes.' Favouring us with a sly look, he added, 'Thank goodness, though, I never got caught.'

Roger laughed nervously but refused to comment. 'The situation is,' continued the colonel affably, 'that Mr Fraser's case is not too bad, not too serious. Provided the money is paid, he will be set free.' He then leaned back and beamed at us.

This was the first time that any of us had been given an inkling that a fine might set me free, although we had always anticipated that it might be an option.

'The company will be happy to pay a fine,' said Roger.

'It is not a question of a fine,' explained the colonel. 'It is simply a question of paying the money.'

Tom, who had been listening attentively broke in to urge, 'Pay the money, Roger!'

Roger's response was to ask the colonel, 'How much, Colonel?'

'Fifty thousand riyals,' the colonel replied (about £7,000).

'I'm not sure about that. I shall have to call the boss,' explained Roger. And I'm afraid he's in England at the moment.'

The colonel's mood changed immediately. He looked at me and said curtly *'callas'* which means 'finished'. I finished my tea and the guards came to lead me back to my cell. Had Roger let a golden opportunity slip?

Tom and Roger, the latter now somewhat abashed, returned next day but this time the meeting was held in the major's office and there was no mention of tea. Tom told me he was sure the Saudis intended to put me in prison and that there was nothing for it but to escape. He said he would help arrange this from the outside. I agreed, that if I were sent to jail and was not released at the latest by 1 November (the day on which one of my nieces was due to get married in England), then I would attempt an escape. However, I felt certain the company would have me released very shortly.

Tom asked the major if he would be allowed to give me some

clothing and a mattress and blanket as well as photographs of my family.

'He can have all those things you mention – except the photos,' replied the major. This was an extraordinarily mean decision I thought, but I didn't bother to argue. At that stage, a mattress was more important to me even than photographs of my children.

We said good-bye and I was taken back to the cell where I lay down thankfully on my mattress. I didn't really need the blanket at that moment for the heat in the cell was such that sweat was running off me so I gave it to Abdul to lie down on. I remained in my cell until ten o'clock on Saturday morning when I was taken up again to the major's office where Roger and Hassan were waiting for the questioning to resume. The cross-examination turned out to be the same old rigmarole as before and I gave the same answers as before. At the end of it Roger asked when I would be moved to a more comfortable place.

'I'm concerned with Mr Fraser's health,' he said. 'He's been in jail now for six days and he hasn't eaten anything during that time. If conditions were better he might perhaps be able to eat the food, once he had got used to it.' I wanted to tell Roger that I'd rather die than eat such filthy food but, on the chance of going to a better jail, I agreed, 'that is so'. The major answered that I would be moved 'soon' and that ended the interview. Back in my cell, I discovered I needed to piss. When I had finished, I moistened my towel under the tap and wiped it over my body; even so when I had finished I still felt that a film of dirt was covering me. This turned out to be my first and only wash in that ghastly cell.

FIVE

The 'interrogation' continued again on Sunday. On Monday, however, the major handed a long statement to Hassan and asked if he agreed with what had been written. Hassan glanced at the statement and then said to me, 'It's only the questions and answers. However, there are more than thirty pages altogether, so I won't read it all. Is that all right?'

I nodded and the major then said I was to sign the statement.

'So be it,' I said and signed my name but I also added, in English, 'I don't read Arabic, so I don't know what I have signed.' The major made no comment but simply handed the statement to Roger and Hassan and asked them to sign as witnesses. When this had been done, the major said I would be taken to see the Sheikh that day. Roger and I both felt good about this, for we imagined that this meant that something would be decided one way or the other.

I was handcuffed again in the chain room and told that a Yemeni prisoner would be accompanying me and that there would be one guard to escort us.

I expected that we would be taken to see the Sheikh in a police car. When we walked outside the station, however, the guard said we were to travel in Roger's car.

'That's a bloody cheek!' I said to Roger. 'But let's not upset him – or at least not just yet. If the court orders me to prison, then we can tell this bloke to fuck off and walk back home.'

'Let's not upset him,' pleaded Roger.

'Don't be daft, Roger!' I assured him. 'I was only kidding.'

The Sheikh's office stood at the back of the Governor's palace, not much more than a hundred yards from the police station.

During this short journey, however, my right handcuff came off again but the guard didn't seem worried about it, so I stuck my hand in my shirt to hide the loose cuff and in this manner we all walked into court. The guard treated the Yemeni pretty roughly but left me alone so that my mood was bright and cheerful when we entered the place. I was sure I would be found guilty all right but I felt confident that instead of being sentenced to prison, I would be deported.

The Sheikh's office was housed in a dirty, two-storeyed building and approached by a set of narrow, filthy stairs which led to a long corridor where a crowd of prisoners sat on the floor all chained together. We followed the guard into a roomy office where there were three desks next to each other and a Saudi seated at each. Our guard approached the first one and handed him a file. The fellow had a quick look at it and then, in Arabic, asked me my name. I answered him and he then passed the file to the next Saudi who again asked me my name and where I came from; I answered again. The file was then given to the next Saudi who asked me my name, where I came from and whether it was whisky. I said 'Yes' to all the questions and the Saudi then asked me to sign my name in a book on his desk. I duly signed my name and the guard put his thumbprint on the page as a witness.

'It's over now,' the Saudi said.

'What's over?' I asked.

'Your trial is over,' he explained patiently. 'Your sentence will come later.'

I looked at Roger who, with Hassan, had come along. He said, 'There must be some mistake, surely.' But there was none.

We were driven back to the police station where both Roger and I asked to see the major immediately. 'What's going on?' demanded Roger as soon as we were admitted.

'The prisoner has confessed to having a still and he will now be sent to Malaz General Prison until he is sentenced,' said the major. 'I have recommended that his sentence be a heavy one.'

'Shit!' I yelled at him. 'I haven't confessed to anything – and certainly not to having a still. I've never had a still. And both Mr Lilly and Hassan have been present at all our interviews. They will confirm that I never admitted having a still.'

'For God's sake, don't worry, Ian,' Roger interrupted, 'I'm

going straight to see the British consul and I'll get him to sort this thing out.'

As I was led downstairs I could hear the major's laughter ringing in my ears.

At 11.30 a.m. on Tuesday I was told to take my mattress and clothes upstairs to the chain room as I was being taken to Malaz General Prison. Three other prisoners were going with me, all Saudis (but as the Arabian media insist that the only criminals in Saudi Arabia are westerners, then this must have been a mistake, mustn't it?). We were handcuffed in pairs and led down to an open pick-up truck. I didn't fancy being driven through the streets like a chained animal and thought of kicking up a fuss but then decided that a ride was better than remaining in jail.

Malaz prison was situated near Humming Bird House, in what we expats like to call Pepsi-Cola Street because the soft-drinks company has a plant there. As we neared the prison I recalled once telling my wife Anne that we lived just down the road from the prison – I never imagined that one day I would find myself inside it.

The road leading to the prison comes to a dead end with the prison itself squatting at the top. A police barracks, manned by 500 policemen, stands opposite it. The dirty brown walls of the prison are twenty feet high and there is a guard tower at each corner with armed guards.

We halted outside the main gate and were told by a guard that it was forbidden to drive inside. So we got down and walked through a small gate which I later found was the visitors' gate. Further on I struggled through a small turnstile, carrying my holdall and my mattress in my left hand – my right hand of course was handcuffed to another prisoner's. We finally reached a courtyard where 60 guards were doing 'bums up' – *salha*. We paid no attention to them, but crossed the courtyard to a double set of steel-barred gates, manned by a guard with a machine gun. When our guards and this fellow had finished kissing each other, we were allowed inside.

Once inside the prison proper we were searched. One guard tried to take away my headache tablets but I grabbed them back. A guard with a machine gun rushed over and stuck the muzzle into my stomach.

'Bastard!' I yelled at him. Perhaps I might have been shot but abruptly a voice speaking English demanded to know what the trouble was. Still with my eyes on the guard, I yelled, 'If he does that again, I'll stick that gun down his throat!'

There was a muttered order in Arabic and the guard walked away. I turned and saw a small man dressed in western trousers and a natty shirt who introduced himself as 'Joseph' and said he was my interpreter. In the meantime, I must sit on the ground, he said. I decided there was no point in causing trouble at this stage, so I took his advice and squatted down where I studied my surroundings.

Malaz prison can best be described by referring to a spider. I was sitting in the centre of the prison, that is in the centre of the spider's body. There were six prison blocks running off this body – the legs of the spider. Spaced round the body itself were four columns, each about eighteen inches in diameter and it was these which immediately attracted my attention. One prisoner was standing against a column with his arms handcuffed around it. At a second column, another prisoner sat on the ground, his feet handcuffed to the column. At the third column a man had been stretched out on the ground face downwards with his arms pinioned above his head to the column. Even as I watched I saw a guard select a cane and start thrashing the last fellow on the backside. It looked a painful ordeal but bearable. I had been told that a guard must hold a copy of the Qur'an under the arm with which he hands out punishment but somebody must have forgotten to tell this guy for I could not see one.

I was eventually called into the office where I was due for a surprise.

'The prison does not want you,' announced Joseph. 'You must go back to the police station.' I didn't know what to make of such nonsense but replied 'Well, that's OK by me.'

It was not, apparently, OK by my police guards. They resolutely refused to return me. The impasse was ended only when a lieutenant came in and said, 'You will try again tomorrow – when there are other guards on duty.' By now I was certain all Saudi policemen, all Saudi court officials and all Saudi guards were not right in the head.

The situation grew even more farcical. Once again I was handcuffed and told to march out of the prison. I did this with my two police guards sauntering behind me. When we arrived outside the prison, I saw that the pick-up which had brought us had vanished. I looked up and down the street, wondering what these guys were going to do now when one of them asked, 'You got money?'

'I have,' I told them. 'Though not much.'

'Right, then. We'll get a taxi – you pay.'

I looked at them astonished. 'You know what you can do, chums,' I said and sat down on my mattress in the roadway.

'No, no,' insisted one of the guards, 'You walk to Pepsi-Cola Street and get taxi.'

'Look, you buggers – if you want a taxi, fetch it yourself and bring it here. And *you* pay for it, not me. Understand?'

They gaped at me; no one, it seems, had ever treated them this way before. I got up from my mattress and walked for about 50 yards from the prison gate, the guards making no attempt to interfere with me. I bought myself a Pepsi and then walked back and sat down on my mattress again. In the end one of the guards went off to search for a taxi and in due course we all ended up back in the major's office. The major could not have been more surprised if Mrs Thatcher herself had walked in. He questioned the guards fiercely, then turned and gave me a little lecture.

'You will return to the prison tomorrow, is that clear? In the meantime, you will pay for the taxi.'

By now I had decided that the best tactics I could use with these malign idiots was to swear at them as much as possible. Each time I did it, I realised, I dented their personal pride.

'Have you finished then?' I asked the major and when he nodded I added, 'In that case fuck off!' And I turned and walked out of the room and went down the stairs to my cell. I was welcomed warmly by my old mates but was told by Abdul that he had heard that the major was 'very angry' with me. I told Abdul the major hadn't seen me angry yet.

I was allowed to rest in my cell all that night but next morning, Wednesday, I was taken up into the chain room at about 11.30 and told I was being sent back to Malaz. I said that that was all right by me but when we got outside the station and I saw the same pick-up that had taken me to prison the day before, I decided it was time to get stroppy again. I pointed to the pick-up.

'I'm not going in that,' I announced. 'I want to go in a car.'

Consternation!

A sergeant came out to argue with me but I answered him in

the same way. Then the major came on the scene and I told him the same thing. Face purple, he shouted at me and I felt sure he was swearing in Arabic. However, I just laughed and told him he was funny when he got angry. He calmed down instantly and turning on his heel shouted, 'Put him in a car!'

I was led to the nearest patrol car where, once again, I was treated to a sample of Saudi pantomime. The driver was sitting slumped fast asleep over his wheel and when awakened, showed his resentment by saying he would not take me. He stood his ground stubbornly, refusing to move and determined to get in more kip until a sergeant came over and shouted at him. After some moments of uproar, the driver complied and so I arrived at Malaz in relative comfort certainly when compared with my trip a day earlier.

Back in Malaz once more, I met with the same reluctance on the part of the guards to allow me to have my tablets as on my first visit. This time, however, I was ready for them and produced a letter from my company doctor. The guard called over an officer who read it and then said, 'You must see the doctor.' He took me across to a window to the doctor's office and both tablets and letter were passed through. We waited for several minutes before the letter and tablets were handed back and I was told I could keep them.

Joseph, my interpreter, reappeared again and explained that I was to go into *Seep* (block) Two, and when I got there, go to room seven. 'Great,' I thought to myself, 'this is better than that blasted police station!' My handcuffs were taken off and I walked jauntily enough to one of the wire cages which enclose the entrances to the *seeps*. A guard shouted for the door to be opened and I stepped – or, to be more accurate – pushed my way into the cage and then carried on into the block. Frankly I had never seen such a sight outside a football ground. Once inside the *seep*, I faced a long, corridor-like enclosed area, about 160 feet long by 14 feet wide, filled with a mass of milling human flesh. Later I learned that there were 450 prisoners crowded into this ghastly place. Along the left-hand side ran seven cells, at the far end of which were four water taps let into the wall and four noisome holes in the floor: the washing and toilet facilities. Along the right-hand side were eight cells and at the far end of the building, up against the wall, lay a pile of mattresses. When I examined these later, I found them to be pieces of foam-rubber about six feet by two and about one and a half inches thick – hardly enough for a comfortable bed, but better than sleeping on the floor.

There were no windows in this extraordinary place – just ten bare electric light bulbs suspended from the ceiling which was about fifteen feet high. My real interest, however, was in the human activity; the hall was more like a *souk* (bazaar or market) than the interior of a prison. Down both sides of the central area Arabs were selling tea, notepaper, Pepsi, clothes and watches. Later I noticed white lines painted on the dark-brown walls and learned that these indicated the spaces which had been allocated to prisoners as sleeping areas. By day, however, prisoners were permitted to 'sell' these spaces to traders.

Room seven was about fifteen by six foot in size and when I arrived it already had three other European occupants – Peter, a Dane, Horst, a German and Pierre, a Frenchman. Peter spoke fluent English but the other two knew hardly any. Peter welcomed me – with a certain touch of irony, of course – and told me to sit on the floor. There were two mattresses lying there but Peter said that they belonged to Saudis and I must not use them. There was a large fridge in the room and Peter asked me if I wanted anything to eat. I told him I wasn't hungry (I had now eaten nothing for ten days).

Peter explained that I was at liberty to use the room until 7 p.m. After that, four Arabs, along with Horst and Pierre, occupied the cell and slept in it. At 7 p.m., I could go along to the end of the central area where there was a 26-inch colour TV which I could watch until midnight on weekdays and until 2 to 2.30 a.m. at Saudi weekends. I should then see the *seep* foreman, a Saudi, who would find me a place to sleep. Peter informed me that he had been imprisoned for being drunk in the street, that Pierre was serving a one-year sentence (he didn't tell me what for) and that Horst had already spent sixteen months in jail for his part in robbing his company of £1 million.

An hour later and while I was still trying to adjust to my new situation, three more Europeans arrived in the cell: two were English, the third German. They had been in a car accident and after blood tests had shown they had a small amount of alcohol in their bloodstreams they now awaited deportation.

For a while we chatted together and the newcomers explained that what they needed most was a change of clothing. Peter said that anything they wanted could be supplied by the traders. A little later a trader entered the cell carrying an assortment of western underwear, socks, towels and pyjamas (which Arabs use as their working clothes) and the newcomers made some purchases. Peter then took us up to show us the four holes and the water taps and to explain how they were used. There was a mat curtain which you could pull in front of you whenever you wanted to use a hole, giving some degree of privacy. You were not, however, to use a hole less than one hour before *salha*. If and when you did use it, you had to slip on plastic sandals which were provided, because of the filth surrounding the holes. He also told me to remember that there were 450 prisoners in the block so I had to be prepared to wait for up to an hour before being able to use the toilet facilities. When he had finished, I realised that at some stage I would have to use one of these awful holes and as we were now just at the beginning of summer, with the heat bound to increase, I had better wash myself as soon as possible. I decided to wait until the middle of the night and wash when things had quietened down.

In the meantime, I thought I would control my intake of tea. Peter said the prison only served chicken and rice and that my friends on the outside would be expected to provide me with other food. As he was talking, an Arab entered the room and said, 'Fraser, visitor.' Peter instructed me to walk up to the cage at the entrance and tell the guard I had a visitor. When I arrived there, however, I saw no guard, so I walked straight on into the cage, crossed to the other side where there was an outer door and shouted to the guard in the compound who eventually came over and opened it. As I entered the big central hall of the prison (the body of the spider), two men emerged from the cage leading to *Seep* Three. When they saw me, they came towards me and one introduced himself as 'Arthur Auger' adding, 'You must be Fraser. We have been expecting you.' He then introduced his friend, 'This is cunt.' I looked at him, baffled. 'His name is Claud,' explained Arthur, 'but I call him cunt because that's what he is.' I recognised the two men as former BAC employees who had been arrested in September 1979 for running one of the biggest automatic stills ever found in Riyadh.

'Who's our visitor?' I asked Augur.

'The British consul,' he replied.

We were led across the central hall and into an office where a prison captain (all Saudi military, police and prison officers wear the same khaki uniforms and are distinguishable only by small badges or flashes) waited along with the British vice-consul. The latter greeted us solicitously and we were invited to sit down in leather armchairs. Auger started off by demanding, 'What's happened to our pardon – it was supposed to come through before all this fuss about *Death of a Princess?*'

'I'm sorry,' explained the consul, 'but I can find no trace of any pardon for you. All I can tell you is that Prince Niaf, the Minister of the Interior, has told me that you have been sentenced to three years' imprisonment and three hundred lashes. However, I'll try to find out more about any possible pardon.' The consul then turned to me and asked if I were all right.

'I'm terrible,' I told him. 'What I want to know is if you can get some improvement in my conditions? Also will the British Government, knowing all the facts about my case, be able to help my company get me released?'

'I'm sorry,' said the vice-consul, 'but the embassy is not able to do very much at the moment. The Saudis are in a touchy mood because of that film.'

'Why? It was all true, wasn't it?' I said. The vice-consul shrugged non-committally. 'Anyway, that's no excuse for them to treat me like an animal,' I continued. 'Are you going to help?'

'I'll do what I can, of course. Someone from the embassy will visit you once a month to see that you're hale and hearty and I'll also see that your family is kept informed.'

'Look, I don't want you or anybody else to bother my family – or bother me, if that's all you can do. In fact, I don't want to see you any more.'

Arthur interrupted: 'Surely Ian's case is different from ours? You must get him out.'

'It's not as simple as that,' explained the vice-consul. He then told us that he would not be coming back again personally as a new consul had been appointed because of an increase in the number of British prisoners in the city.

The interview ended and we were led back to our *seeps*. Before we split up, however, Auger said he would get my name 'shouted out' tomorrow and then we could get together for 'a good talk'. I didn't understand what he meant, but nodded agreement anyway.

Back in cell seven, I explained to Peter and the others that my visitor had been the British vice-consul. Horst, who up to this stage had not said a single word to me, now said, 'Shit consul!' I looked at Peter in surprise and he told me something more about Horst. Apparently he and his two mates had been given sentences of five years following their robbery and had also been sentenced to have their right hands chopped off. For thirteen months the three of them had been incarcerated in 'murderers' room' among prisoners, everyone of whom was a convicted killer. During this period, they were allowed out of the room on only three occasions, each time to see the German consul. They had not been allowed to write or receive letters, to smoke or have any reading material and, as the ultimate punishment, had been forced to pray as Muslims five times a day.

In protest, the three men had staged a nine-day hunger strike which had, at least, got them out of 'murderers' room.' At the same time, the German Government had brought pressure on the Saudis over the hand-chopping sentence. The Germans insisted that if the punishment was proceeded with then all three men, along with their chopped-off hands, were to be rushed to the international airport where the German authorities would have a plane waiting, with three medical teams aboard, ready to sew the hands back on. In face of such German determination the Saudis had given in and remitted the hand-chopping sentence. 'But they put these men through thirteen months of intolerable mental torture,' said Peter. 'They do, of course, deserve prison. They did steal one million pounds, the biggest theft ever known here – that is, if you don't count the amounts stolen by the Saudi Royal family and their sidekicks. But they didn't deserve that.' Horst and his chums, it seemed, were now awaiting new sentences. I thought I now understood why Horst looked so quiet and grey – and I imagined *I* had been having a rough time!

Two Saudis entered the room and asked us to leave. It turned out that they owned the mattresses and by day ran the main shop in the prison. Five of us Europeans, therefore, picked up our belongings and like a herd of lost sheep staggered out of the door and into the maelstrom that was the central hall of the *seep*. The noise was ear-splitting. The TV set was going full-blast. Then there was the noise made by 350 Arabs – and Arabs never speak, they shout. Peter advised us to go to the other end of the *seep*, away from the TV set and find a place to sit in the cage near the exit. Two Egyptians there, he said, would find a place for us to sit until TV was finished.

The Egyptians introduced themselves as Farouk and Hassan and both spoke excellent English. They made us very welcome and Hassan even bought us tea from a trader. After a while he got up and went to the side of the cage and spoke to a prisoner outside. When he came back he told us how the system worked. Six Saudi prisoners were permitted to stay in the central hall of the prison in order to carry out errands for the prisoners jailed in the blocks. You told a man what you wanted, pushed your money under the wire (there was a three-inch gap) and he brought you back cigarettes, chocolate bars, cheese, or even Pepsi in a plastic bag. If you could eat Arab food, he would also purchase whatever you wanted. For these services, he took 10 per cent commission – but out of this he had to pay the prison guards 2 per cent. The prison shop itself in turn paid the Governor a commission on everything it sold. All in all, it seemed, that for some Saudis, a prison spell was a godsend as they could end up making a lot of money.

Farouk asked me why I was in prison and I told him about the whisky. Then I enquired about my sentence – when was I likely to hear about it? He said it would take six to eight weeks.

'As long as that?' I asked, suddenly depressed.

'Yes. As to the sentence itself – well, if you had much whisky, you will get three years. That is the sentence all British and Americans are getting at the moment.'

'What about an appeal?' I asked.

'I would not advise an appeal. In all cases I've heard about, when anybody appeals he has his sentence doubled. But these people were Arabs and it may be different for you, you are British.'

'How would I appeal?'

'Don't sign for your sentence.'

'Sorry, I don't understand.'

'Well, when the Sheikh gives you your sentence, he will ask you to sign a book accepting it. If you refuse, then that is your appeal started. He will then ask you three times to sign and if you still refuse, he may grant you your appeal. He also has the right to say no, however. But I warn you – as I said before, if he grants you the appeal, it might lead to a doubling of your sentence.'

I gave thought to this point but the more I considered it, the more it seemed to me that I had nothing much to lose. I had made up my mind that I was not going to spend three years in a Saudi prison. If I won my appeal and was set free, well and good. If not, it made little difference whether my sentence was three years or six – I would break out. Indeed, even as Farouk was talking to me, I had begun weighing up my chances of getting out of Malaz. I had to admit that they scarcely looked good. Each cell had only one tiny window and even that was heavily barred. If I did manage to get through a window, then there was a considerable drop to the ground outside where it would be easy enough to break a leg (or even a neck). Perhaps the greatest difficulty of all was that I was surrounded by Arabs every minute of the day – and if anyone saw me trying to escape, they'd probably shout the house down. I decided to have a long talk with Arthur and Claud and see if they had worked out any good ideas.

I spent the rest of that evening in the cage meditating quietly on my problems and talking in a desultory fashion to Farouk and Hassan. When TV had finished, Peter fetched the *seep* foreman and Farouk explained that sleeping space had to be found for four newcomers. The foreman said that the only space available was in the centre of the floor as the sides of the hall were already occupied with other prisoners who were sleeping toe to toe. In the end I was given a 'lucky' space – next to Farouk and Hassan. Hassan gave me a blanket to sleep on as there was not enough room for me to lay down my mattress. I then stretched out with other people's feet pressed up against both sides of my body. All through the night there was constant traffic up and down the block which made my position extremely uncomfortable. That discomfort grew almost intolerable when I suddenly realised I needed to use the hole but all I did was to lie there and pray that the need would soon wear off.

Waiting for things to quieten down so that I could bear using the hole, I noticed an Arab praying.

'Why is he praying?' I asked Hassan. 'Has he missed his prayers earlier or what?'

'No. He is praying as a punishment. He does this every night after TV is finished and he goes on praying until five o'clock in the morning. But don't worry about him – he's crazy. He only says his prayers in the hope that Allah will forgive him.'

SIX

That first night in Malaz prison turned out to be a nightmare. It was almost impossible to sleep, due to the constant passage of people to and from the toilets. As people tried to step over me, they even stood on my feet or planted themselves on my body. I lay awake until about 2.30 a.m. and then decided to try the toilets. I took a small plastic cup along with me which I filled at the first tap I came to and I then gave myself a cup shower – the first wash I had had since my arrest. Then I finally used one of those awful holes in the floor!

I had hardly laid my head down again before it was 4 a.m. and I was awakened by loud calls for *salha*. I did not have to get up as the prayers were being said in the other half of the hall, but as there was a constant flow of prisoners past me and I was in some danger of being trampled to death, I sat up until they had finished and everybody had settled down again. Then at 8 a.m. we were all awakened again by names being called out over the tannoy system.

I got up wearily, then noticed that most of the Arabs were already fully dressed. I asked Hassan why this was so and he told me, 'This is women's day. You will be called out – all westerners are called out.'

'Not me, mate,' I told him, 'I've got no woman to visit me.'

My name, however, was duly called and feeling curious, I went along to the cage and told the guard that my name had been called out. He indicated a line of prisoners who were filing out through another door and told me to follow them. I joined the line and found myself in a large yard between Blocks Two and Three which was already filled with black-clothed women and their menfolk. The women, however, were sitting apart in small groups while their husbands or male relatives sat together separately, some distance away from them. This seemed to me to be the daftest way of having a visit from your wife ever invented as it ended up with all the men kissing each other instead of kissing their women.

In the middle of the yard I spotted some western men and women standing together so I walked over to a guard nearest to them and, giving him my name, explained that I had been called out. I heard a female voice call out, 'Hello Ian – I'm Joan. Come and join the gang.' I glanced across and saw a pleasant-looking woman waving to me, so I joined her.

'I'm sorry you weren't called out sooner, Ian,' apologised Joan, 'but some of the other ladies were late turning up and as I had already called out four of you, I couldn't call out any more – the guards get a bit uptight if one woman calls too many.' I said that was all right – I had just wakened anyway.

I spotted Arthur and Claud and they waved to me so I went over and they introduced me to some more of the women and some other western prisoners. One of the prisoners was a giant six-foot-six American called Bill Shunk who wrote down my name and other particulars in a notebook. Some of us then sat down on Pepsi boxes and chatted. I learned that the women, who had brought us newspapers and flasks of coffee as well as bags of food, were members of a Christian friendship group who visited western prisoners every Thursday. They seemed to be a remarkable bunch of women – British, American, German, Italian and Portugese ladies who moved around from one prison to another to bring warmth and comfort into the lives of men unfortunate enough to find themselves in my predicament. To me they seemed real angels of charity because they had not only to arrange their own transport (women are not allowed to drive in Saudi Arabia) but had to purchase most of what they brought along to us with their own money.

The visit proved a real treat so far as I was concerned; almost like having a picnic and made all the more enjoyable because of the conditions we were in. Just being outside and not jammed in that sardine-like crush inside the *seep* was worth a great deal. Time passed quickly, however, and soon it was noon and the Saudis began calling prayers. Bill explained to me, 'When they finish prayers, the visit finishes.' He added that many more women used to visit the western prisoners but for some reason the number had been declining recently and rumour had it that soon only wives would be permitted.

'Let's hope it is only a rumour,' I said, for apart from anything else I had already thought of a way of getting out of prison which involved dressing up as a woman. With my face, of course, I could hardly get away with pretending to be a western woman, but I could probably smuggle myself out as a Muslim woman for they kept their faces covered. I was still mulling over ways to get hold of the robes of an Arab woman when prayers ended and we were ordered to return to our blocks. We said goodbye to our visitors who promised to return the following week. I sauntered back with Arthur who told me that Peter had got my share of the food brought by the visitors and so I would be OK for something to eat but that I ought to try and find some means of getting into his block so that we could talk. I promised him that I would try, although I couldn't think immediately of any way of doing so.

Back in the cell we all felt a bit depressed, a reaction, I suppose, to the pleasure of the visit. Peter and Horst, however, busied themselves emptying the bags of food brought by the visitors into the fridge. Then Peter said, 'Look, as there are now four more of us than last week, we've no choice but to eat some of the prison food too.' Not me, mate, I thought, I'm not going to eat any of that junk. Besides, I wasn't hungry. So I said, 'Listen, I don't need a share of your food. But please don't take offence, for none is intended.' Peter looked at me doubtfully but did not argue and I was sure he understood. Later I found out that he himself had not eaten any of the 'welfare ladies'' food until he had been in a position to contribute his share – so he obviously knew how I felt.

I was awakened again at 4 a.m. for *salha* and to the abysmal realisation that this was a Friday and therefore the big day for Muslim prayers. I knew also that the whole palaver would be repeated again at 10 a.m. and would last until twelve noon. At ten o'clock I saw a distinguished-looking Arab with a white beard approaching down the block, followed by the block foreman and several other prisoners. The man was wearing a rather special-looking brown cape with gold interwoven at the edges. I stared at him curiously as he came up to me. He looked down at me and asked, 'Are you English?'

'No,' I replied shortly, 'Scottish.'

'Why are you here?' he demanded.

'It's none of your business mate – but it's whisky,' I told him.

'You are a bad man,' he accused me. 'You corrupt Arab youth.'

When I heard him taking this tack, I knew that our conversation was over. 'Fuck off, mate,' I said.

I have rarely seen a man look more surprised or insulted. As for his followers, there was complete consternation among them. Peter hurriedly intervened to say that I had better get into the cell – 'Prayers are starting now,' he said, 'and this is a big session – going on for two hours.' So I got up and went along with him and we walked into the cell which had just been vacated by the four Arabs who had squatting rights there.

'Who was that geezer?' I asked Peter.

He told me the man was a *matela* who had killed somebody and who, as a result, was now serving a sentence of eleven years. He lived in a little hut in the front courtyard and was only asked to mix with the other prisoners when he led them in Friday prayers.

'My God, you mean that that was a killer telling me I'm a bad man,' I said. 'That's like a bank robber telling a speeding driver he's a criminal!' This made me feel a whole lot better that I had told the fellow to fuck off. I felt even better when the bloke began on his sermon. The service came over the public address system and what with the noise, the praying and wailing it all sounded quite awful to western ears. When the man began on his sermon I had no difficulty recognising its theme – whisky. Listening incredulously I heard him say whisky was bad. And so, too, were westerners. And the worst of all westerners were Scotlanders. 'Be on your guard against them all times; they are here to corrupt Arab people and to destroy the Muslim faith, to destroy all true believers.'

I am not what you would describe as a true believer – certainly I do not subscribe to any organised faith. But the idea of a killer preaching this load of rubbish struck me as blasphemous.

'If that's Muslim thinking,' I growled to Peter, 'then it'll be a long time before he catches me bowing to Mecca.'

I survived Friday somehow or other and was surprised when, at eleven o'clock on Saturday morning, my name was called and

I was told I had a visitor. Going to the office where I had been interviewed by the vice-consul, I found our boss, Ian Wylie, who had just returned from England, accompanied by Roger Lilly.

'Are you OK?' asked Ian, at once concerned with my well-being.

'I'm all right, thanks, Ian. But I do need some decent food – can you arrange for some to be sent in?'

'I'll see to that, of course. But what about Anne? She hasn't heard from you for several days now and she's bound to be worrying. Shall I telephone her and tell her what's happened but not to worry?'

'OK. I suppose it's time she was told. But tell her that under no circumstances must she worry. Tell her the company is doing all it can to get me out.' Then I asked, 'But what about getting me out, Ian? What's happening?'

'There's no need to worry, Ian, I think I can guarantee that you won't be here for long. We know too many people and we have a lot of influence. I'm seeing the deputy Governor of Riyadh tonight.'

'That's great.

'Don't worry anyhow, Ian,' said the boss. 'We'll get you out all right.'

'One other thing,' I interrupted, 'if I'm still here on pay day, will my wife get my pay all right?'

'Of course, absolutely. I'll guarantee that. The company will definitely see you all right.'

'That's a plus at any rate,' I told him. 'I wouldn't want to worry about my wife and children.'

'Well, don't,' Wylie assured me.

I told him about Thursday morning visits from the welfare ladies.

'Next Thursday both my wife and Roger's wife will come here and they'll bring you anything you want.'

'I need easy food,' I said. 'Anything pre-cooked would do. Also I want a cotton sheet to sleep on.'

'I'll see to that at once,' promised Ian. 'And, of course, Tom will be seeing you on Tuesday.'

I returned to my cell feeling slightly better and certain that between them Ian and the company would soon get me out. I was in the middle of telling Peter and the others this good news when further prayers were announced. At the same time the Saudi who ran the prison shop came in and asked us to vacate the cell as he wanted to pray. All five of us Europeans, therefore, walked out and went up to the sleeping spaces occupied by Hassan and Farouk where the latter again made room for us. We sat down and waited quietly, not even speaking, while the Arabs droned through their rituals which seemed interminable, at least to me. I was bored out of my mind and thought of this as an additional form of punishment. However, I felt it right that we should respect Muslim customs; and not because of any fear of retribution or anything like that.

When prayers had finished, I walked over to the *seep* foreman and told him I wanted to see the warden. Soon my name was called out and I was taken to see the warden, who held the rank of captain. I told him that I would like to be moved into *Seep* Three along with the other two Englishmen who were there.

'No,' he replied brusquely, offering no explanation of his refusal.

Once again I tried but all he would say was, 'No.' When I realised I was not getting anywhere, I simply boiled over.

'OK, Captain,' I said icily, 'you're a cunt.'

Immediate uproar.

Yelling blue murder, he called on the guards and ordered them to chain me to a pillar. I realised then that I was in trouble but, determined always to do the opposite of what the Saudis expected of me, I laughed. I was still laughing, indeed, when the guards took me outside and chained me up. And I kept on laughing until they had gone away. When they left I found that the handcuff on my left wrist had slipped off and I was free. But I had nowhere to go; if I tried returning to my *seep* without being ordered I might easily find myself in even more trouble. So I sat down quietly and lit a cigarette.

Some minutes later the captain, emerging from his office, saw me still sitting there. He yelled at once for the guards and bawled them out.

'Why isn't he chained to the pillar?' he demanded. The guards replied that they had chained me up so the captain ordered me to stand up and then personally handcuffed me to the pillar.

'Now,' he said, 'just try and get out of that!'

Even as he spoke, the handcuff came loose again. So I reached down, took a cigarette from my shirt pocket and putting it to my mouth, asked him coolly, 'Have you got a match?'

His face went a dark purple and for a moment I thought he was going to attack me. He thought better of it, however, and turning to a guard, said *'callas'*. My handcuffs were taken off and I was led back to the *seep*. The captain, of course, never twigged that the handcuffs were faulty and instead regarded me as a Houdini.

I was visited by Tom and Ian Wylie on the following Monday morning. We met again in the captain's office and I was delighted to see my younger brother once more. He had brought me a bag of food and a shaving kit but the captain refused to allow me the shaving things and on this occasion I didn't argue. Tom assured me that Ian was doing everything he could to get me out and the latter added that he was certain I would be freed within the next two weeks. He had telephoned Anne; everything was all right in that quarter and I was not to worry. Tom, too, said he was keeping Anne informed, but that I ought to write to her. If I wrote her a letter that day, he would pick it up when he came next day and make sure that it was posted.

'Don't worry, Ian,' said Wylie, just before they left. I'm right behind you one hundred per cent; all the way. We'll soon get you out.'

Next day I was sitting quietly minding my own business when the *seep* foreman came into the cell and told me that all westerners must leave because the Muslims wanted to say prayers. I was no longer in the mood to stand for such nonsense and told him straight, 'Look, I'm not going to be shunted about every time somebody wants to say prayers. All I ask is that you buggers leave me alone and don't bother me and I won't bother you. So, now, run away please, will you?'

'You must move,' yelled the foreman, furiously.

'Oh, fuck off!' I told him, losing patience.

He at once ran off to the cage and returned a few moments later with two guards. They told me that I must move, so I told them to fuck off also. There was a debate about my disobedience for a moment, then I was told that I must accompany them to see the captain and be punished.

'Good!' I said smartly, 'that suits me fine.' And I went with them.

That day, for reasons known only to himself, the warden had

decided that he was no longer speaking English and kept me waiting until Joseph, the interpreter, had been fetched.

'What is the trouble?' enquired Joseph when he arrived.

'Certain Saudis do not want us in the cell during the day because they want to pray,' I told him. 'But as there are Muslims praying the whole length of the block, where am I supposed to sit? Wherever I go, they are all around me.'

'All right,' interrupted the captain impatiently, 'so what does he want?' Obligingly Joseph 'translated' for me.

'Tell him I want to be put in the same block as the two Englishmen,' I replied.

To my astonishment, the captain agreed immediately and as I walked out of his office I realised I had the beating of them. All I had to do was act in unexpected ways and show that I was not afraid of the guards. I knew most Saudi guards rarely hesitated to beat-up or rough-handle any prisoners who did not stand up to them. Even westerners, when they refused to assert themselves, had been made to take part in Muslim prayers, for example.

I returned to my block to collect my belongings and to say good-bye to Peter and the others and was led off to *Seep* Three. I was delighted to find that Block Three was less crowded than Block Two. A German called Hans was sitting just inside the cage and directed me to cell six, which turned out to be a room about fifteen by nine. When I entered, Arthur, Claud and Bill, the big American, were squatting on the floor eating. They were surprised to see me and when I told them I was there to stay, asked how I had managed it. When I told them the story they roared with laughter. Arthur warned me to be careful, however; much more of that behaviour, he said, and I could find myself in the punishment block – hardly a suitable residence for a Scotsman.

Arthur wanted to know if I had heard anything more about my release. I said I thought that we British were being made an example of and the whole thing was all due to that blasted film, *Death of a Princess*.

'I still think you'll be released, all the same,' said Arthur. 'That raid was a mistake. There was no still – and the police know damn well that there was no still. They know where every bar in Riyadh is, and what's going on – so why pick on you?'

'I hope you're right,' I replied, 'but I'm not pinning any hopes on that thought. In all cases where westerners have been arrested for whisky offences, they've got at least a year's imprisonment – and sometimes five.'

'My advice to you is to press your company to pay you a large lump sum of money now,' suggested Arthur. 'Just in case somebody in London decided to stop paying you your salary after a month or so.'

'The company's not like that,' I told him. 'They won't let me down.' (Nor did they – Anne received my salary cheque once a month.)

We discussed the sleeping arrangements for that night and Arthur said I would have to sleep outside in the main hall, at least to start with.

'Not in the middle of the floor again,' I protested.

'It's not that bad – not as bad as what you've been used to,' replied Arthur. 'We're less crowded in this block. However, there are twenty-nine men sleeping in this room already and every bit of space, except for that taken up by the fridge, is occupied. During the day, of course,' he added, 'you are very welcome to stay in the cell itself and we are happy to have you as a member of the group.'

The routine in the cell, Arthur explained, was that he usually prepared the food while Bill and Claud did the washing-up – they had been given plastic plates and cutlery.

'You'll have to take your turn, of course,' said Arthur, 'but I hope you're not like that lazy cunt there.' And he nodded towards Claud. I soon discovered that there was very bad feeling between these two old partners in crime. I never heard Arthur address a single word to Claud and when the latter spoke to Bill or me, Arthur always turned his head away. I didn't want to pass immediate judgment on Claud, for my philosophy is to accept people as I find them. So when Claud asked me if I would play chess, for instance, I told him that although I had never played the game before, I was willing to learn if he were prepared to teach me. We spent a whole hour playing the game and I must say I found him an excellent teacher.

Claud, of course, was only too happy to tell me something about himself. He said he came from Stockport and had been working in Saudi Arabia for seven years now; indeed, his two children had been born in Riyadh. Before he came out he had been a tropical fish dealer in Manchester and had also supplied all the BAC men in Cheshire with home-grown tomatoes and mushrooms.

'You must have been a busy man,' I commented.

'I wish he was as busy here,' interrupted Arthur, 'and took his turn at washing up.' Claud ignored the jibe and went on talking. Then I noticed that Bill never spoke to Claud, either; if Claud addressed him, he would answer all right, but he would never initiate a conversation.

While I was still wondering how it was that two men who were locked up together could not, for some reason, get along together, I heard my name called out again.

'Men's visit,' explained Arthur. Hoping that Tom would be waiting for me, I rose quickly and walked eagerly towards the cage. I had expected to be allowed outside the block as before but instead I found that the arrangements for ordinary visiting were different. Prisoners, in fact, were not allowed outside the cages at all and had to talk to their visitors through the wire mesh. When I entered the cage, the place was like bedlam. Prisoners were fighting each other to get to the mesh and the noise was overwhelming as everybody bawled and shouted to make himself heard. Using my shoulders to good effect, however, I rapidly cleared a path and got to the mesh. Then I saw Tom and Harry Hall. I shouted at them but because of the uproar ordinary conversation was impossible. I saw that Harry had tears in his eyes as he shouted, 'How can you stand all this?' I bawled back, 'I can stand anything the Saudis care to throw at me – and then some!'

Tom asked me if I had written my letter to Anne and I nodded and slipped the letter under the mesh. He then said he had telephoned her the previous night and that she sent her love and the message was that I was not to worry about her or the kids.

The visit was brief, over in less than five minutes because we found it impossible to talk to each other. Tom promised to return the next day with Ian Wylie and said he would bring me all the food I needed.

Both Arthur and Bill also had visitors that day but Claud's name was never called and Bill told me later that Claud's wife had left Saudi Arabia, and nobody ever visited him. I felt sorrier for the bloke then than ever.

Later that day Arthur prepared a meal, based on the cooked meats, bread, cheese, tomatoes and fruits brought by our visitors.

Our first course was soup, cooked on an electric ring which had been smuggled into the prison. Then we had meat, tomatoes and a salad, followed by fruit. I said that this was the first food I had eaten since my arrest and when they asked me why I had not eaten earlier, I explained I had been reluctant to use the holes in the floor. Bill said the holes in block three were not too bad, although you still had to wear sandals when you used them; if I wanted a wash, I should take along a bucket. Once the meal was over, I inspected the facilities and was delighted to see that in this block at least, the holes were accommodated in cubicles with proper doors in front of them.

We ate our dinner sitting on the floor and were joined by two other westerners – Hans, a German lorry driver who had been in prison for 22 months (and had yet to be sentenced) and Gunter, a Swiss, who had worked for Volvo and who had managed to buy himself out of prison and was awaiting release. I asked Gunter how he had done this and who had done the fixing but all he would tell me was that it had cost him 65,000 riyals. When he reached home, he promised, he would write to Arthur and tell him how he had done it. I was disappointed as I felt sure Tom could raise that sort of money, even if the company refused. But Gunter, although I pressed him, refused to reveal his secret.

Following the meal, Bill got up and prepared to take our plates away to be washed. 'No, here let me do it,' I volunteered. Claud, I should mention was already lying down, ready to fall asleep.

'No,' roared Arthur, 'it's that cunt's turn – he hasn't washed a dish all week.' I insisted on being allowed to wash up, however, pointing out that I was a new boy and it was as well if I learned the procedures; Claud could do his turn tomorrow. In the end Arthur agreed and I went along and washed the dishes. Afterwards, I tried out one of the holes and then with the help of a bucket, had my first proper wash since my arrest. Afterwards I felt like a new man.

My sleeping place proved to be a great deal more comfortable than my cramped quarters in *Seep* Two. I had at least a foot of floor space to spare on both sides of me and in addition, there was very little traffic. For the first time since my arrest, I think, I slept soundly and undisturbed. At 4 a.m., however, I was awakened by a kick in the ribs and saw a prayer-caller standing over me telling me it was *salha*.

'Look,' I said to this guy in the ugliest tone I could summon up, 'if you ever do that again or ever disturb me again in any way while I'm sleeping, then you'll get this bunch of fives,' and I made a fist and waved it at him so that he would understand. He apologised at once, saying he thought I was an Arab.

'When the hell did you last see an Arab with fair hair?' I roared and he beat a hasty retreat.

The snag with sleeping in the main hall was that I had to rise early and move my mattress and blanket to make way for the other prisoners. I had to rise at 7 a.m., an early start when one has a whole day to put in. I crept quietly into Arthur's room and found the floor still littered with sleeping bodies, for prisoners lucky enough to have space in cells did not have to rise until 9 a.m. Big Bill was awake, however, and cheered me up by telling me that I should be able to get into the room within about three months. Arthur soon woke up also so I went and sat on his mattress and talked. He told me that if I took a thermos flask to the cage and shouted for Joseph, the latter would get us hot water and then he, Arthur, could make us tea. I was happy enough to do this as my contribution to our joint efforts on the chores.

While we were enjoying our cuppas, Arthur gave me a quick run-down on the do's and don'ts of the prison regulations, and in particular told me what visitors were allowed to provide. I asked him if he had tried the prison food and he said he hadn't as both he and Bill gave the welfare ladies 50 riyals a week each to buy them food on top of what the women themselves brought along as gifts. Other friends also kept them well supplied. I said I didn't think I'd have any trouble getting supplies and I hoped not because I couldn't stand the prison food which was simply rice – and then more rice.

I asked him if he expected to serve his full three-year sentence?

'No. Claud and I have actually been given a pardon but that's now gone down the drain because of that film being shown on TV and then the row that's followed with the ambassador being asked to leave and all that.' His opinion was that the decision to show the film had been daft.

'I don't agree with that,' I told him. 'After all, what it said was true and I don't think Saudi Arabia has any right to control what appears on our TV programmes.'

'Well, it's certainly wrecked our chances. We'd have been out by now.' Arthur added that he was preparing a series of articles for publication in the British press. In these he would 'take the lid off' the Saudi Royal Air Force and the problems it had with drink, drugs and sheer inefficiency.

I asked him if he knew Group Captain Paddy King who was the RAF's chief representative in Saudi Arabia. Arthur said he did and I mentioned that Paddy was a frequent visitor to our club because his wife worked for my company – and this despite the fact that it was supposed to be illegal for women to work in Arabia except as teachers, nurses or doctors. 'But then, as we know, all the companies, including the Arab ones, employ women in their offices.'

Eventually we returned to the topic of food. I told Arthur that my brother Tom and my boss were due to visit me that day and that if I made up a list of the kind of foodstuffs we wanted, they would see that Ian's wife, Lillian, brought along all we needed when she visited me next day. We then spent some time making up a short list.

Tom and Ian when they came, had good news for me. As Ian put it, 'The wheels are turning – and you'll soon be out.' The staff had demanded a meeting with him the previous night to find out what he was doing to get me released and he had assured them that success was imminent. In the meantime, they had brought along a few things I might need: some food, a change of clothing and a pillow. Lillian would bring whatever was on my list and also some of her home-baked apple pies and sausage rolls which she knew I loved.

That night, we westerners had a bucket wash in anticipation of a visit by the ladies next day – the day when we could all begin to feel like men again. Everybody was looking forward to laughing and joking with the women, one or two of us even wishing we could be alone with one of them – although common-sense told us that as they were all happily married women, it wouldn't do us much good.

That night, indeed, the chat took on the colour of the barrack room. The talk was about women. As the 'new' boy, I refused to state my views other than to remark that I wouldn't refuse any of them.

At nine o'clock next morning, my name was called and I went to the courtyard and saw Joan. The other British and American prisoners were already out but as I took my seat on an upturned

Pepsi case, the German and Portuguese prisoners also joined us. Then I saw Lillian Wylie and Roger Lilly's wife, Cherry, accompanied by the American wife of one of our sub-contractors walking towards me. Although I got on well with the welfare ladies, I found it easier, naturally, to chat with women who I already knew pretty well. Lillian did not disappoint me, either. Among the goodies she had brought was a special home-made apple pie. We talked about Ian's efforts to get me out and Lillian said she was confident he would manage it but as I listened to her talk and began to count the days I had been inside already – seventeen altogether – I got the feeling that we were both whistling in the dark. Despite these doubts, I realised that there was no point in spoiling the occasion and so I tried not to let the three women see that I was worried. Before the end of the visit, there was some trouble with the Arab prisoners; only four of them had bothered to *salha* at midday and when the guards began to cut up rough, the men complained that they did not like saying their prayers while being watched by western women. It all sounded daft but I wondered if it would lead to the limiting of visits by the welfare ladies or our other women friends. The visit over, the three women kissed me on the cheek and left. As I watched them go, I once more pondered on my chances of getting hold of an Arab woman's clothes.

Back in the cell, Arthur whooped with joy when he unwrapped the frozen steak, ground beef and assorted vegetables which Lillian and Cherry had brought. 'With this lot, Ian, you don't owe the kitty anything. This is better than anything we usually get.' Having made a contribution, I no longer felt guilty about eating the communal food. Arthur then asked Bill and me what we fancied for supper and I said, 'So far as I'm concerned, anything will do,' but I added, 'How does Claud feel?'

'Claud will eat whatever we eat – and he'll like it!' snapped Arthur.

Before we started our meal, a Lebanese American came into the room and invited us to join him for supper as his sister had brought him a whole parcel of Lebanese food. We weren't too keen because although Lebanese food is much better than the usual Saudi diet, it was hardly our cup of tea. We didn't want to offend the chap, however, so we agreed. He went away and returned with a variety of pots stuffed with food, which Arthur carefully ladled out. I found myself picking at the stuff, however, although the food itself was quite interesting. Claud, on the other hand, scoffed five full plates of it and I realised then one of the reasons for Arthur's antipathy.

On Saturday morning, I had another visit from Tom and Ian. The latter told me not to lose heart; he was still confident he could work the trick and get me out.

'Listen, Ian,' I told him, 'if you don't get me out soon, I'm going to get out myself, and damn the consequences!'

'And I'll make sure he gets out,' chipped in Tom.

An alarmed Wylie said, 'For God's sake, Ian – don't do anything hasty. I'm certain I can get you out – otherwise you could ruin everything.'

'So long as you get me out before November, that's OK,' I said. 'That's when a niece of mine is being married in England – and whatever happens, I intend to go to that wedding.'

I gave Tom a letter to send to Anne along with a short note for himself explaining that I planned to escape dressed as an Arab woman and asking him to see if he could get me some robes; he was to make sure, however, that any woman who helped me would not get into trouble herself.

Rumours abound inside prisons and that weekend we were deluged with them. One rumour had it that all prisoners in for drink offences were to be released to mark the fact that the Arab calendar had just reached the fifteenth century. (As I remarked, 'That's probably why the Saudis are so backward.') Bill's 'rumour' appeared to have more substance as it originated with Joseph, our interpreter; according to Joseph all westerners were to be transferred to a villa. We thought this pretty sound stuff if only because there were now too many western prisoners in Malaz and, if nothing else, we were all proving a nuisance during *salha*. Arthur and Bill made a special trip to the cage to see if they could learn anything more from Joseph and returned to say that the move was definitely on – we were to be moved either today or tomorrow. Even as we were talking the Lebanese came in and said he hoped he would be going with us. After all, he explained, he was a Christian and held an American passport. The trouble was, however, that the prison authorities had so far refused to treat him as anything but an Arab; they ignored his American passport and would not allow him a visit from the American consul, on top of which they made him take part in Muslim prayers. We tried to reassure him but the fact was that all we were thinking of was ourselves. We only cared about getting out of this hellhole and it was every man for himself.

Ian Wylie arrived around one o'clock to tell me again that he had been working night and day to secure my release and that he could definitely promise me that he would have a result for me within the next week. I told him that was good news but asked if he could please find out if I were being moved from Malaz to a villa. Ian asked the captain who confirmed that a move was definitely on and would take place that day. We were to be taken to a villa on the Industrial Estate just behind Riyadh University. I recognised the place immediately; it was a building known to all expats as 'The Pink Tit', due to its colour and size.

I went back to the cell pretty excited and confirmed the good news to the others who then started packing. I had almost nothing to pack but the others had so much stuff that they found it hard to get everything into their suitcases. There was a decision to be made about the food, too – should we take it or leave it? In the end we decided to take everything, hoping that there would be a fridge in the villa; if not, in that heat, the stuff would not last longer than a couple of hours.

SEVEN

We assembled in the main hall of the prison where we were handcuffed. Altogether there were ten westerners: Bill, Arthur, Claud, Hans, Peter, four Portuguese and myself. Peter and I were made to share a pair of handcuffs, which left us each with one hand free to carry our baggage. Outside, an open truck was waiting for us and we were told to dump our belongings in this. Having done so, we were then led to a minibus.

'What's the betting they'll expect us to pay the fare?' I joked to Peter.

'Perhaps the driver will settle for a tip,' he replied.

We settled down inside the bus and then I 'noticed that we were being escorted by an unusually large number of guards.

'If we're merely going to a villa, why are there so many guards?' I asked Arthur.

'I suppose it's because they like to feel important,' he suggested. 'After all they like waving their guns about and all that.'

'I don't know,' I said doubtfully. 'I have the distinct feeling that we're being conned in some way.'

We drove out of the prison, the truck carrying our clothing just ahead of us. One bundle fell off (later we found it belonged to Hans) but our driver drove straight over it as the guards guffawed, and no attempt was made to retrieve it. We were so relieved to be outside the prison, however, that none of us protested.

We soon noticed that we were driving down very narrow streets with ancient mud-walled houses rising on either side and were taken aback to realise that we were now in the old quarter of Riyadh. I think we all spotted the dark grey prison walls with the guard towers at the corners almost simultaneously and were surprised because we had the impression that there was only one prison in the Saudi capital. This, however, *looked* like a prison and could hardly be anything else. Then the big double gates swung open and we drove into a courtyard with high walls all around us and we knew that we were back in a prison all right.

'Saudis certainly do have some queer ideas about what a villa looks like,' somebody said.

Within minutes we were imprisoned in a large room (which we later discovered was called the 'visitors' room') looking out through a wall of steel mesh into an inner square where we saw some prisoners. The striking thing about all these prisoners was that they were *bald!*

'What kind of a barber do they have around here?' I asked.

'Short, back and sides be blowed!' said Arthur. 'This fellow really believes in getting down to the bone.'

We were nattering away like this, still adjusting to our new surroundings, when a Saudi in full Arab robes came into the room and ordered us all to huddle down on the floor. The others dutifully obeyed him and even Peter, beside me, went down on his haunches, but I stood there and refused to move although I was still handcuffed to him. The Saudi walked over to me and repeated the order. I still refused to budge.

'I can't,' I lied to him. 'I was injured some years ago and I get a bad pain in my leg. Besides I'm not an Arab and I prefer to stand.'

The guy looked at me as if he were going to burst a blood vessel. His face contorted with anger, he quickly turned on his heel and left the room. The others immediately implored me not to rock the boat.

'If they stop trying to treat me like an Arab, I'll behave myself,' I promised.

'They might release us if we don't give them trouble,' said somebody.

'Shit!' I said. 'The Saudis have no intention of releasing us. This is just another prison – and there's no point in kidding ourselves.'

The furious Saudi returned, this time accompanied by a corporal wearing a shiny black holster at his side. As the corporal approached me he opened the flap menacingly and then ordered me to huddle down.

'What difference does it make whether I crouch or stand?' I asked him. 'Anyway, British prisoners don't crouch – only Arab prisoners do. Besides, I have a bad leg.'

The two Saudis looked at each other nonplussed, clearly not used to such defiance. They left the room again. While they were out, the other chaps again begged me not to cause trouble, arguing that the Saudis might make it harder for us.

'How the hell can it be any harder for you?' I asked. 'Some of you have been stuck in jail for months, even years – and without being properly sentenced. It's time some of you tried to change the system.'

We were interrupted by the arrival of two guards who took off my handcuffs and then led me outside the room. There I was confronted by a sergeant who began by warning me that he was a member of the Secret Police. 'You must do as you are told – or else we shall punish you,' he told me.

'If you make a reasonable request, I'll obey it,' I replied. 'If I don't think it's reasonable, then I won't.'

Not knowing what to make of this, the man's mouth opened and shut like a fish's as he tried to think of something to say. Then he said, 'The warden will punish you tomorrow,' and ordered me to return to the room. I found the other chaps still crouching down on the floor but I stood there and lit a cigarette. The guard in the room bawled at me to stop smoking but I ignored him and carried on. When the other fellows saw I was getting away with it, they too lit up – and soon the whole room was a cloud of smoke.

We were kept waiting for some minutes before two guards came in and led out two of the Portuguese prisoners. Then they returned and took out the other two. Then it was the turn of Peter and me. We were taken out into the yard where we saw our belongings scattered on the ground. The guards removed our handcuffs and ordered us to pick out our stuff and place it in front of them so that it could be searched. We did this and when they had finished poking through it, they told us we were to take our clothing with us but to leave all pens, writing materials, washing gear and books behind, and that included my paracetamol tablets. The guards then shoved these items back into our bags and left them there.

We were then led through into the prison square and Peter and I were conducted into Block Two which was about 70 by 12 feet in area and contained 9 cells, each about 18 by 7 feet square. Two English-speaking guards were on hand here and they ordered us to enter room four. Inside we were delighted to find five double bunk beds.

'Well, this is a bit of all right,' I remarked to one of the guards.

'No, you don't sleep here,' the fellow replied with some satisfaction. 'One year before you get bed. You sleep on floor outside.' He then briefly lectured us on the prison regulations and it seemed to me that if Malaz had been bad, this place promised to be a damn sight worse!

First, he said, this was called Al-Ould and it was Saudi Arabia's maximum security prison. Second, it was a long-term prison mainly for drug offenders; there were two Americans here on such charges but I was the first drink offender. Third, we would not be allowed to have anything brought in from the outside – and this included food. Fourth, there would be no visiting days by women. Fifth, discipline was very strict and everyone would have to pray regularly – whether Christian or Muslim.

This seemed a bad start, but at least the Arab prisoners made us welcome and even offered us some of their food, which I declined, I hope politely. They told us it was possible to buy food from the prison shop which like the one in Malaz, paid 'commission' to the warden and to the guards; however, there was no *souk*-style trading allowed because of the drugs problem which was taken very seriously by the government which was determined that no drugs should find their way into the prison.

The Saudis were certainly keen on TV. Inevitably there was a TV set near the block entrance and the foreman told us that we were welcome to sleep in that part once the programmes were finished. That night, Peter and I dossed down on blankets where we smoked and chatted before attempting to go to sleep. Then the foreman came up and informed us that it was forbidden either to talk or smoke so we stopped talking but I carried on smoking. This made the foreman angry and he rushed away to return with a guard who warned me that I would be punished in the morning.

'Look, chum,' I told him. 'From my point of view, you seem to be determined to make me live like a wild beast – so what more can you do to me? You're not frightening me in any way, see?' And so I sent him off with what I hoped was a flea in his ear.

At 3.30 a.m. I was prodded awake and saw Peter sitting up. He said it was prayer time, but I just laid my head down again and decided to ignore the disturbance. I was still lying there, eyes closed and beginning to feel drowsy, when the prayer-caller came up and shouted *'Salha'* at me. I sat up and said quietly 'Fuck off! I'm a Christian and so is my friend here, and we'll pray whenever we feel like praying.' Visibly shocked the man disappeared while in the meantime other prisoners gathered round me and tried to explain that 'everybody has to pray'. I told them, 'Not us, mates – we Christian, savvy?' The prayer-caller then returned with a guard who was carrying a cane and who threatened to whip us if we did not pray. I got up quickly and yelled at him, 'Try it, mate – just try it.' He backed away at once muttering something about the fact that we would be punished. When he had gone, Peter and I went back to sleep again, ignoring the interminable invocations of the bums-up brigade.

As at Malaz, those of us forced to sleep in the main hall had to rise at 6.30 a.m. while those lucky enough to have bunks in the cells were allowed to sleep on for another two hours. We spent most of the intervening time trying to keep out of the way of four Arabs who, armed with hard brushes, had the task of keeping the block clean. At 8.30 a.m., we were called for breakfast. Peter was prepared to eat what the Saudis handed out – Arab bread, black beans and a concoction that looked like mildewed Scotch porridge, I boldly announced that I had no intention of 'eating that muck'. Sabri, one of the two English-speaking Arabs who had greeted us kindly on our arrival, told me, 'But you must eat, Fraser.'

'I'll eat when I can get food from outside.' I declared.

'But that will never be allowed,' said Sabri.

'OK, then,' I answered him, 'in that case, I'll die.'

Hans, the German from Malaz and Pierre, the French thief, arrived in our block a couple of hours later. Initially they had been put into Block One, along with five other westerners, but somebody it seemed, had decided that if too many westerners were put together it would mean trouble. I didn't particularly like Pierre – after all, he was a thief and not my type of person, whereas Hans was merely in for a whisky job; he had smuggled 1400 cases of whisky into Saudi Arabia in a truck. So I felt sorry for Hans but not for Pierre, reckoning he was a real villain.

A little later we were called into the yard and told we were to have our hair cut. This upset Peter as he felt certain he would be released within a few weeks and did not want to go home looking like a billiard ball. He said he would refuse to have his hair cut and I told him I'd also refuse. Our stand led to the appearance of the warden himself. He came out of his office and quietly explained to us that because the prison was filthy, cutting our hair was a hygienic measure to avoid lice. We would only have our hair cut once, he promised. Reckoning that he knew something we didn't, we both finally agreed to have our heads shaved. It was an odd experience to look round and see everybody looking like Telly Savalas.

While the warden was still there, I seized the opportunity to ask him about my headache tablets which had been taken away when I entered the prison. He didn't give me a chance to explain the problem but ordered a guard to take me to see the doctor. I was led along a narrow corridor in the office block and into a room where I saw a small, fat Egyptian doctor to whom I explained that I had a plastic plate in my skull, suffered severe headaches and needed paracetamol tablets. The doctor looked at me and then at my skull and then asked me what the trouble was. I repeated that I suffered constant terrible headaches and needed my pills. He mulled over the problem for a moment and then said he would give me an aspirin three times a day.

'But aspirin's no damned good to me,' I burst out. 'These aren't ordinary headaches. The pain is almost continuous and I need something far stronger than aspirin. I have headaches at all times of the day, so I need to carry tablets on me.'

'I cannot give you tablets,' he said. 'You are a drug addict.'

'Who on earth told you that?' I exploded.

'That's why you are in prison,' he said.

'I'm in prison because of whisky – not drugs,' I told him.

This seemed news to him. Nevertheless, he still wouldn't allow me paracetamol tablets and it was only when I insisted that I had to have something there and then, that he even consented to hand me an aspirin. I swallowed this, hoping against hope that it would afford me slight relief. Then I went back to my block. I remember that as I walked back, my head throbbed with pain and I had no idea how I was going to cope with the awful din in the block. This would become unbearable after a while and I would be driven insane unless I was helped. Yet somehow

I managed to retain both my sanity and my temper. I was due for a visit from Tom on Friday afternoon and I hoped he would be able to help but when I walked into the entrance cage, there were over 100 prisoners fighting to get to the wire and the shouting was so loud and sustained that we couldn't hear each other. Tom managed to yell that he would return next day along with Ian Wylie and then left.

At 11 a.m. on Saturday I was called to the warden's office and there I found Tom, Ian and Lieutenant Abdul Azziz, the warden, waiting. Ian asked me how I was and I told him I was not getting any medical treatment and that I had refused to eat the prison food. Azziz explained that I could not be allowed drugs as this was a prison for addicts and peddlers and it was not permitted to bring food in from outside because drugs could be smuggled inside in food. I told him my tablets were merely for headaches and could be bought over any counter in any chemist's shop. As for the prison food – surely he didn't expect me to live on rice twice a day and a ghastly gruel in the morning? Azziz looked thoughtful, even concerned, but finally said that there was nothing he could do, and thus washed his hands of the problem.

'What about books?' I demanded. He said he would arrange for these (and incredibly, he provided me with a copy of the Qur'an – and in Arabic at that!). What about prayers? Why should I pray if I didn't want to? Well, everybody prayed but if I didn't wish to, then I needn't; I was a guest of Saudi Arabia and therefore I would not be forced to pray.

'If I'm supposed to be a guest in this country,' I snapped, 'then I'd like to leave it.'

'I'm sorry but I cannot agree to that,' he replied.

While Ian and Azziz talked about my problems, Tom seized the chance to slip a note into my hand. When I got back to my cell I read it. The note said that Ian was still trying to get me out and my brother Bob in Singapore was trying to pressurise London to take more positive action on my behalf but Tom thought that the only way I could get out of prison in the foreseeable future was to escape. He was prepared to help in every way and in the meantime he intended to remain in Saudi, although his contract finished the following week, in order to help me.

On 2 June my name was again called over the tannoy. I went to the warden's office where I found Arthur and Claud along with two well-dressed Britons who were introduced to me as

Mr Richard Northern the British vice-consul and the personnel manager of BAC. I told Northern he could do nothing for me, that it was a waste of my time talking to him and I walked out of the office.

The guards came after me. Abdul also followed, shouting at me, and in the end, I was physically marched back into Abdul's office. Abdul found it difficult to accept the fact that I had walked out on a government official – a heinous, unheard of crime in Saudi Arabia! 'This is your consul,' he protested as though talking to a child. 'You *must* talk to him. It is *important*.'

I gave the vice-consul a long look and then said, very deliberately and without heat, 'Fuck off!' and walked out of the office again. This time nobody followed me and I was allowed to return to my cell.

Next day I was again called to Abdul's office where Ian Wylie and the vice-consul were waiting.

'This is a waste of time,' I told Ian. 'I don't need the embassy to tell my wife that I'm hale and hearty.'

'But the vice-consul can help you,' insisted Ian.

'How can he?' I demanded. 'Will he get me proper food? Will he get me a bed to sleep on, instead of having to lie on the floor? Will he see that my conditions are improved?'

'He can do nothing for you just at the moment as diplomatic relations between Britain and Saudi Arabia are still very bad. Our ambassador has been kicked out and things are very difficult. But the consul knows all about your case and is trying to pull strings behind the scenes. You must have patience. And in the meantime you must eat – there is no point in dying in here – and if you don't behave, the guards might beat you.'

'Nobody's going to beat me,' I told him. 'And I'm not going to eat this damned prison food. I want to change my conditions and I don't want to be treated as an animal. I want a bed, daily exercise and food brought in from outside every day.'

'Is there any chance of him getting a bed?' Northern asked Abdul.

'In about a year's time,' said Abdul. 'But no prisoners except Saudi prisoners are allowed exercise.' He then went on again to explain about drugs being smuggled into the prison in food.

'In Malaz I was allowed food from outside,' I told him. 'Send me back to Malaz, then.'

'No,' he said. 'This is a better prison. And the food here is very good.'

'Well, I'm not going to eat it – and I'll go out in a wooden box before I'll eat it,' I shouted at him.

To my surprise he then suggested that if Ian brought the food into his office, he would allow me to eat it there.

'Not bloody likely!' I told him. 'I'm not an animal in the zoo at feeding time!'

'Oh, don't make trouble, Ian,' Wylie said. 'What's the point when you may be out soon?'

'Abdul for one, doesn't think I'm getting out soon. And anyway, even if I were, I'm not going to eat that swill. The Saudis expect the world to treat them as civilised people and yet here they are not even prepared to treat me in a civilised way.'

'It won't help you in any way if you insist on upsetting the warden,' advised the vice-consul.

'Look, Ian,' said Wylie, 'I'm going to talk to the deputy Governor of Riyadh again and see if at least he won't do something about a bed for you and about better conditions. In the meantime will you cool it, for God's sake! I'm still trying like hell to get you released.'

'Well, we'll see, Ian, we'll see.'

That was the end of the visit. On the way back to the block I was subjected to search no fewer than three times, despite the fact that I was wearing only a pair of shorts. I became so fed up with this that when the third guard tried to search me, I searched him back. This made him shout at me so I shouted back at him. And then I smiled – I heard laughter coming from behind the gate leading to my block and turning round I saw a crowd of fellow prisoners enjoying the pantomime. The guard stopped searching me, flung open the gate and ordered me inside, at the same time yelling at the other prisoners in an effort to restore his authority. For once, however, the prisoners refused to be cowed and as I walked among them they shouted, 'Fraser, good!'

Later, Sabri came to tell me that the guard was furious because he had lost face and intended to punish me that afternoon by beating me with a cane. I told him to pass the word on that it would take more than one guard to handle me and that if the fellow wanted to try anything he had better bring along plenty of his chums.

That afternoon, as Sabri had predicted, my name was called out.

'They will beat you now, Fraser,' said Sabri.

'Then they're in for a surprise,' I told him.

As I moved towards the block gate, I hunched up my shoulders like a fighter keying myself up, trying to decide whether to start punching the guards as soon as I spotted them or wait until they had their canes raised over their heads before hitting them. Instead I was led out into the reception area, where I was surprised to see Roger sitting on a large carpet which had been spread out on the ground and sitting beside him, two guards. There was no sign of any canes, however, and as I walked up a guard pointed to some food which had been placed on the carpet and invited me to sit down and eat it. I looked at Roger dumbfounded.

'You don't surely expect me to sit down and eat here?' I demanded of him. 'I'm not an animal you know, so you can tell these buggers I'm not going to eat anything until I'm allowed to have proper food and allowed to eat in my cell in the proper way!'

'But what about your health, Ian?' protested Roger.

'Roger, I know what I'm doing. In the end the Saudis will have to let me have food from the outside – otherwise I'll die on them. Anyway, I'm not hungry, and really I'm quite fit. I'm not going to weaken in my attitude. If I start to weaken, then they'll know they have me.'

'You talk as if you've given up hope, Ian, but the boss is trying desperately to get you out, I assure you.'

'Well, it doesn't look as if he's getting anywhere, does it? So if he doesn't succeed soon, I'm going to escape.'

'But how on earth can you escape?' demanded Roger. 'And even if you did, how would you get out of the country? You'd be nabbed long before you got anywhere.'

'Well, that's my problem isn't it?' And I changed the subject.

I asked him what was happening otherwise and he said everything was pretty well back to normal at Humming Bird House although the lads were missing their booze badly; most of them were having to go along to the Tarmac Club for a snifter. He himself had been out to the vice-consul's villa where he and Richard Northern enjoyed the odd glass of beer (as the embassy was British territory, no problems were involved).

'Don't tell me you and Northern have been drinking your heads off when you should have been trying to get me out of this hellhole!' I said angrily.

Roger looked taken aback. 'Everybody's doing what they can – '

'Well, they're not doing enough!' I told him. I quickly realised I was being unfair to him. But when you've all the time in the world to brood on your troubles, the niceties in a situation tend to escape you.

Next day I demanded to see the doctor again. My headaches were getting worse and three aspirins a day were proving useless. The doctor said he would speak to Abdul and arrange for me to go into hospital where I could be examined to see if I had a plate in my head.

'If you feel the top of my head, you'll feel it for yourself,' I told him. No, no, that wouldn't do – finding out if I had a plate in my skull was the hospital's job, not his. I decided that, under the circumstances, he had to be one of the most useless doctors I had ever come across; the only medicine he ever prescribed for anybody, anyway, was an aspirin which is why we eventually christened him the Aspirin Kid.

Despite the pain and general discomfort, I decided not to let my headaches get me down and to be as patient and understanding with my fellow prisoners as possible – after all, it wasn't their fault I was in prison and suffering the tortures of the damned.

The Arab prisoners spent most of their day in the hall of the block either talking, reading the Qur'an or playing backgammon (they used the plastic tops of water bottles and bits of soap for dice). Peter and I whiled away many hours talking but Hans the German was very quiet and withdrawn, brooding, I suppose, on his dreadful situation – two years in prison already and not even sentenced yet. His mood brightened, however, when we were joined by an Austrian called Manfred who was in for selling whisky to an Arab. Manfred was keen to improve his English so he jollied Hans along and they both encouraged me to teach them; which is why there are now two Teutons running around somewhere speaking English with a strong Scottish burr.

Two weeks were to pass before I had another visit – this time from Roger Lilly and Tom. Tom had some promising, if surprising, news; he had managed to make contact with a Saudi princess who, he said, had promised to use her influence on my behalf. He had already visited her twice and believed she would be able to do something. Roger urged me in the meantime to cool it and eat something.

'I am *not* going to eat Arab food,' I told him. He said he was worried about my health, so I told him again I was quite fit and well, and suffering no ill effects from my prolonged fast. I wasn't giddy nor was I getting spots before my eyes, or even suffering a craving for something like filet mignon. The heat, I thought, was also helping me as well as the general prison inactivity, by dulling my appetite.

Before the end of the visit, I urged Tom to go back to England but he refused.

On the nineteenth day of my hunger strike, the scene changed dramatically. I met Tom and Roger in Abdul's office where the latter announced important concessions which the Governor of Riyadh had decided to make to western prisoners. We were to be allowed books and newspapers and to have our food brought in (Roger interrupted to say that the company would see to it that I got food daily which had been prepared in the company kitchens). We were also to be allowed visits by welfare ladies. In addition, continued Abdul, beds were to be provided for all western prisoners though it would take a week or two to purchase these. As for exercise, due to the possibility of us attempting an escape this, unfortunately, would be restricted to one hour every two weeks.

'Well, it's a start anyway,' I admitted. 'But I'm warning you – I'll be round to see you every day until I get a bed.'

To his credit, the bugger smiled, a smile which I wiped off his face almost at once by asking about my headaches. The aspirin treatment, I told him, was absolutely hopeless and I needed something better.

'Is there any reason why our company shouldn't examine him here, in your presence?' Roger asked Abdul. It was a sign of the change of attitude that Abdul at once agreed.

'Yes, that will be good,' he said. 'Perhaps Fraser will now be happy as our guest.'

'Listen,' I told him bluntly, 'I'll only be happy when I'm on a plane carrying me back to England!'

Tom, with Abdul's agreement, returned to prison that afternoon bringing sandwiches and cakes meant to tide me over while he tried to set up a proper schedule so that I would get three

good meals a day. Back in the cell I shared the stuff out with
Peter, Hans and Manfred and was happy enough to break my
fast.

As is usual in Saudi Arabia nothing, of course, worked out as
was promised. During the first week of the de-restriction, the
guards on duty would often not allow in any food at all. On
other occasions, when I went to reception to collect the food, I
found the guards poking their dirty fingers in it. The scene often
became farcical. When I caught the guards at their dirty habits,
I yelled at them to keep their 'fucking hands off'. When they
continued to do it, I dashed into Abdul's office and demanded
he control his men. Usually the guards followed me, shouting at
me to come back. For several minutes there would be bedlam; I
would shout at Abdul, the guards would shout at me and finally
Abdul would order the guards to shut up. He kept telling them
that the food was to be allowed in without inspection but as
the dirty practice continued, I decided this was mere window-
dressing.

Tom arranged that my food should be brought into me in half-
gallon ice-cream cartons. He provided me with scrambled eggs
and sausage for breakfast, followed by cooked meats and salads
for lunch or dinner but as time went by he managed to increase
the diet, adding cornflakes, frozen milk, bread and even apple
pie. The cartons usually arrived in large cardboard boxes which
I was not permitted to take into the block. Usually, the guards
took the cartons out of the boxes and then lined them up until I
arrived at reception. One day, however, I got there to find a
carton containing apple pie which had been covered over with
silver foil, with a hole in the foil where a guard had stuck his
finger in. I saw one of the blokes smiling as though he had just
got away with something clever.

'So you're fond of apple pie, are you?' I asked him.

He giggled stupidly.

'In that case,' I shouted at him, 'you'd better have it properly
hadn't you?' And with that, I pushed the pie into his face twisting
and turning it so that he would get the full benefit. At once the
other guards ran towards me, but I made for the nearest wall
where I turned my back and put up my fists, shouting, 'Come
on then. Hit me if you dare.'

They gathered in a menacing semi-circle and slowly advanced
on me. Almost certainly I would have been beaten up if I had

not been rescued by Abdul who came out of his office to see what all the hullaballoo was about.

The sergeant told him about the pie – neglecting to mention, of course, that someone had stuck a finger in it.

'Why did you do that, Fraser?' asked Abdul.

'Because one of these cunts put their finger in it, that's why.'

I saw Mohammad, my old driver, who had brought the food, standing there trembling. I knew why he was in such a state, of course. According to Saudi logic he was a party to the crime; he had brought the pie to me and if he hadn't done so, then I wouldn't have pushed the pie in the guard's face, would I? I wasn't prepared to accept such oriental-style reasoning, however, and asked him to confirm that a guard had stuck his finger in the pie. As I could have guessed, he refused to speak.

'Listen, Mohammad – if you don't tell the truth, I'm going to belt you. And none of these buggers is going to stop me.' Under threat he quickly told Abdul what had happened. Having then got the guard to admit what he had done, Abdul said quietly, 'It's time you returned to your block, Fraser.'

'I'll go,' I said, 'but may I take the food in its cardboard box, to avoid more trouble?'

'Yes,' he agreed.

The news of what I had done to the guard had already spread like wildfire, but Sabri came up to me with a warning, 'Some prisoners are taken into the punishment block and are spread-eagled and then whipped – just because they give a guard a bad look. This has not happened to you yet because most of them are afraid of you but I know they are determined to get you into a punishment cell, and may Allah then help you!'

'I know, Sabri, I know. But I'm not going to change. If you see me changing, then you'll know I've resigned myself to being in prison – and I'm not going to do that.'

On his next visit, Tom had more news of the princess and his belief that she would turn a few of the right wheels for me. He also repeated, however, that if I could think of some way of escaping, he was all for it. The company was still trying to help me through some Englishman who was the right-hand man of one of the royal princes but he had no idea what the chances were there. In the meantime he had telephoned Anne who wanted to cancel a trip to the USA which I had already arranged for the whole family.

'Tell her not to do that,' I told him.

'She insists she won't go without you, and the rest of the family, and that goes for mum and dad too, take the same view.' I became aware, almost for the first time, that my imprisonment was proving not only a torment for me personally but was also affecting the lives of the people I held most dear.

Tom's worry was that I might do something daft and get ill-treated by the guards and possibly seriously hurt.

'Don't worry about that,' I told him. 'If I can't control these guards, then that would mean they were controlling me – and the one way I'll prevent that is to make them scared of me. Believe me, Tom, they're shit-scared right now.'

There was hardly a detail, indeed, which Tom overlooked. He made sure newspapers or a fresh book arrived for me every morning with my food parcels. He also spoke to Wilson, the company's new chef, who as a result took the greatest care to select the right foodstuffs for me and to vary them as much as possible. It may seem that I'm making a big fuss about food, but selecting the right food in a climate like Saudi Arabia's is vitally important. The temperature inside the prison, for instance, often rose to 140 degrees during the day and the only way I was able to keep the meat and salads fresh was by wrapping them up in a wet towel. All fresh food, too, had to be consumed on the same day.

Despite our misery and angry resentment at being held so arbitrarily and (in some cases) without a proper trial, we soon developed a sense of camaraderie. It would have been easy to become entirely selfish and self-centred but on the contrary, adversity seemed to bring out the best in us. The food I got was sufficient only for one person, for instance, but I always shared it with the other Europeans in the cell. Peter, who received food parcels twice a week, also shared everything he had in a most generous way. Neither Hans nor Manfred ever received any parcels but I am sure that they, too, would have contributed had they been able to.

One day I mentioned to Ian Wylie that Hans was a cell-mate and he remembered that when he had spent a day in jail himself after charges had been laid against the company, that Hans had been there and had generously shared whatever food he had.

'If you're sharing with him, then I'll see if I can get your food ration increased,' he promised. From then on I got two portions every morning instead of my usual ration.

EIGHT

At nine o'clock on the second Saturday of July 1980, my name was called out over the tannoy. But when I went to the guard at the gate he turned me back saying I was to put on my trousers and shirt as I was going out. I asked the man where I was going but he refused to tell me.

Back in the cell, Sabri said he thought I was going to be released. Peter and Hans said they also thought this, but I pointed out that I had not been asked to bring my belongings with me, which I would if I were going to be set free. They said it had to be that for if I were going to be sentenced I should have been told about it the previous night at eight o'clock which was the time set for telling all prisoners that they were to attend court the next day.

'Well, I'll soon find out, won't I?' I said. 'But my good old sixth sense tells me that this had nothing to do with being released.'

At the reception desk I was once more handcuffed and a guard signed for me as usual by putting his thumbprint in the book. A land cruiser then drove us quickly to Chop Square. We halted outside the building where my 'confession' had been registered – at the Sheik's office – and I was led up to a large waiting room where there were already about 30 prisoners, some chained in pairs, others handcuffed together like a chain-gang all squatting on the floor. I sat down with the rest of them and began asking two prisoners from my block whom I did not know but who knew me apparently – word of Fraser's exploits having got around, it seems. Why hadn't I come along with everybody else at 7 a.m? they asked me.

'Because I wasn't called until 9 a.m., that's why,' I replied.

'You must be here for sentencing, then.'

'Let's hope so,' I said. Roger Lilly had told me that the company was pressing for a quick sentence in the hope that once the Saudis had registered their disapproval, they might be prepared to commute the term.

I sat there for three hours, awaiting my turn. In the meantime prisoners who had been led from the room were announcing, on their return, that they had been sentenced to two, three or five years in prison as the case might be. It had been warm in the room to start with but as the Arabian sun rose higher and higher in the sky, the heat grew so unbearable that even the Saudi prisoners complained. They called out 'Water, water,' and eventually a guard brought in a large steel bowl of water for everybody to drink. Although my throat was parched, I decided to put a brave face on it and pretend that the heat didn't bother me. Hell, after all, I was British, wasn't I?

Following some of the most miserable hours I have ever spent in my life the two prisoners from my block and I discovered that we were the only people left who were due to be sentenced that day. I expected to be called next when a guard entered the room, I rose to my feet and prepared to follow him. Instead he told me, 'You are too late to be sentenced today. Maybe tomorrow.' As tomorrow to a Saudi could mean next year or the year after or even never, I was angry – although I had no reason to suppose that getting a sentence was likely to make me feel any better. That, however, is how the way the mind works at such moments.

I was conducted downstairs with the other two prisoners and we were made to halt in the doorway while the guards looked around for a conveyance to take us back to the prison. Finally, one said to me, 'We will have to walk out into the street now and find a taxi.'

'Not on your life, mate, I bristled, 'bring the taxi to the door.'

Suddenly everybody was shouting at me and then a guard took off his army webbing belt and raised it in the air and made as if to strike me. I didn't wait to find out what he really intended; instead I stuck out my hands and found the handcuffs were just loose enough to allow me to grab the fellow by the throat. I squeezed and saw his face gradually turn blue.

Anywhere else in the world, I suppose, a man's comrades would have immediately rushed to his aid. Not so in Riyadh, however; the other guards merely stood back and watched like uninterested spectators at a bad bullfight. I still recall the thoughts that went rushing through my head. Will I kill this man? I asked myself; no, that would be stupid. But then why not? Fuck it, yes! And I squeezed the man's throat even harder.

I have no idea whether I would have killed him or not but as we were still grappling outside the front door, I heard a cultivated Oxford accent behind me, ask, 'What is the trouble?'

I glanced past the guard's shoulder and saw a distinguished-looking Saudi standing at the foot of the stairs. Instinctively I released the guard and explained, 'There's no trouble – except that this man has some trouble with his breathing.'

'Can I help in any way?' asked the newcomer, concerned. He looked like a Mr Big for the guards hung back deferentially.

'No,' I said 'I'm all right – now.'

'You were attacking the guard?' he queried. 'Why were you doing that?'

'I'm not an animal,' I replied. 'I'm not going to be paraded in handcuffs in the streets of Riyadh just so that these policemen can get a taxi. And nobody's going to hit me.'

'Who was going to hit you?'

'This man was going to hit me, and with that belt.' And I pointed to the floor where the belt was lying.

Mr Big stooped down, picked up the belt, and handed it back to the guard. Then, in a complete change of mood, he suddenly let fly with a flood of vituperative language at the unfortunate guard. He spoke too fast for me to grasp all of what he was saying but I understood enough to gather he was telling the man he was a disgrace to Saudi Arabia, was giving the country a bad name and that he was to go immediately and find a taxi and bring it to the door. The guard, his face a mixture of embarrassed blues and reds, rushed away while the rest of us, including Mr Big, waited patiently for him to return.

'Who the fuck is this guy?' I asked myself but I was more than grateful to him because if he hadn't come along I might easily have found myself up on a murder charge. Soon the guard returned with a taxi and I walked over to get into it.

'Good-bye, Mr Fraser,' said Mr Big as I stepped inside the vehicle.

I looked back blankly at him. I didn't know what to say for there was little love lost between me and any Saudi, however cultivated his accent. Still, he might have saved my life.

'Thank you,' I stammered. 'I'm much obliged.' And with that I sat down in the taxi.

As we sped back to the prison, I started worrying about what had happened. There was no way I was going to get away with it this time. Meantime, the air-conditioning in the taxi was working full blast and after the awful heat in the Sheikh's office I began to feel I was sitting in paradise.

It wasn't long, however, before I ran into more trouble. When we arrived at the prison gate, my guard calmly demanded that I pay the taxi fare. I looked at him dumbfounded.

'You must be kidding,' I told him. 'I'm not paying any taxi fare.'

It may have something to do with the heat, but Arabs do love shouting. Almost before I was aware of it, I was in the middle of another uproar. The guards shouted at me, then they shouted at the other two prisoners, then the two prisoners shouted back and then everyone shouted at me. I just sat there and ignored the lot of them. In the end, the other two prisoners had to fork out £20 while my guard, bristling with anger, told me that I must go to the warden's office right away.

'Lead on,' I said, hoping I looked convincingly unperturbed.

By now, of course, I was thoroughly fed up with the treatment I had received that day. Useless hours spent in the shrivelling heat in the Sheikh's office; then the fracas with the guard which had set my nerves pretty much on edge; then the uproar over the taxi fare – in short, I was in a mood to declare war on the entire Saudi Arabian nation. When a guard tried to search me at the prison gate I could contain my anger no longer.

'You stupid cunts!' I roared at them. 'That's what you are. Stupid cunts!'

Perhaps I should have tried smiling when I said this, for nobody seemed to see my remark as a side-splitting joke. Before I quite knew where I was, a guard had grabbed his MI rifle and rammed the barrel in my belly. You've gone too far, this time, Fraser, I told myself. Then I laughed and deliberately turning my back on him, marched to the door of the reception area and headed straight for the warden's office. When the guards saw where I was going, they shouted at me, ordering me to come back. I ignored them and walked straight in on Abdul who looked up in surprise when I appeared.

I had decided that my best tactic in the situation was to create a diversion. So before a guard could appear to complain about my assault, I launched into a complaint about the taxi fare.

'Why the hell should I pay the taxi fare from the Sheikh's office?' I demanded.

'All prisoners must pay for taxis,' replied Abdul patiently.

'Why?'

'To show respect to the guards.' It was an explanation, I may say, that mystified me as much as anything I had come across in Saudi Arabia.

I turned and looked at the two guards who had escorted me from the prison and who were now standing sheepishly at the door. 'There is no way I'm going to respect those two fuckers,' I told him.

The inevitable uproar followed, with everybody shouting and trying to make himself heard above the din. I kept on harping about the taxi fare, hoping that Abdul would be persuaded to see this as the main issue, while the man I had attacked at the Sheikh's office kept trying to show Abdul his injured throat. Other guards kept coming in and out to complain that Fraser had tried to kill a guard. It was all pure bedlam but I still wondered how I was going to get away with an attempt on a guard's life.

Nothing, however, ever resolves itself as simply as that in Saudi Arabia. Trivial affairs may bring unexpected retribution; serious crimes may be passed over as though they never existed. Abdul suddenly stood up, ordered all the guards, save the two who had escorted me back from the Sheikh's office and a desk sergeant out, then closed the door and quietly sat down to sort out the situation.

The first item on his agenda was to take a look at the guard's throat. After inspecting it, he ordered the man to see a doctor – and that was that! Then he turned to me and said, 'All prisoners must pay for taxis. You are a guest, Fraser, and you must do as you are told.'

The word 'guest' almost broke me in two. 'Guest!' I said and roared with laughter. I don't think Abdul actually understood what the word meant for, to my surprise, he laughed back at me. To my further surprise, he invited me to sit down and in good humour ordered the guard to bring 'Tea for Fraser'.

I waited while Abdul dealt with other business. All sorts of Arabs, none of them prisoners, kept trailing in and out of his office and God knows what kind of business he was supposed to be transacting. However, he was clearly trying to be fair, even decent, to me. My tea arrived in a miniature beer pot, served with no milk but lots of sugar and I sipped it slowly, taking advantage of the air-conditioning. Finally he turned to me and asked quite affably, 'Have you any complaints?'

I was prepared to manufacture a dozen on the spot if necessary. However, I did have a list of genuine complaints. 'First, my food gets delayed, so when I eventually get it, it's uneatable.'

'I'll speak to the sergeant about that,' he promised.

'Also, I want a bed.'

'You must wait until your turn comes, Fraser,' he said patiently.

'I am not prepared to wait for a year,' I said.

'All right, I understand,' he said. 'I will talk to the *seep* foreman about this problem.'

He was as good as his word, ordering Said, the block foreman, to see him right away. I was beginning to revise my ideas about the bloke until he started talking to Said. I had never, of course, revealed to any of the Saudis that I knew a little Arabic, believing this a card I should keep up my sleeve.

Abdul started off by asking Said, 'When is there likely to be a bed?'

'In one year,' answered Said.

Abdul seemed put out. 'Oh, no, don't say that. Don't tell Fraser that. Just tell him "soon", so that he is made happy. Fraser, as you know, has no brains.'

I pretended not to understand and tried to look as pleased as punch when Abdul told me that Said had assured him I would get a bed 'soon'. The problem of course, was that I did not want a bed – if they had given me one, that would have been merely one less complaint. My strategy was to pile complaint on complaint until they got sick of me and ordered me out of the country.

The bed complaint having been disposed of, I switched to the problem of exercise. I needed exercise, I told Abdul. I hadn't had any since I had been hauled into jail.

'You will be allowed exercise next week,' he said.

I decided I had used up my ration of complaints for the day and rather pleased at the way things had turned out, walked happily back towards the block. To my surprise I was stopped, outside the punishment cell which lay on the way. Incompetent as usual, however, the guards found they had no key and I was made to wait while they sent back to Abdul for the only one available. Abdul himself came out, key dangling in his hand. He walked straight up to the door of the cell, then stopped and looked at me. I did the only thing I could think of in the circumstances and smiled.

'*Seep* Two,' he barked at the guards and turning on his heel, strode back to his office.

Back in the block, I found that news of my attack on the guard had preceded me and Peter said I had become quite a hero among the Arab prisoners, 'because they regard you as brave and not afraid of the guards'. I was pleased about this, feeling that my tactics were having some effect. My tactic of swearing at the guards was obviously unsettling them, because Muslims like to pretend that swear words do not exist in Arabic.

That night my name was called out at eight o'clock with the news that I was to attend the Sheikh's court the next morning. Peter warned me that I should accept any sentence I got, repeating the argument I had already heard, that if I refused it, I was liable to have it doubled.

'That's a yarn put about by the Saudis to con prisoners into accepting their sentences,' I told him. 'I'm not accepting any sentence, anyway – whatever the risk.'

At 6.30 a.m. next morning I was taken into the yard and made to sit with six other prisoners, three Arabs and three Americans (two blacks, one white). The white American was nicknamed 'Ski' and the blacks Jim and Joe. I asked them what they were in for and they said for whisky. I remember Bill Shunks, who worked for 'Ski's' company telling me about him. He was an office manager who, while driving home with two British passengers, a doctor and a nurse, was caught by the police with seven bottles of *siddeeky* in his car boot. The doctor and nurse were released next day and at once sent a message to Jim and Joe who were 'Ski's' suppliers, telling them to get rid of everything they had as 'Ski' intended to name them in the hope of escaping prison. Jim and Joe were duly arrested but as they had got rid of their booze, the police were unable to link them with 'Ski'. Undeterred, the police threatened them with torture (a nice case of colour prejudice as the Saudis normally do not torture westerners in drink cases) and under this threat Jim and Joe had confessed.

In the reception area, the three Arab prisoners were handcuffed together and then Jim and Joe were also. 'Ski' and I were handcuffed to each other and then a guard, having fixed an ankle shackle to 'Ski' attempted to attach the other end to me.

'Fuck off!' I shouted at him.

'You are a troublemaker, Fraser!' said the guard.

'Well, *I'm* not a troublemaker,' chimed in 'Ski', 'so please don't shackle me.' Then, to my astonishment he began to plead with the guard.

'Do shut up, "Ski"!' I bawled at him. 'And stop whining like a kid.' I turned to the guard. 'If you shackle me, then I won't go to the Sheikh. Tell that to Abdul, will you?'

To 'Ski's' astonishment the guard dutifully trotted off and eventually returned with the warden. Abdul took one look at the shackles, announced 'No shackles', and turned and went off again.

In the big room at the Sheikh's office where I had spent a terrible three hours the previous day, some 30 prisoners were already waiting, including the chain-gang from Malaz who had been there yesterday. To get into the room, we had to stumble along a corridor packed with black-robed Arab women, surrounded by a horde of children who were sitting as quiet as graven images. Babies only a few months old gurgled so softly that you could hardly hear them. I was so struck by this that I mentioned it to an Arab prisoner and he said that the Sheikh's office was respected in the same way as a mosque; it was considered a holy place and because of that, if a child made a noise, an Ayatollah would thrash him.

'All I can say,' I remarked as the heat began to grow unbearable again, 'is that it's more like a hot holy hell.'

I noticed that when prisoners were called in to see the Sheikh their handcuffs or shackles were removed first. 'Ski' had the handcuffs taken off when it came his turn as had Jim and Joe. When my name was called, however, I was told I must remain handcuffed to 'Ski'. I said I didn't give a damn but 'Ski', who had spent 30 years in the US Army and should have been prepared to put up with anything, began to complain again; he insisted he didn't want to get into trouble.

'Listen, mate,' I told him, 'nobody's going to get into any

trouble except me.' I felt livid with him for being so lacking in drive.

He didn't want to be dragged into the Sheikh's office again, still handcuffed to me. Nevertheless, in we went and I saw along the back wall two desks, one occupied by the Sheikh and the other by his clerk. 'Ski' and I were told to sit down in front of the Sheikh and we did so. An Egyptian who told me that he was the translator sat down on the seat on my right.

He began by apologising. 'My English is not too good,' he said.

'Don't worry, mate,' I told him, 'I'm Scottish, so my own English isn't all that hot either.' Then I added, 'Perhaps I should get my company's translator here – and someone from the British Embassy?'

The Sheikh wore very thick glasses and had a long grey beard, looked a nice old gentleman but when the translator had interpreted this for him his whole demeanour changed and I saw that he wasn't a nice old gentleman at all. He simply blew his top. 'No translator!' he raged. 'No one from the embassy!'

'In that case I want a lawyer,' I demanded.

The translator somehow stemmed the flow of invective from 'the nice old gentleman' long enough to explain my new demand. This time the old bird nearly hit the roof! Under Qur'anic law, he declared, there was no question of any lawyer. And my sentence was three years in jail!

The clerk quickly leaned across and said something to the Sheikh which I couldn't catch but the Egyptian advised me to keep quiet or otherwise, 'we'll all get into trouble, including me.'

It turned out that what the clerk had apparently told the old geezer was that my 'confession' should have been read out first before sentence was passed. This had the effect of calming the Sheikh down but he still sat there simmering and threatening to explode as my 'confession' was read out. When the clerk reached the part which stated that I had operated a still, I immediately objected.

'That is not true – I have never admitted it. Nor, so far as I or my company witness, Mr Roger Lilly know, was that ever written down in my statement. Anyway, the statement was in Arabic, not English, which I don't understand.'

The clerk held up the bit of paper which was my 'statement' and showed me a signature.

'Is that yours?' he demanded.

I said it was. I had signed all the sheets and so had Mr Lilly and we agreed to everything read out to us by our company translator. But I had never admitted having a still – and I still didn't!

By now it was 12.30 p.m. and perhaps I had been keeping the Sheikh from his prayers for he suddenly stood up and still in a rage, announced, 'Three years' imprisonment and three hundred lashes. The sentence to be published in all Saudi newspapers and broadcast on TV and radio. This evil crime, this corruption of young Arab youths by you and by other western criminals must be stopped.'

I was completely taken aback by the vehemence of the Sheikh's denunciation and by his obvious anger but when the clerk handed me the sentence book to sign, I put on my best English accent and said, 'I wish to appeal. I will not sign this book or agree to this sentence.'

This created more uproar. The Sheikh started to yell at me, telling me what a dangerous criminal I was. He and the clerk then threatened that if I did not sign the book, my sentence would be doubled. When they saw me stand my ground, however, the clerk bawled that I would be tortured and made to sign. 'In the end you will sign because all you westerners are shit,' he declared.

I leaped to my feet instantly. As I did so, the chain of my handcuff caught on the open arm of the chair in which I had been sitting and dragged it forward. I grabbed at the arm to get the chair out of my way and then changing my mind I grabbed the chair firmly, raised it in the air, and hurled it at the Sheikh. I didn't intend to hit him, of course. I wanted to hit the wall behind him, as a sign that I could get as angry as anybody else in that room. But the chair splintered behind his ear and all hell broke loose. Guards swarmed all over the place but oddly enough, nobody tried to touch me. Instead, they pounced on 'Ski' and hauled the two of us back into the big waiting room. When Jim asked what was wrong, 'Ski' almost wept.

'This guy Fraser will get us all shot,' he protested.

'What happened was that a chair flew out of my hand,' I told Jim, and tried to turn away in disgust from 'Ski', an impossible feat as I was still handcuffed to him. 'Anyway, he'll tell you what happened when he stops crying like a baby,' I said.

This time there was no argument about the guards hiring a taxi to return us to prison (although it meant they could not claim 'expenses'). In their view I was no longer just a troublemaker but a really dangerous criminal. One of them telephoned the prison and asked that the minibus which had brought us to court should come back to fetch us. I was sure that this time I really had gone too far. I had heard that it was not unusual for Arab trouble-makers to be taken into the desert and shot and I envisaged a similar fate. Not that I was afraid of death – or at least not at that moment, for life was proving so damn awful in Saudi custody that even death seemed a relief. Nor did I regret the way I had behaved. The Saudis had every right to object to alcohol in the club but the correct punishment, in my opinion, should have been deportation – not the degradation of an Arabian prison. I *had* baited the guards – and indeed, every other Saudi with whom I had come into contact – but I had a purpose behind this. I wanted to show the Saudis that I was a 'Scotlander' and therefore not a man to be pushed around like a coolie; I also wanted the Saudis to realise I was more trouble than I was worth, in the hope that they would release me.

When we returned to the prison, I was taken immediately to see Abdul. There was an American prisoner already in the office, a young 21-year-old called Christian who had already served two years of a five-year sentence for drug offences. Also there were Christian's father and stepmother who had just flown in from America to see their son. Abdul interrupted his conversation with them to ask why I had thrown the chair.

'Because I don't think much of your justice,' I replied.

'Sit down,' he said curtly. I held up my handcuffed hands and he gestured to the nearest guard to release me.

He then turned to Chris and asked him if he would translate for him. Chris, I should explain, had been the only westerner in Malaz prison for some time and as a result had been forced to learn Arabic in order to survive.

'Don't bother, Chris,' I said. 'If Abdul wants to talk to me, tell him to use his limited English – I'll understand.'

'Cool it, Ian,' advised Chris. 'Abdul is really a nice guy.'

'Shit to that,' I replied. 'I don't want to talk to him,' and I began chatting to Chris's parents, asking them what part of the United States they came from and other questions of that kind.

Abdul decided it was time I was hauled out of there so he

called a guard and, although I couldn't catch what he said, I decided he was ordering me into the punishment cell. I said good-bye to Chris's parents and began to trudge back to my *seep*. As we walked down the long hall, the guards suddenly called 'Halt' and again stopped me opposite the door to the punishment cell. Once more, of course, nobody had a key and so a guard had to go back to Abdul's office. Once again Abdul appeared in person, this time handing the key to one of his men who opened the door. Without hesitation I boldly strode in – and then wished I hadn't. The cell was no more than two metres square and there were two sets of handcuffs bolted high up in the wall. In the middle of the floor was another of those noisome holes which pass for an Arabian water closet, this one overflowing with indescribable filth. I decided it would be bad enough to be strung up to those handcuffs, but a hell of a lot worse to be forced to stare at that awful hole all day. I stood there waiting to be pinioned while Abdul watched me from the doorway. Then I smiled at him as much to say, 'Do your worst' and he suddenly turned to the guards and said 'Finish'. To my surprise, I was told to return to my *seep* which I did. I couldn't understand it, really. Was it because of the presence in the prison of Chris's mother and father? Or was it because he liked me or admired my spunk – or simply realised that I was being treated badly? I never found out – yet the fact that I was able to get away with outrageous behaviour when other prisoners, both Arabs and westerners, were punished for the slightest misdemeanour was extraordinary.

There was more pantomime at the *seep* gate when the duty guard began his routine attempt to search me. In return I attempted to search him which raised hoots of laughter from the other prisoners who were quickly dispersed by the irate guards.

When I walked back to my cell, it was like the return of a conquering hero. Prisoners gathered from all over the block to stare at me, rumours of my behaviour having already reached them on the prison grapevine. Peter, Hans, Manfred, Ibrahim and Sabri greeted me eagerly and when I confirmed that I had thrown a chair at the Sheikh. Sabri translated the details to a delighted audience from the whole block and there were loud murmurs of approval. Sabri said to me, 'The Arabs say "Fraser good." '

Peter had collected my food for me while I was in court and I had my first drink of water since early that morning; as the temperature had by now risen to over 100 degrees, I was in need of it. I had, in fact, refused water offered me in the Sheikh's office, again as a way of showing the Saudis that I was not like them, but was a very special man. I had overheard one of them say that I was like a camel, which at least meant that I was getting through to them.

For the rest of that day I remained a hero to the Arab prisoners. Later that afternoon, the atmosphere took a less agreeable turn. Some Arabs came up to me to say that they had been told by the guards that the authorities intended to shoot me – I was proving too troublesome.

Peter and Hans were concerned about this and Manfred urged me to make sure I took one of them with me – he would see that Austrian newspapers printed the full story.

'Thank you for the kind thought,' I replied, 'but I don't intend to get shot. However, if you'd like to take my place and get yourself publicity, then you're welcome.'

We laughed but underneath all the grins and smiles I realised that the possibility that I might be shot was not at all farfetched.

Next day, 'women's day' all western prisoners were allowed into the visiting room and I finally got a chance to talk to such friends as Arthur. Arthur also took a gloomy view of my chances and said he was sure I'd be taken into the desert and shot. Indeed, the reaction of the Saudi authorities so far was baffling everyone. I ought at least to have been bunged in the punishment cell – or even tortured, if not shot. Instead I was being allowed to behave as though I were in some way privileged. Nobody could understand it and could only guess that the Saudis were preparing to boil me in oil.

The welfare ladies were, as usual, sympathetic and even suggested that they should visit Abdul to explain that it was my headaches that were at the root of the difficulties. I was rather rude to them, I'm afraid, and bluntly told them to 'mind their own business', but quickly added, 'it might only get you into trouble also'.

I did not, in fact, find it easy to carry on a sensible conversation with these good ladies who obviously had such excellent intentions towards us and whose visits undoubtedly helped to lift our morale. But as my morale was already as high as I wanted it to be, I did not feel I was benefiting much from their ministrations.

Besides, their visits did arouse a definite sexual interest. I had never even thought of touching one of them, of course, or of wanting to affect the relationship but I found myself regarding them as alarmingly flirtatious, especially as some of them carelessly undid the top button of their dresses when they walked into the waiting room. One woman, indeed, eventually had an affair with a Frenchman after he had been released. Anyhow, I still looked forward to their visits, if only because it gave me a chance to talk to Arthur and Bill.

Tom turned up during this visit, as usual with a welcome parcel of food. He had heard about my sentence and said that both Ian Wylie and Roger Lilly intended to visit me on Saturday. They believed that now that I had been sentenced, it should be easier to get me released.

'But I still believe the only way you'll ever get out is by escaping,' insisted Tom.

'OK. If I'm not free by October, then I'll go along with that,' I promised him. He assured me that he would help in every way and would never leave Saudi Arabia without me.

On Friday afternoon, which was 'open visiting' day, I had a visit from four members of the company staff. On these occasions we were not allowed 'private' interviews. Instead, as at Malaz, we were forced to crowd up to the wire and to talk to our visitors through the mesh. I joined in the general shouting as the lads did their best to make themselves heard but it was hopeless. However, it was good for morale and helped to keep my spirits up. One of the chaps called out, 'There's no bar in Humming Bird House now, Ian! We're all getting mighty thirsty!'

'Try it in here for a while,' I called back. 'We've the same trouble here!'

Bill Hunter, our site clerk, shouted to me that three years was a ridiculous sentence and had to be a mistake. He had been charged with drink offences himself, five times in four years – mainly for being drunk – and had always got away with a nominal sentence. As for the club, the Saudi authorities had always condoned the existence of such places provided no Arabs were involved.

'I know that, Bill,' I told him, 'and you know that. But the Saudis don't seem to know it.' And we laughed. After all, it might be me who was behind bars today – but if the Saudis continued to behave irrationally, any of the other fellows might be in jail with me tomorrow.

On Saturday morning I was taken alone to see the Sheikh and brought straight into his private office without a preliminary wait in the big room outside. This time, however, I was not placed opposite the great man as on my previous visit but instead made to stand just inside the doorway where I was surrounded by six guards. The nearest chair, I noted, was a good ten feet away from me.

The proceedings opened with the Sheikh placing the sentence book on his desk and again asking me to sign it.

'I wish to appeal,' I said.

'There is no appeal,' replied the Sheikh, 'and if you don't sign this you'll stay in prison until you do.'

'Does that mean if I sign, I'll go free then?'

He glared at me angrily. Clearly he didn't like people who argued with him or twisted his words.

'No. It means that your sentence will start. Your sentence cannot start until you sign – which puts your release back that much further.'

'Why is it important for me to sign?' I challenged him.

'Because it is Qur'anic Law,' he replied.

'But I'm not a Muslim,' I pointed out.

'That is not Allah's fault,' he snapped. 'You are a misguided person – but with Allah's help you will change.'

I'd had enough of this sort of stuff so I shouted at him, 'Nuts!' and turned to walk out of the office.

The result was another terrible flap, the interpreter shouting at me that I must stay.

'This conversation is at an end,' I told him and stalked out of the room without anybody hindering me. No one, it seems, had ever done such a thing before and now no one knew what ought to be done. I walked straight into the big waiting room which was full of other prisoners and stood with my back to the wall waiting to see what would happen. The ball, as I saw it, was now in the Sheikh's court.

Some minutes later, two guards came into the room and prodded me towards the exit.

'Where are we going?' I demanded.

'To prison,' I was told.

'Tell me,' I enquired, 'how are we going back – in a taxi?'

'Yes.'

'And you're paying?'

'No, no, you paying, Fraser.'

'In that case we're staying put. Do you understand? Fraser no money. Fraser not pay for taxi.'

It took them some minutes to make a decision about this and it then turned out to be in my favour. Rather than risk another row, they decided to fork up themselves. When the taxi-driver saw that the prisoner was a westerner, however, he refused to take us so one guard had to go and hunt for another taxi, leaving me alone with only a single guard.

We were scarcely alone before the fellow began to flatter me. 'Fraser is good,' he told me.

I stared at him in astonishment. 'I'm a good man, I know that.'

'Yes, Fraser is good,' he repeated and I then twigged that he was scared stiff I might boff him and run off. I wanted to tell him that the only thing that prevented me doing it was the presence of my younger brother in Riyadh but I decided to let the bloke sweat it out.

Back in prison again, I was taken straight to Abdul's office where Roger Lilly was waiting to see me. Wylie, it seemed, had gone back to England on urgent business. Roger said he had been instructed to do everything he could to get me released now that I had been sentenced and that he hoped to see Prince Khalid and get him to intervene. 'Thanks, Roger,' I replied 'but all this is the kind of stuff I've been hearing since my arrest. I'll believe something when something happens.'

'Well, Lillian's going to visit you on Monday and she wants to know if there's anything special she can bring you?'

'Some of her apple pie, tell her. Indeed, any of her home baking.'

I then asked him about Ramadan. During the 40 days of Ramadan, Muslims fast during the hours of daylight and abstain from such pleasures as sex. I wondered how this would affect all the queers in Al-Ould. 'I've been told that even non-Muslims are expected to observe these abstinences,' I informed Roger. 'Now, if anything like that happens to me, Abdul is going to have a lot of trouble.'

Roger crossed over to Abdul's desk and took up the matter at once. The latter shrugged, 'Why worry. It is only forty days, after all – and soon passes. The problem is that we have no place in the prison where we can put non-Muslims.'

Roger quickly showed he was not satisfied with this limp explanation. 'I'm sorry,' he said. 'We will immediately let our embassy know about this and our company in London will certainly raise the matter with the British Foreign Office as a matter of urgency.'

Abdul wasn't looking for a fight. 'Well,' he said casually, 'if there is going to be an objection, I will speak to someone about it. I will let you know the result on your next visit.'

I chipped in at once to add to Abdul's little burden with a request that I be allowed to share my cell with the two Englishmen, Arthur and Claud.

'That is not possible,' said Abdul, shaking his head.

'In that case,' said Roger doughtily, 'I shall speak to the Governor of Riyadh.'

Before the end of the interview, I managed to ask Roger what Richard Northern, the vice-consul, was doing for me and he said he was trying to find out the technical situation following my refusal to sign the sentence book and whether my appeal had been allowed.

When I returned to the block it was in time to see a right old punch-up in progress, and for once I stayed out of it. The Arabs were constantly fighting between themselves and we westerners had long ago decided that it was not in our interests to become involved. I steered clear of the fracas and walked into the cell to find that Peter had received some excellent news. He was to see the Sheikh the next day and as his 'crime' was a minor one – he had merely been drunk in the street – his company anticipated that he would be released and deported. Hans and Manfred insisted that as they had been in prison for several months and their 'crimes' were hardly more serious than his that he was bound to collect three years rather than be released. The gap between Peter's hopes and Hans's and Manfred's expectations was so great that I decided to run a 'book' on it, with stakes of £2 each. Peter's own fancy was deportation; I guessed he would get six months and 50 lashes; Hans said he would be sentenced to six months; and Manfred plumped for one year and 100 lashes.

The idea of a bet raised our spirits and we were all in a state of high good humour and excitement when Peter returned. He kept us waiting for a moment to allow the tension to rise.

'Six weeks – and no lashes,' he said finally, 'so all bets are off.'

'Good on you, Peter,' I said. 'As you've already done eight weeks that means you'll be released right away.'

'Perhaps,' said Peter. 'Perhaps not. This is Saudi Arabia, after all.'

'Yes, fuck it,' I said.

In the event, the wheels of Saudi justice ground almost as slowly as the mills of God. A week later, Peter was transferred to Malaz prison and four weeks after that he was finally released, which meant, all in all, that he had served out a thirteen-week term for only a six-week sentence.

The Saudis, of course, have a saying that covers this sort of thing – 'What does it matter?'

NINE

I continued to carry on, almost as though I were running the prison and not Abdul. When anybody left the block, for instance, he was not supposed to take cigarettes with him. When the guards tried to prevent me, however, or take away my cigarettes, I simply shouted at them 'Fuck off!'

If they remonstrated, I pretended I didn't understand them and to pile on the agony, would pull out a packet and offer them a cigarette. Usually they held up their hands in horror but when I knew other prisoners were watching, I added insult to injury by offering them a lighted match.

'Go away!' one fellow finally shouted at me. 'The other prisoners see that we cannot control you. We do not want them to see our shame.'

The following Monday, we were finally allowed into the court-yard to exercise. This minor relaxation on the part of the authorities was interpreted by most prisoners as the direct result of my complaints and throughout the whole of the exercise period, prisoners kept coming over to me and saying, 'Fraser good, Fraser good.'

Indeed, conditions were improving to such a degree that, when I added everything up, it looked as though I might have difficulty finding any other complaints. Sunday was a visiting day, as was Monday sometimes; then there was women's day on Thursdays and finally all discipline was relaxed on Fridays, the Arab Sabbath. In each period of a fortnight, there also appeared to be at least one or two other days when we were simply left to get on with life as we pleased. In a sense it was the life of Reilly, although my experience was hardly typical of the other prisoners.

I, after all, was the only one to enjoy the privilege of interviews or visits in Abdul's office or in the reception room. I also got fresh food every day. Even canny old stagers like Arthur had to spend all their time in the *seep* and except for the odd visit from the vice-consul or this new hour of exercise in the courtyard, had to remain behind bars all the time. I had much to be thankful for – which was not, however, the way I wanted to view it. I was still smarting with indignation at my incarceration and the sheer injustice of it all.

Soon after the exercise period, ny name was called out and I was told to go to Abdul's office where I found Lillian Wylie waiting along with a fellow Scot called Don. Lillian had worked hard to prepare several nice little things for me and had brought me an apple pie as well as Scottish scones, home-baked sausage rolls and other goodies and general foodstuffs. Don was a good raconteur and his flood of funny jokes put everybody, except Abdul, in good humour. Unfortunately it was my last visit from Lillian for she was forbidden to visit the prison again by the Saudis.

At the end of the visit, I strolled with my two visitors towards the prison gate. We were at the gate, saying good-bye when I heard a sobbing noise behind me and I saw Claud being led across the yard by two guards who were helping to hold him up. When they reached me, the guards released him and he dropped to the ground where he lay moaning and crying as though he had just been tortured. I went over to him and asked him if he had been beaten up.

'No,' he replied and I was surprised to see tears running down his cheeks, 'I've got toothache.'

I stared at him in astonishment. 'You mean you're not dying?' I demanded. 'You've simply got toothache?'

'Yes,' he mumbled and I saw the guards laughing at him.

I turned to Don. 'This is Claud,' I said. 'He is *supposed* to be *British*. There's nothing wrong with him except toothache.'

I was so ashamed by this bloke's conduct that I turned away and went back to my block at once. 'If he's British,' I told myself, 'then from now on, I'm going to call myself *Scottish*.' Back in the block, I found several Arab prisoners still chortling at Claud's performance. I decided they were laughing at a westerner's discomfiture simply because he was a westerner.

'Listen, you geezers,' I warned them, 'I'm no Claud – so never try and treat me like him. Otherwise, it's a punch in the mouth. Is that clear?'

I was beside myself with anger and it was only later that I realised the Arabs were not laughing at me (or, indeed, westerners in general) and had intended no disrespect personally. I should have joined in their laughter and in that way, I suppose, they would have forgotten Claud. The worse thing, I felt, was that I had revealed part of myself and for some days after, I felt uncomfortable just being near them.

Tuesday afternoon was usually 'men's visiting day' so when I heard Arthur's name called from the next block, I went along to our gate and told the guard that my name had been called and without checking he allowed me into the yard where I strolled over to the visiting room, some 30 yards away.

Both Arthur and Claud were there. The visitor, it seems was Arthur's but every time Arthur had a visitor, Claud went along too.

'Hello,' I said to Arthur, pointedly ignoring Claud. 'So what was his trouble yesterday?'

'He's a cunt, that was his trouble,' said Arthur venomously.

Claud having been disposed of, I asked Arthur about the conditions in his block. I told him Roger Lilly hoped to get me moved in along with him.

'Don't you let him,' advised Arthur. 'Ours is a dreadful block.' He said it was filthy and incredibly noisy, and every time the Arabs said *salha* everybody had to get up and join in. I'd be far better off staying where I was, he advised.

While we were talking, my block guard came running up and started yelling at me. I looked at him as if he were a lunatic and then he called two more guards and I was told to go back to my own block. As the noise in the visiting hall at that moment was so bad that you could hardly hear yourself think, I decided to go quietly, but I had hardly got back when my name was called out so I again trotted off to the gate where the guard, convinced that I was once more trying to con him, refused to allow me out. I called Sabri and asked him to translate but he was so scared that he would be punished if the guards didn't like what he translated, that he refused. So I grabbed the guard's wrist, squeezed it very tightly and then hissed at him, 'I'm going to have my fucking visit!' I then released him and walked over to the wire mesh where I saw Tom. The entire effort, alas, turned out to be a waste of time because neither of us could hear each other because of the din. As I walked back to my block, I vented my ill-humour on the guard by searching him. The guard just stood there staring at me unhappily but making no attempt to resist me. Back in the *seep*, the Arab prisoners crowded round me to tell me again 'Fraser good.'

Ramadan was due to begin the following Saturday. On Wednesday, I had a visit from Roger Lilly and Richard Northern who confirmed that I had been sentenced to three years' imprisonment along with 300 lashes and that the judgment would be announced on Saudi TV and radio. However, my appeal had been allowed, despite the chair-throwing incident and would go to Prince Niaf, Minister of the Interior, who would either confirm or reject the sentence or perhaps double it. Northern would do everything he could to have me released. He hoped I might even be released during Ramadan – but everything depended on the way I behaved.

'Behave?' I queried.

'Be like the other prisoners,' he said. 'Don't complain.'

'You mean live in filthy conditions. Lie on the floor. Have lice crawl all over you. Take any beatings the guards wish to dish out. No, thank you. I'll not give any trouble provided I'm treated properly – but otherwise . . .'

'You're making it hard for the company to help,' interrupted Roger.

'What help?' I demanded to know. Actually I knew I was being unfair because I had no way of knowing what strings the company were trying to pull.

'That's not fair,' he objected, as though he had read my thoughts.

'Perhaps I'd understand better if you'd tell me exactly what you are doing?' I said.

'Well, one of the company's top Arab contacts is going to see a Sheikh in Jeddah who has enormous influence and it is hoped that he can either release you himself or act as an intermediary.'

'What about Prince Khalid, our sponsor?' I asked. 'Why can't he do something?'

'I'm sorry, he can't,' said Roger. 'He cannot get involved as this is a drink offence.'

'Ian Wylie told the staff that Prince Khalid would get us out of any offence,' I said angrily. 'Was he lying?'

'He wasn't,' said Roger. 'The prince could handle something like a driving offence but he can do nothing about drink.'

'A fat lot of good that does me,' I said. 'I'm not in for a driving offence.'

'Changing the subject,' I said to Roger, 'Ramadan's coming up – I don't suppose these heathens expect us Christians to take part in their prayers, do they? If they do, there's going to be trouble.'

Northern at once turned and addressed Abdul. The Saudi captain explained that all Christian prisoners would be put in a double cell in Block One and, indeed, would be kept there for the rest of their sentence.

'Will we get beds?' I asked.

'Yes,' said Abdul.

'What about food? Will we get it every morning, even during Ramadan?'

'Certainly.'

'And exercise. Will we get exercise?'

'I'm afraid not. All the guards will be fasting.'

'What about night-time, then?'

'The guards will be eating, then. It will not be possible.' He glanced at his watch impatiently. 'I'm sorry, gentlemen. But the time is up.'

On Friday I was visited by Bill Hunter and two other members of the company staff. Bill confirmed that Farouk, our company Arab, had gone down to Jeddah to see the Sheikh and to try to secure my release.

'You'll be out in a week,' he promised. 'Ian Wylie has been telling the staff that they are only waiting for the papers to be signed.'

'I'll believe everything when I see it,' I told him.

Bill said he would visit me on Thursday morning as Tom had been sent to Hofuf. He would bring me whatever food I needed. Wilson, the chef, wanted to know if there was anything special I needed?

'Well, if he could increase the amount of stuff during Ramadan – I'd like to help out some of the other western blokes here.'

'I'll arrange that,' promised Bill.

On Saturday morning the big move to Block One took place. At first the guards refused to allow Sabri and Ibrahim, who though both Arabs were Christians, to go with us but eventually they agreed. There were plenty of bunk beds in the block – each cell had its quota of fourteen double bunks – and there were others outside in the hall. Altogether, there were 26 of us Christians in the block. The Arabs who had been occupying the bunks, of course, were determined not to give them up and there was a shouting match; in the end, indeed, the guards had to force them out. Once the squawking Muslims were cleared out the Christians from Blocks Three and Four were allowed in, among them Arthur and his fellows.

The double bunks were crowded so tight that it was an easy matter to step along the top from one bunk to another. Hans and I managed to grab top bunks as did Arthur and Claud but poor Bill Shunks had to put up with a lower bunk. My bunk proved to be very comfortable with a twelve-inch space on one side and about two feet on the other. At ground level, however, there was an illusion that the bunks were crowded closer together; from my bunk the guys at the bottom looked like sardines in a tin. I had a box of 50 paperback books with me and as I surveyed the cell, I felt I had done pretty well. It reminded me of being in a hostel somewhere in Europe; there were four Germans, four Portuguese, one Italian, one Frenchman, two Greeks, one Austrian, seven Americans, two Sudanese, one Swiss and two Arabs, besides we three British.

A guard told us about the rules: no smoking or drinking outside the cell, so as not to tempt the fasting Muslims. An Arab who was being allowed to stay in the cell demanded that we made no noise during the day as he would be sleeping but I gave this character short shrift. If he didn't want to put up with us I told him, he could leave. So he shut up.

Soon the other fellows worried about food – were they going to be forced to eat prison food during Ramadan? Claud, in particular, was very worried about this. 'I don't know,' I told him. 'Anyway, I've never eaten it and I don't intend to eat it. If you're so worried, why don't you ask yourself?'

'You have powerful friends,' he told me. 'They help you.'

'Oh don't be such a cunt, Claud.'

However, as the other chaps were also worried about food supplies, I agreed to go and see Abdul on their behalf.

The sergeant at the gate stubbornly refused to allow me through to see him. So I shouted at him and then threatened that he would 'be sorry' if he didn't change his attitude. The bloke was soon on the run and he eventually ran off to the warden only to return to open the gate for me.

Abdul, in his own way, appeared pleased to see me. Was I happy in the block? Oh, yes, I replied. Then, on a sudden thought, I put in yet another complaint – the first thing that popped into my head.

'There is only one roof fan, however,' I told him, 'and we need two.'

Obligingly, he made a note of this on his little pad of paper. 'What we want to know is what about food during the day for the Christian prisoners?' I asked.

'You get your food, Fraser. Why do you worry about the others?'

'We are friends, that's why. They have asked me to speak to you?'

'Well, go back and tell them you have spoken to me, Fraser. However, there can be no government food during the day. I have no power to do anything about it. The food is not prepared in this prison.'

I realised he was telling the truth and to be honest, I was not all that interested in the other fellows' food anyway. So I wished Abdul a nice Ramadan and returned to the block where I told the fellows that they would have to eat at night like the Arabs. Claud got very upset at this but I calmed him down by telling him I'd give him some of my food, although I said I couldn't promise to feed the whole 25 Christian prisoners.

'When do we eat, then?' demanded Claud.

'Hold on there, friend,' I said, 'I'll have to see how I can stretch it out – after all, I have to consider Arthur, Hans, Manfred and Bill.'

'I thought you meant just you and me,' accused Claud.

'Claud,' I said to him, 'you really are a glutton aren't you?'

We had been told that during Ramadan, the prison shop would sell us orange squash along with water to dilute it. I told Arthur I'd try and get ice sent in which would give us a pleasant cold drink in the morning.

That night someone outside the prison spotted the new moon and hurried to register his find with the Moon Spotting Office in Riyadh so that Ramadan could start officially. (We had asked if we could join in the race but were told it was not permitted – a pity because we knew the exact time and exact evening when the new moon would appear, which the Muslims didn't.) The Muslims in the block seemed surprised by the news but were happy enough to reverse their daily routine – sleeping all day and eating and doing their other chores at night. Arthur and I were baffled by the procedure; to us the whole thing made no sense.

Next morning, after some trouble wakening up the block guards, I collected my food as usual. I despatched my compliments to Wilson the chef and asked if he could increase the supply as I wished to share some with my fellow prisoners. Back in the block, I prepared the usual breakfast of one carton of frozen fresh milk, green salad and cheese, plus some sliced meat. Then I placed an old newspaper which Wilson had sent to me at the foot of my bunk and set out some egg, sausage and bread. I then cut six sausages into twelve pieces and told the fellows they could each have a sandwich – first come, first served. Claud, as I had expected, was first on the scene and grabbed two halves of a sausage.

'Don't be so greedy, Claud!' I shouted and told him he was only supposed to take half a sausage.

He then reached out and grabbed an egg!

'Listen,' I said more fiercely, 'a sandwich means a slice of bread with a half-sausage or with an egg – it doesn't mean sausage *and* an egg! For Christ's sake, behave yourself.'

After that, the meal proceeded harmoniously. I completed the repast with some cold orange and handed out whatever ice cubes were left. We agreed that next day Bill would buy the water and orange drink and Hans said he would do the buying the day after that. So we suddenly found that we were a little group prepared to cooperate and to pay, each in turn, for whatever little luxuries we wanted.

Conditions in the cell, however, were too crowded. If four men lay down on the floor at once, for instance, there was no room to move. So, except for visits to collect food or to go to the toilet or to wash, most of us spent the six weeks of Ramadan lolling on our bunks reading or chatting to each other. As a result we got to know each other fairly well. Arthur, I discovered, was unhappy at being in prison while Claud actually liked it and Bill felt philosophical. Hans, for his part, had given up all hope of ever being released. I was the only one, it seemed, who had decided to escape (although because I was surrounded all the time by Muslim prisoners, I still couldn't see a way of managing it). I wondered if Arthur would join me in an attempt.

'Would you try to escape if you could, Arthur?' I finally asked him.

'You can bet I would,' he said fervently, 'but it wouldn't be easy.'

I said nothing and let the subject drop for a moment. However, I now knew that Arthur would be prepared to take part in an attempt but as I hadn't made any plans yet, I didn't tell him I was determined to break out.

About a week after Arthur and I had this interesting conversation, a sergeant entered the cell and ordered out both Sabri and Ibrahim, announcing that both were being released, which came as a surprise to everybody. We gathered round to congratulate them and tell them how sorry we were to lose them, but they had hardly gone when we discovered the truth – Sabri had been put in Block Three and Ibrahim in Block Two on the excuse that they planned to escape. Everybody knew that this was rubbish for the chances of an Arab escaping were nil. We decided it was one of Abdul's nasty little tricks. All along he had been opposed to treating Christian Arabs like westerners but he obviously wanted to assert his authority and prove to us that he, Abdul, was in charge of the prison.

'So that's his little game,' I said to Arthur. 'Every dog has his day, I suppose. But I'd have thought him above that sort of thing.'

The next pin-prick came from the block foreman who turned out to be a nasty little runt who stubbornly refused to leave us alone. He came into the cell to complain that we made too much noise when we went outside into the hall during the day to eat more comfortably. In fact, we only left the cell, as I have already said, to collect food parcels, visit the toilets or wash – and, after a day or so of our crowded conditions, to eat our meals; when we did so, too, we tried not to disturb the Muslims. So when this little brute started to stir up trouble, I told him to fuck off.

He must have known about my reputation but like an idiot decided to pursue the matter. He hastily backed out of the cell after I had sworn at him but returned within minutes to tell me that I must go to the guards for punishment.

'Look, mate,' I told him, and as far as I can remember, I even wagged a finger at him, 'fuck off! And furthermore, tell the guards to fuck off also!'

You've never seen a man's face change so quickly. The tough, authoritative little air suddenly vanished and, instead, I found myself looking at a frightened rabbit. Without another word he scurried from the room.

'Silly little bastard,' commented Arthur. 'Doesn't know his arse from his elbow?'

I found that Bill Shunk had managed to escape from Saudi police custody while he was being interrogated in a police station and had been able to remain at liberty for six days. I cornered him and asked him to tell me his story.

When his mother died of cancer, Bill had gone back to America for the funeral. When he returned to Riyadh, a policeman was waiting for him at his rented villa. Due to the hurry of his departure, he had forgotten to pay his rent and when the land-lord turned up to demand payment and found the place empty he had entered the premises. There he had found a *siddeeky* still which Bill had been operating on the quiet.

Bill made no attempt to resist arrest, but on being taken to the police station asked to go to the toilet where he escaped through a window. During his six days on the run, he walked the streets of Riyadh, sleeping rough at nights until he contacted some Arab friends who promised to get him transport to take him out of Saudi Arabia. He steered clear of all western friends so as not to involve them, believing he could trust his Arab contacts. This trust was not misplaced – with the exception of one man who telephoned the police and told them where he was hiding.

'Your mistake, Bill, was that you trusted Arabs,' I told him. 'No westerner should do that!'

'What else could I do?' he asked. 'I had no car. There was no way I could get away without help. I had to take the only course open to me.'

'I reckon you score four marks out of ten for escaping at all and for staying free for so long. But you trusted the wrong people.'

This conversation gave me much to think about; at least I now knew what I should and shouldn't do. So I lay on the bunk, patiently trying to evolve a plan of escape. My advantage over Bill, of course, was that I had Tom on the outside.

Conditions inside the cell, despite overcrowding, were so

much better than I had previously experienced that I soon began to feel much better physically and much more alert mentally. The noise in the cell, too, was almost as nothing compared to the din outside; it was like sitting in the Garrick or Savage instead of in the middle of Petticoat Lane. As a result, the constant hammering in my head had eased off and I could take fewer paracetamol tablets. I hoped I would be allowed to stay in this cell during the rest of my stay in prison.

A day or two later I had a visit from Bill Hunter and two other members of the staff who came along to give me the latest news and to cheer me up. I was rather taken aback to find out that Tom had gone to England to see my father and mother and Anne and to tell them what the company was doing to obtain my release. At first I felt hurt by Tom's 'desertion' – he had not told me he was going. Then I told myself I was simply being stupid. After all, Tom had made sure that visits from the staff continued and that my food also still arrived on time. Wilson the chef had given him a promise that he would not let me starve and had proved as good as his word.

One day however, my food box did not arrive until 5 p.m., when it was brought to me by Mike White. Mike apologised for the delay, particularly as the meal had been a special one – turkey. At lunchtime that day Wilson the chef had announced to the staff that he intended sending whatever remained of the bird to me. When the staff heard this, they refused to eat any of the turkey and insisted that the whole bird, neatly sliced, be sent to me – a gesture which I much appreciated. The chef had first taken the turkey into the office of one of the bosses where it was left, unfortunately forgotten. It was not until late afternoon when Mike visited the office that he discovered the turkey. He grabbed it immediately and brought it straight to me as fast as he could.

Mike said I appeared to have lost weight, but otherwise that I looked OK. I told him it was because of the quiet life – it was proving good for me. He told me he had taken over my job and that work on the contract was going smoothly. Everybody on the site missed me but the buildings were still going up.

'You mightn't believe this – but I'm glad,' I told him. 'Really, I still think of it as my contract, you know. I'm proud of what I did.'

'I know,' agreed Mike sympathetically.

I was allowed to accompany him to the main gate. As we

neared the guards, I called out, loudly enough for them to hear, 'You know, Mike, these fellows wouldn't mind it a bit if I went out and you stayed in my place.' I turned to the guards, 'Isn't that so, fellows?' Like the dumb geezers they were, they laughed and nodded agreement.

'There, I told you so Mike! Now, all you have to do is to let me walk ahead of you.'

Mike gave me a long and strange look. Even if the guards didn't realise it, he knew I wasn't joking. He laughed nervously, quickening his pace and rapidly getting on the right side of the gate before I could do anything 'foolish'. I waved good-bye to him and went back to the block, carrying my turkey and with a plan of escape now beginning to formulate in my mind.

The turkey was greeted with delight by my cell-mates and Arthur took much pleasure in cutting up the bits that had not been already expertly sliced by Wilson. These pieces were placed on the end of my bed and divided up as equally as possible and then I called out, 'Grub's up' and invited everybody to partake. Again I caught Claud trying to take twice as much as anybody else and warned him that if he didn't behave I'd make him eat his share in solitude. I grew even more incensed with him when he refused to do his share of the washing up.

Claud, in fact, was turning out to be an incredible glutton. Food for the Arab prisoners arrived at 8 p.m. and 1 p.m. and although, of course, all westerners were entitled to share in these rations if they wished to, none of us except Claud would touch them. I saw him scoff down this slush with relish and said, exasperatedly, 'Is there nothing you won't eat?'

'Your company isn't providing enough food,' he retorted.

'What do you mean?' I asked him.

'Well, the British Embassy is paying your company to provide us with food. And you're giving it away to people who aren't British.'

'You absolute clot!' I told him. 'We're only getting that food because of the good offices of my brother Tom and Wilson the chef.'

'I tell you, your company is being paid by the embassy to feed the British prisoners.'

'If you believe that, you'll believe anything!' I shouted at him.

Arthur said to me, 'Now you know why I won't speak to him.

And, if you like, I'll now tell why I keep calling him a cunt and won't have anything to do with him.'

'I'd like to know, Arthur,' I replied and climbing back into my bunk, I lay down cupping my hands under the back of my head.

'When we first arrived in Al-Ould,' Arthur began, 'I wrote an account of all I knew about the Saudi Air Force – its problems with drugs and drink and how inexperienced Saudi airmen really were; it was the real inside dope, and I sent it to a friend of mine who works on newspapers in England in the hope that he could get it published. I was daft enough to tell Claud about this and he immediately wrote letters to the boss of BAC in Saudi Arabia, to the Governor of Riyadh, to Prince Niaf, to the British Embassy and finally to his wife saying that I intended to have these defamatory letters printed in England and declaring that he, Claud, was in no way involved in such disclosures and did not want to be punished for them.'

I looked at Claud and then back to Arthur.

'He wouldn't do that – there must be a mistake.' I said.

'There's no mistake,' replied Arthur darkly.

'Did you really do that, Claud?' I asked him.

'Of course, I did,' he retorted. 'Why shouldn't I? I wasn't involved in this ridiculous idea.'

'But you were informing on a fellow prisoner,' I pointed out. 'And a friend of yours, who was your partner in crime so far as the Saudis were concerned. Wasn't it up to you to stick together?'

Claud shrugged. 'I've done nothing wrong,' he insisted. And I had to leave it at that. If the man couldn't see where he had gone wrong, what was the use of arguing?

TEN

When I was next called to Abdul's office, Richard Northern and the personnel manager of BAC were waiting to talk to Arthur, Claud and me.

The BAC fellow began by pressing Arthur hard about the notes he had sent out to England. 'What do you think you'll gain by having such letters printed in the press?' he asked.

'Freedom!' replied the latter crisply.

'No, it won't,' said the manager. 'It won't help you at all.'

I was fascinated and wanted to hear more but just at that moment, a guard came into the room and told me that my daily food parcel had arrived. Reluctantly, I got up and went to collect it.

When I returned, the argument was still raging. As I walked in carrying my hefty parcel, Arthur, however, suddenly attacked the personnel manager: 'Look, that's how Ian's company looks after him. And what do we get from you – nothing!'

I showed Northern the food parcel. 'That is very good of your company,' he observed. I glanced at Claud, as much as to say 'Yah, so who's paying for food parcels?' but let the matter drop rather than let Abdul know that there was friction among the British prisoners.

The BAC representative eventually agreed to send food to Arthur twice a week but reiterated his view that Arthur was wrong to send the letters to Britain and that he should do everything he could to make sure that they were not published.

'I think he was right,' I butted in. 'I only wish I knew enough about the Saudi Air Force so that I could write about it!'

'Calm down, Ian,' advised the BAC chap.

'Don't tell me to calm down,' I exploded (although I normally considered him a nice chap). 'When you two fellows leave here, you'll trot off to a bar somewhere and have a gin and tonic while we're in here paying the penalty for doing the same. But it's OK for you lot – one of you is a diplomat and the other can drink on the air force base where the Saudi police aren't allowed.'

'Try and accept the situation, Ian. You are only making trouble for yourself and everybody else!'

'There is no way I'll ever accept this situation. As for the British Government – they should tell the Saudi Government in no uncertain terms to release us or otherwise they'll send in the boy scouts – which is all we would need to beat the Saudis. Or they could even send in a couple of Israelis to take over the country.'

'You're being silly, Ian.'

'Maybe. But I'd be a lot sillier if I accepted prison the way that cunt there is doing.' And I looked at Claud. Northern and the BAC chap exchanged glances and I could see they agreed with me about Claud. I may have been a troublemaker but my behaviour was more in the old-fashioned British tradition.

Following this visit, Arthur and I lay down on our bunks and ruminated on our plight. Finally I said to him, 'Look, old friend, obviously there's going to be no early release for either of us. I'm going to try and escape. Do you want to come along?'

Arthur considered this for a moment or two, then said, 'All right.'

'Good,' I said and I suddenly felt quite excited. 'After the "men's visit" on Friday, there is always a lot of activity in the reception room with the guards handing out whatever goodies our visitors have brought and giving out clean clothing to the Arabs. There's always a good crowd there and a lot of confusion. My idea is that we should add to those crowds and that confusion.'

'How?' asked Arthur.

'Well, we get every westerner to make sure he has a visitor that day and that the visitor brings a parcel. I reckon, what with westerners queuing up for their parcels and Arabs for their clothing, there should be about one hundred prisoners in there, all milling about. You and I will then make a run for the main gate where we'll both jump the guard. You'll grab him and hold him as a sort of hostage so that the guards on the watch-towers can't fire while I open the gate. Once through the gate, we can duck into the buildings opposite and keep out of the line of fire.'

'It sounds all right up to a point,' agreed Arthur. 'But what then?'

'Tom will have a car waiting for us. Then all we have to do is to leap into the car and he'll drive off. He'll have a safe house ready and we can lie up there as long as it's necessary before trying to get out of Riyadh.'

'Well, I'm game,' said Arthur. 'Anything's better than rotting in this hellhole.'

'Right, then. I'll work out further details. We mustn't be caught whispering together, or some of the others may cotton on to what we're up to. We need to keep this thing as quiet as possible.'

'That's OK by me,' agreed Arthur.

'I know plenty of British who will be happy to let us use their place as a safe house. Tom ought to be able to arrange with a British truck driver so that we can travel out of the country with him.'

'A container lorry's a good idea – we could hide in the container,' suggested Arthur.

'It may be asking a lot of some unknown lorry driver to smuggle us out,' I pointed out. 'Why should he risk it? Anyhow I'll write to Tom and put the idea up to him. He may be able to think of a better way.'

I wrote the letter that night and had it all ready when I was called out to pick up my food parcel next morning. Unfortunately the caller was Muhammad, our driver and not Tom himself who was working on the site. I didn't know whether or not to trust Muhammad who could read English but he had always been a good and faithful bloke so I decided to risk it. I told him he was to go straight to the site and deliver the letter to Tom as soon as possible. In the event, he did exactly as he was told.

Tom turned up in person with my food parcel on Sunday morning and handed me a letter in which he said that there would be no trouble arranging a car and a safe house. But he added that to ask an unknown truck driver to run the risk of smuggling us out of Saudi was a tall order. I told him I agreed with this and that I'd try and think of something else.

I returned to my cell and waiting until our cell-mates were busy about their own affairs, told Arthur what Tom had said about the truck driver.

'It seems to me that the only way out of Saudi Arabia is by truck,' said Arthur.

'No, it isn't the only way,' I objected. 'For instance, we could arrange to have ourselves flown out of Riyadh as cargo.'

'How do you mean?' asked Arthur, puzzled.

'Suppose Tom were to arrange for two big boxes to be made and then when we escaped, we climbed into them and were taken straight to the airport and loaded aboard as cargo. We'd be home in twenty-four hours.'

'No, I don't like it,' said Arthur adamantly. 'I don't fancy being locked up in a box. As to being tossed around with a lot of cargo – you could get your neck broken.'

'I'm sorry, Arthur. But unless you can think of a better idea, I'm going to see if this will work.'

Without help from Arthur, I then proceeded to make a sketch of a suitable box and asked Tom to arrange for two to be made, each four by three by two feet in size which I decided would allow us to sit comfortably. Twenty-four hours of being cooped up inside one would certainly not be comfortable but I decided that any discomfort we suffered, physically or mentally, was worth going through in exchange for our freedom. I then carefully wrote out a set of directions to Tom. He was to arrange for a gallon of water to be put into each box, as well as a gallon container each for us to piss into and finally a hammer and a blanket. I also asked him to secure sleeping tablets from the company doctor. As I saw it, we would fall fast asleep at Riyadh airport and wake up to liberty at Heathrow.

Arthur was still not convinced but I felt sure that once we were out of Al-Ould, he would be quite happy to climb into a box in order to get free.

On the following Thursday morning, Tom turned up with my food parcel and I was able to take my escape plan one stage further. I handed over the sketch of the boxes along with directions about the water containers and so on. I also asked him to give me an opinion on the feasibility of the scheme. Tom glanced at the sketch and after a quick study agreed that the idea seemed possible. I then told him I wanted him to get in touch with Anne and get her to send me £2000 to cover any expenses during the escape. I gave him a letter to this effect, confirming the request and explaining that although the scheme might seem dangerous,

I was prepared to take any risk in order to see her and the kids again.

Back in my cell, I lay down on the bunk and for the rest of the day ran over every aspect of the proposed break, hoping to foresee the snags that might occur. I told Arthur we would have to postpone the break until the nights grew darker, for we'd then have a better chance of succeeding. Besides, I explained, Tom would have to be out of the country at the time, otherwise the Saudis would pick him up in my stead. I said Tom was due to go on leave in early October, so we would plan our escape for 26 October. Arthur said that this was OK by him.

'I'm just trying to think what they'll all say when I walk into my niece's wedding in England as promised,' I remarked. (And, indeed, Anne, who attended the wedding, brought my clothes along with her, hoping I'd be there.)

Two days later, our hopes were savagely dashed. Tom arrived with a food parcel and said he had reconnoitred the airport to see if there would be any trouble getting through. The box idea would not work, he said. He had spent a whole night in the airport cargo section to check what happened there and saw that the Saudi customs opened all boxes. There was no sign that they were lax and he could only suggest that I think of some other idea.

Arthur was delighted to hear the news – he clearly feared claustrophobia. I told him, 'Fine, but the truck idea won't work, either.' I decided the best thing to do was to leave the transport question aside for the moment and instead figure out the point at which we should leave Saudi Arabia. Any attempt to get out via Bahrain seemed out of the question, because there were lots of troop movements along the east coast as a consequence of the Iraqi-Iranian conflict. Our best hope appeared to be to make for the port of Jidda on the west coast. If we could then arrange for a rubber boat, we could cross the Red Sea and make landfall in Egypt.

Arthur was sceptical. Crossing the Red Sea he said, would not be as easy as it sounded. By his reckoning we would have to sail some 300 miles and that would be difficult in a rubber dinghy.

'There are ships passing up and down the Red Sea all the time,' I pointed out, 'It's like being on a motorway in fact; all we'd have to do is to get into the shipping routes and hail a ship going towards the Suez Canal – we'd be home and dry.'

'We'd need luck – and lots of it,' objected Arthur. 'Suppose we pick on the wrong ship?'

'You're a Jeremiah,' I told him. 'Why should we pick on the wrong ship? Anyway, what else do you suggest?'

'We could sail up the Saudi coast, moving by night and hiding up by day, and make for Israel.'

'But that's a thousand miles,' I objected. 'And we'd be sailing in Saudi waters all the time.' I hesitated, then added, 'I'd prefer to take my chances on the open sea – there's no reason why a rubber dinghy shouldn't work. Anyway, Arthur, this is my escape. You can either do it my way or not come along. Is that fair?'

'OK,' he agreed doubtfully. 'You're right, I suppose.'

We finally decided that we would rush the main gate of the prison on the evening of 26 October 1980. Once out, we would take immediate cover in the buildings opposite the prison gate and so avoid the fire of the guards; then we'd jump into the car provided by Tom and drive like hell for Jidda.

'What about road checks?' asked Arthur.

'You're right – I hadn't thought about them. But we'll get past, somehow or other,' I said. 'At Jidda, we can buy the rubber boat.'

There were still further details to be thought out, however. What about footwear? I had only one pair of sandals which would be useless if I had to run or get involved in anything like jumping in and out of a boat or sailing it. I obviously needed shoes but how could I persuade Abdul of this? Apart from anything else, any demand by me for shoes might arouse his suspicions. Then the thought struck me; why not get the help of the doctor?

Some years earlier, I had broken the big toe on my left foot and it had never set properly. I could still not bend it. If I saw the doctor and complained that my toe was hurting, he might agree to order me new shoes.

The idea worked like a dream. The doctor began by apologising about the headache tablets, claiming that it was not his fault that he could not prescribe anything stronger than aspirin, but having looked at my toe, he was sure he could arrange for me to have proper shoes. He left me to go and see Abdul and when the latter called me to his office and inspected the offending member for himself he declared, 'Yes, I can see the trouble. I am happy to arrange for you to have a pair of shoes,' I marched out of the office grinning all over my face and thinking, 'You stupid bastard, Abdul – if only you knew.'

A new problem suddenly surfaced, however; Arthur had no shoes either. He had only a pair of old flip-flops which were of less use, indeed, than my sandals. The chances were that, particularly in the early stages of the escape, we'd have to run like hell, possibly ducking and weaving, as the guards in the block towers opened fire with their machine guns. There was no way Arthur could ever get clear, running in his old flip-flops.

'The hell of it,' he said, 'is that I actually have a good pair of shoes in my baggage.'

'Why can't you get hold of them, then?' I demanded.

'My baggage is in the storeroom. But look here, Ian, even if I can't get hold of them, I'm quite prepared to run barefoot.'

The next morning it was like bedlam in Al-Ould and when I woke up I couldn't understand what was going on at first. The Arab prisoners were all dressed in their Sunday best and were dancing madly around the main hall.

'Has somebody told them they're being released or what? Or are they all gay?' I asked.

'It's the end of Ramadan,' said Arthur. 'This is the Arab equivalent of Christmas.'

Our cell was filled all morning with celebrating Arabs. They came in to shake our hands and wish us well and in general to exchange cordial greetings. Out in the big hall the dancing continued as if it would never stop. The end of Ramadan, of course, was a terrific release for them. They could now eat, drink, or smoke if they wanted to; all fasting and restrictions were ended. With the celebrations, also came a whole new spate of rumours, the most feasible being that all drink prisoners were to be released. I found it hard to believe a word of this but when Hans, the German, was called out and told that he would be released, Bill Shunk said he now felt certain that most of us would soon be set free also. He said that every American imprisoned in Al-Ould had written to his congressman or senator back home and every man had received a reply – some were from men like Edward Kennedy and George Bush. None of the replies had been optimistic, but they gave the prisoners some hope that something might be done for them. (In February 1981, after the American Government had agreed to sell spare parts to the

Saudis for their F16 planes, all American prisoners were, indeed, sent home.)

There was also some bad news, however. Our relatively easy-going warden had suddenly disappeared (he had gone on a course, but we weren't told this) and had been replaced by a western-hating deputy called Abdullah. The first time I saw anything of this character was when he entered our cell on the second morning after his appointment and proceeded to dress us down over our 'dirty habits'. It was due to our 'dirty habit' of wiping our arses with tissue paper that the drains had become blocked, he said. In future we were to do as the Arabs did and use our hand.

'Fuck off!' I told him.

'You are shit, you westerners!' he screamed. 'And your mothers are shit!'

To the credit of our Muslim fellow prisoners, none of them was prepared to put up with this kind of abuse which they considered undeserved and so they, too, told him to buzz off. He departed, rather shame-faced, obviously having expected the Muslims to side with him. Fifteen minutes later, the *seep* foreman entered our cell to propose a compromise: we could continue to use the tissue paper but we were then to deposit them in the waste bins. We gave the bloke the same flea in the ear we had given Abdullah and off he went.

It was a bad start to the new regime and things rapidly grew worse. We heard over the grapevine that now Ramadan was over, we westerners were to be split up and sent back to our separate cells and blocks. When Roger Lilly came to see me that day, I asked him to speak to Abdullah about this and explain that we had been promised that all westerners would be kept together. Abdullah's reply was uncompromising. He was now in charge of the prison, he said and he would do as he wanted. He had heard all about Fraser and intended to show Fraser who was boss in Al-Ould. Roger told me he would immediately go to see the vice-consul and find out if there was anything he could do for us.

I broke the news to the other fellows and Arthur said that there was only one answer to this sort of behaviour and that was a hunger strike. We all agreed to this and so I took my box of food down to the guard at the gate and handed it to him. He looked at me and then at the box in astonishment and obviously didn't understand. I didn't bother to enlighten him, but turned and walked back. Back in the cell, the other fellows were busy getting rid of all their food. All, that is, except Claud. Claud stood there with an apple and an orange in his fists and when I walked in, asked, 'When does the strike begin?'

'It's begun,' I said. 'It began five minutes ago.'

'Why didn't you tell me?' he complained. And with that, he began eating both the apple and the orange as fast as he could.

'You *are* a cunt, Claud,' I said. 'Nobody can force you to strike – but you're either on hunger strike or you're not. You'd better make up your mind pronto.'

In due course Abdullah, accompanied by four armed guards, walked into our cell. It was time to move, declared Abdullah. We ignored him and lay there on our bunks.

'Fraser – move to *Seep* Two!' he ordered.

I lay back on my bunk, cradling my head, legs crossed comfortably, and without even looking at him, repeated 'Fuck off!'

He shouted to one of the guards who jumped up and tried to pull me off my bunk. I saw this dark face loom above the side of the bunk and with a quick movement, I bonked the guy on the nose. I didn't intend to hit him hard or destroy his male beauty, but he fell back with a startled yelp. Abdullah himself leaped back as if stung and then gave me a frightened look and bundled both himself and his guards out of the cell.

The other fellows immediately remonstrated with me. Why had I hit the guard? Now everybody would get into trouble.

'For God's sake, stop worrying,' I said. 'I'm the guy who hit him and I'm the only guy who's going to get punished – if anybody's going to get punished. What we must do is stick together and not allow ourselves to be separated. If Abdullah gets us on our own, he'll do what he likes with us.'

The block foreman suddenly arrived and informed Chris, the young American, that Abdullah wanted to see him.

'Go ahead,' I said. 'We're not starting a revolution.'

Chris was back within minutes carrying a stern warning from Abdullah. Chris, who had done only two years out of a five-year sentence, would lose all his remission, for example, others would also lose remission and on top of that the Saudi National Guard would be called in to force us out if we did not clear out voluntarily.

Faced with this threat, both Bill and Arthur argued that we

had no alternative. 'Resistance means bloodshed,' argued Arthur, 'and it isn't worth that.'

'I have a lot of respect for both you and Bill,' I told Arthur, 'but I think you're both wrong. Conditions have only been improved in Al-Ould because of the way I have been behaving. If we cave in now, it's back to square one.'

'We can carry on the hunger strike in the other blocks,' argued Bill.

'You're missing the point, all of you,' I said. 'I *want* the National Guard brought in. I *want* to see if they'd shoot us. Supposing they did shoot one or two of us – imagine the stink? They daren't do it.'

I could have argued until I was blue in the face, but it was clear that there was no support for my view. When Abdullah's guards returned and asked me if I was prepared to move, I gave in 'Yes – but under protest,' I said.

After confirming that everybody would keep up the hunger strike, I went back to *Seep* Two where I had been imprisoned before the start of Ramadan. I was not allowed to return to my cell, however, because the other prisoners did not want me it seemed; they were 'afraid of me'. I think this really meant that they were afraid I would get them into trouble. Anyhow, this didn't worry me too much. I wandered around the hall until I found a vacant spot and then lay down, intending to have a kip. At once the foreman arrived and told me that I could not lie down there during the day. I gave him my usual answer, 'Fuck off!' and away he went.

Ibrahim, the Christian Arab, who had also been moved back into Block Two, told me that the guards had warned all prisoners not to be friendly with me or they would be punished.

'Well, this is a good start to another spell in Block Two,' I told him. At that moment Manfred the Austrian came up and told me that he was 100 per cent on my side. He was due to be released within a day or two but despite this, was prepared to show solidarity and keep me company on the hunger strike.

'I really appreciate your gesture,' I told him, 'but I don't want *you* to go on hunger strike! There's no need – you're getting out in a day or so.'

'I know, Fraser. But I'm going on strike, anyhow. I'll start eating again only when I leave this prison or when you yourself start to eat.'

Once again I thanked him and repeated it was not necessary for him to continue with the strike. But I was absolutely delighted with his gesture.

That night Manfred went to the gate to see how the hunger strike was going. He chose a time when food was being handed out to Arab prisoners and those westerners who were not receiving special food parcels. He returned to report that all the westerners in Block One had eaten food. Claud, who was in Block Three, had also eaten. Altogether this meant that out of 26 westerners in Al-Ould 12 were not observing the hunger strike; it was only being kept by the chaps in Blocks Three and Four. Manfred was very angry about this but I told him it was up to every man to make his own choice and that, so far as I was concerned, it made no difference.

At 9 a.m. next morning, a Wednesday, I heard my name called out and I was told to take all my belongings with me. The Arab prisoners crowded round me to assure me that this meant I was going to be released. I said I'd believe that when I saw it. As I walked through the gate of my block, I spotted Arthur and Bill standing at the gate to their block, watching me. Arthur was trying to mouth something to me but he was too far away for me to make him out, particularly as there was the usual din going on. He seemed to be saying 'You are going to be released.'

I yelled back at him, 'I don't think so. More likely they're going to take me into the desert and shoot me. If they do, make sure that Tom finds out about it.'

In the reception area I was informed that I was being taken back to Malaz prison. I was told to stick out my hands and when I did so they snapped a pair of handcuffs on me. I was then told to walk outside and get into a waiting minibus.

I shook my head. 'I'm not leaving here until I get my holdall,' I said. 'I have certain valuables in it.'

'Where is this holdall?' enquired the senior guard.

'In the storeroom,' I told him.

I did want the holdall, and not merely because I wanted to be a nuisance. It had my precious silver cigarette lighter in it. However, when I was allowed to go to the storeroom and open the bag there was no sign of the lighter. Angrily I grabbed it and walked back to the reception area. On the way I had to pass Abdullah's office and when I saw the fellow sitting there, I shouted that he had stolen my cigarette lighter.

'You're a thief!' I roared at him. 'All Saudis are thieves.'

He came rushing out of his office, eyes blazing with anger. 'Saudis are not thieves,' he shouted. 'No Saudi steals.'

'Tell that to the Marines,' I shouted. 'If Saudis don't steal, why are sixty-five per cent of the prisoners in this jail Saudis?'

He did not reply to this but shouted to the guards to take me away. Three or four guards moved in on me but I warned them, 'Don't touch me! If one of you touches me, he'll regret it.' Then I turned and walked to the reception room, went through and then got into the minibus. I was certain of at least two things by now: I was not being released and I was not being sent back to Malaz for my health.

That the Saudis clearly meant business was apparent almost as soon as I reached Malaz, for I was greeted by a posse of armed guards who had clearly been told to handle me firmly. I decided to go along with the game until I found out what they intended to do with me. I was escorted straight to the centre of the prison where I was ordered to leave my baggage, then I was taken to a large office where three senior police officers awaited me.

'Sit down,' invited the most senior officer, a major. He addressed me in a friendly way, and then turning to a guard he said, 'Fetch Joseph the interpreter.' I decided that this was more of the old Saudi baloney as the major himself obviously spoke English as well as I did.

As soon as Joseph arrived, the major started off quite crisply. 'You have been transferred here for torture,' he informed me. 'After that, you will be taken to Tief prison (Saudi's mental prison) and kept there.'

I tried to show that I was unconcerned by jumping to my feet and saying, 'OK, let's get started then. But I insist you wear kinky boots.' They must have thought I was, indeed, really mad, for in addition to this nonsense, I grinned at them like a prize idiot. I think I must have been the first prisoner in the whole history of Malaz to have received the news that he was going to be tortured the way I did, by laughing at it.

'You won't be grinning when we've finished with you, I promise you,' warned the major. He then shouted at his sergeant to bring chains and the man returned shortly, carring a whole string of handcuffs hanging down from his left arm like Spanish onions and another string of leg chains in his right. I gave an even louder laugh than before which took everybody by surprise.

'I'm already handcuffed,' I pointed out, 'Why bring more? And what on earth do you intend to do with all those chains?'

I think they had trouble deciding whether I was mocking them or not but the major's face suddenly turned a dark colour and I thought he was about to burst a blood vessel.

'This is very bad,' whined Joseph at my elbow. 'They will break you this time, Fraser.'

I stopped laughing and jutting out my chin aggressively, hoping to look as pugnacious as Churchill, I told Joseph, 'No one will break me. As for torture – I'm not worried about that. These clowns will break before I will, I promise you.'

The major turned and dismissed his sergeant. Then he turned back to me and to my surprise, said mildly, 'Fraser, would you like some tea?'

'What in hell?' I said. 'One minute you're threatening me with torture or sending me to a mental prison; next you're asking me to have tea. What's the game?'

'You will take tea?' asked the major.

'Yes, but I want milk in it,' I said, determined to be as awkward as possible.

The major told a guard to fetch me tea with milk in it. Then he settled down for what he obviously hoped would be a confidential chat.

'Now, Fraser,' he began, speaking in impeccable English, 'why do you cause trouble? Why did you get the western prisoners to go on hunger strike?'

'I am not the ringleader,' I told him. 'I decided to go on hunger strike and then some of the others joined me. But it was their own decision. I didn't make them.'

'I do not believe you, Fraser,' said the major.

'It's all the same to me, major – have it your way.'

'What *is* your complaint, Fraser?'

'My God,' I said. 'I have so many complaints that we could be here until Christmas.'

'But what are your main ones?' he persisted.

'Well, there are no beds,' I said. 'And I never get any exercise.'

'Listen, Fraser,' said the major, trying to sound reasonable, 'if you will stop your hunger strike and tell the others to stop as well, then I'll come and see you all on Saturday morning at eleven o'clock and sort out your complaints. But you must come off the hunger strike.'

I said I would think about it.

'All right,' he concluded. 'You will go back and speak to all the other western prisoners and tell them that their worries will be over when I have been to see them on Saturday. In the meantime, I'll arrange that you are moved back into Block Three with your two friends – the Englishman called Arthur and the big American, Bill, I think?'

'Right,' I said. 'I'll accept your word. But I can't promise you that everybody will do as I say.'

'I'm sure you'll do your best,' smiled the major and then ordered the guards to take me back to Al-Ould.

On the return journey I noticed that the guards looked quite a disappointed and even worried pair. Arab prisoners later told me that Abdullah had told all the guards that they would be pleased to know that I was going to be tortured at Malaz and now here I was, being brought back to Al-Ould unscathed. They were worried that they would be considered to have lost face; not only that, they were scared stiff that Abdullah would blame them because I hadn't been tortured.

Back in Al-Ould again, I was taken at once to see Abdullah. He had not been warned that I was coming back and when I was pushed unceremoniously through the door, his eyes bulged. He yelled at the guards who, scared almost witless, rushed to him and handed him a letter from the major, giving him written instructions as to what to do with me. The major was so angry at first that he ignored the letter and, fury all over his face, glared at me so that I felt certain he was going to attack me physically; I steeled myself to meet his onslaught. Instead, he quickly pulled himself together and still angry, ordered me to Block Two.

'I am to be moved to Block Three,' I told him.

'Block Two!' he roared at the guards, but I again interrupted him, 'I am to speak to the western prisoners about the hunger strike. It is in those written instructions if you open that letter.'

He stood there as if transfixed. Then, recovering himself, he yelled, 'Take this man to see the western prisoners!'

I was led first to Block One where, of course, there were no western prisoners on strike. I said 'hello' to one or two and mentioned that the hunger strike was off and was then led to Block Two where I broke the news to Manfred.

'So there's no need for you to jeopardise your release,' I told him. 'Thank you for standing up for us all, all the same.'

'I'm glad for all your sakes,' said Manfred.

The first thing I noticed about Block Three, to which I had asked to be transferred, was how dark and filthy a place it was compared with the other blocks. I found Bill and Arthur there and also Claud, of course, and a German called Horst and a Filipino called Manny who was squatting on the floor when I went in. I told them what had happened and added that I thought the major was telling the truth and meant what he had said. Anyway, all we had to do was to wait until Saturday and then we'd find out whether he was lying or not. In the meantime, I said, I thought the hunger strike should be abandoned.

Claud immediately chipped in to say that we should at once write down all our complaints.

'Shut up, you cunt,' said Arthur. 'You weren't on hunger strike anyway. You've no business putting forward complaints.'

'I was ill,' complained Claud. 'I had to eat.'

When I finished with Block Three, I went to Block Four where there were six westerners – an American, a German, two Greeks and two Italians, all of whom had joined in the strike. I explained the situation to them and they agreed to eat again, pending the visit of the major on Saturday.

While I was busy explaining all this to the chaps in Block Four, Abdullah arrived on the scene and told me to hurry up and finish talking. I told him I had finished what I had to say but before returning to my block, I wanted to make a telephone call to my company to ask them to recommence my food parcels.

Abdullah replied by shouting at me, so I told him to fuck off. Then I turned and went on speaking to the other prisoners. Furious, Abdullah stalked out of the block.

'You could be in trouble again, Fraser,' warned Dieter, a German. 'Let's wait and see, shall we?' I replied. 'I'm always supposed to be in trouble.'

The block foreman turned up and said I was to go to the office. When I arrived in Abdullah's office, he merely pointed to the telephone and said, 'Ring your company.' I did so and got Roger Lilly on the line and told him to start sending food parcels again as we had come off hunger strike. Would he also arrange for the British vice-consul to come along on Saturday morning when we were meeting some senior prison officers? I had just time to hear Roger say, 'Yes – ' before Abdullah pressed down the receiver and cut me off. Instead of reacting angrily, I just laughed at him.

In Block Three, we westerners had only a space seven by four feet in which to sit most of the day. Until I arrived, everybody was expected to pray whenever the Muslims said prayers but I made it clear I had no intention of doing so. I had also noticed that at nights westerners slept all over the place, so I suggested that we should all sleep next to each other, forming a group. Big Bill said he'd prefer it if I did not 'create any problems' and as I had grown fond of Bill, I agreed to wait until everything was sorted out on Saturday. Arthur, too, was not keen 'to make waves', so rather than create difficulties for the others I decided to go along with things as they were for the time being.

Conditions in Block Three were a great deal worse than anything I had anticipated. For twelve to eighteen hours at a time the block had no water supply and the smell from the privies became overpowering. Bill said I would get used to it but I never did. My 'reputation', of course, had preceded me. The *seep* foreman, indeed, approached me early on and enquired if I were 'going to cause trouble'?

'For the guards, yes. For the prisoners, no,' I said and he went away seemingly satisfied.

The next morning Tom arrived with my first food parcel since I had ended my hunger strike. As this was not 'a visit' in the proper sense of the word, he had just time to exchange a quick word with me. He said Roger Lilly had refused to hand over my passport (which had been passed on to him by Harry Hall) but he would get me proper shoes and anything else I needed. There was one new possible development. There was a chance he might be able to buy me out of prison. However, he didn't have time to tell me anything more then.

Back in the block, Arthur took charge of the food and announced that we would all eat together immediately after prayers at 4.30 p.m. Just before 4.30 the prayer-caller came up to me and asked me if I were prepared to join in the prayers. I said no westerner would pray but we would respect Muslim feelings and remain as quiet as possible during the service.

'That is good,' he replied. 'But, still, it would be better if you all stayed out of sight in one of the cells until prayers are over.'

Bill Shunk chipped in to say, 'I'll go along with that. Then let's see what the meeting on Saturday brings.'

Bill, in fact, was taking great care to see that I did not explode again and cause trouble. That night, he gave up his sleeping space to me so that I would not be disturbed by the TV. The *seep* foreman had allocated me a space near the TV set and I had made up my mind to switch it off as soon as I was ready for sleep, whether or not the programmes had finished. Bill reckoned that if I had done that, there would have been a riot. So far as he was concerned, then, it was anything for a quiet life!

So far as I was concerned, however, a quiet life was the last thing anybody apparently wanted me to enjoy. At 3.30 a.m., somebody kicked my feet and I awoke to find the prayer-caller standing over me.

'You must get up for prayers,' he announced.

I gave him my ritual answer and the next moment I was surrounded by several irate Muslims ready to lynch me. I had my fists at the ready when I heard Bill Shunk say, 'OK, Ian, let's move into the cell while they're praying. After all, it's only until Saturday.'

'Sure, Bill,' I agreed and followed him into the room. To my astonishment, at least nine Muslims were sleeping soundly on the floor.

'What the hell?' I asked Bill.

'Prisoners in cells don't have to pray at 3.30,' explained Bill. 'Only those sleeping out in the block halls have to do *salha*.'

'Do you mean to tell me these bastards are allowed to sleep on while somebody walks up to me and kicks me awake? Why do you allow it?'

'What else could we do?' asked Bill, surprised.

'You could fight the bastards, that's what!' I said angrily. 'These buggers will keep on pushing at westerners and refusing to treat us properly just so long as we let them. You've got to fight the buggers.' And with that, I began kicking at the dozing Muslims shouting 'salha! salha!' They had no idea what the hell was going on, and kept telling me they did not have to pray. The uproar continued until Arthur and Bill calmed me down by reminding me that we had to wait only a short time until Saturday. I didn't need reminding, actually; my trouble was that I wasn't sure if I could keep my cool until then.

ELEVEN

It was half past eleven on Saturday morning before Bill, Arthur and I were called out and told to report to the visitors' room. When we arrived there we found four Americans from Block One already waiting along with Dieter the German and Len, an American from Block Two. Dieter said that one of the Saudi guards had told him that there were some western visitors waiting in Abdullah's office and as the news of the hunger strike was all over Riyadh by this time, he guessed that the visitors must be western consuls. I said I hoped they were and also that they were laying into Abdullah good and proper.

Two Saudi captains whom I had never seen before then came into the room and began to interview us. Both spoke excellent English and there was no nonsense about an interpreter. They asked Chris what his problem was and he said he thought he should have been sentenced only to two years' imprisonment not five. One of the captains said he would look into his case.

'What the hell is all this about sentences?' I asked Arthur.

'They're supposed to be here to do something about our conditions.'

'I don't know, Ian,' shrugged Arthur. 'We'd better wait and see.'

Next thing I knew, two of the black Americans were complaining about lack of proper medical treatment.

'These guys weren't on hunger strike,' I protested. 'What's going on here? They already have beds and better conditions than we have. We're the guys who have real complaints. We're the guys who went on hunger strike about them.'

One of the black Americans, a bloke called Morrison, turned

and said to me, 'Listen, we guys don't care how you live. If you want to know our attitude, it's "fuck you". '

The whole interview turned out to be a waste of time. None of the officers seemed interested in our complaints and I decided the entire operation was simply a whitewashing exercise. Those of us who had genuine complaints were never given a chance to put our case. I said to one of the captains, 'This whole thing is a waste of time. I'm disgusted. Absolutely disgusted!'

The officer shrugged and the other one made no attempt to interview me or any of the other hunger strikers.

'You're a great lot!' I told them, fed up with them and with the fact that prisoners who shouldn't have been there at all because they were enjoying reasonably good conditions had been given a long hearing. After all the promises made by the major in Malaz, we had been allowed exactly 30 minutes of Saudi time and even then we hunger strikers had not been permitted to state our case.

Arthur decided that the proper thing to do was to make sure that a list of our complaints was published by the British press. I told him I thought this was a good idea but I didn't want my own name to appear; however, I'd be only too happy to help him in every way I could. I would arrange for Tom to post any letters and I would also get him to telephone the London newspapers from Riyadh. Following this, Arthur sat down and wrote a letter to his mother.

In this, he listed the following complaints by the strikers: No beds; terrible smell; dreadful noise; no exercise – and locked up in the block all day; lice and bugs everywhere; no proper medical treatment and no proper utensils.

We agreed that publication of such a list would jeopardise any chances we had of being released but we also felt that it might lead to a genuine improvement in our conditions, because the one thing the Saudis do not like is criticism in the western press. I eventually decided that the right thing to do was to add my name to the complaints – although I didn't want publicity – and for once Claud also came up trumps, adding his signature. Next morning, when my name was called out to collect my daily food parcel, I brought the letter with me intending to hand it to Tom. Unfortunately, Tom was not able to make it that day and Roger Lilly turned up in his stead. I told him what we were doing.

'You are at liberty to read the letter we are sending, of course,' I told him.

Roger didn't seem at all happy, however. 'I think it may be only stirring up more trouble,' he advised me. 'Although I understand your feelings and the feelings of the others. However, I'll post it today and make sure that Richard Northern gets a copy.'

When Tom turned up the following morning, he told me that Roger had shown him the letter and that, so far as he was concerned, we were doing the right thing.

'It can only help your position,' he said. 'It can't make it any worse.'

'By the way,' I told him, 'remember, when you're talking to London that the police are liable to tap your telephone.'

'I'll take that chance,' he replied. I told him we had decided to escape on the evening of 26 October and that Arthur badly needed shoes and clothes. Tom promised to see to these and said all he needed to know from me now was how I proposed to escape from Saudi Arabia once Arthur and I got clear of Al-Ould.

Three nights later on 6 October, we were chatting idly in the cell, when two Arabs came running in to tell us that Arthur was on the BBC Arabic News.

'Yes, we know,' I replied quickly, although I was taken by surprise. I didn't want to give the impression, however, that any of us westerners were curious about the broadcast or, indeed, that we had anything to do with it. But next morning, as I was walking towards the reception area to pick up my parcel, some Arabs from the other blocks began shouting to me, 'British on BBC'. When I saw Tom, I asked him what had happened and he said that Arthur's mother had appeared on TV and that the British newspapers had run big stories about 'our hellhole'.

'Was my name mentioned?' I asked.

'No. It appears the company got in touch with Anne and advised her to keep quiet and say nothing to anyone.'

'Well, that's OK by me,' I said. 'After all, the company's still paying my salary and providing me with food and pocket money and still trying to get my release. So I've got to go along with anything they advise.'

When I went back to the block I announced to all and sundry that we were stars. Our story, I said, had been on TV and in all the newspapers.

'What will happen now?' asked Claud.

'Let's wait and see,' I replied. 'Maybe they'll try to make us suffer for it – but what more can they do?'

'They could take Arthur away – perhaps they will punish him,' suggested someone.

'Well, they won't take him alone,' I promised. 'If they take him, they'll have to take me also. By the way, Arthur, I'm sorry that my name was not mentioned but that was all the company's doing.'

I learned later that originally Anne had wanted my name mentioned on both TV and in the press but she had been persuaded to change her mind by the company and had decided to telephone Arthur's mother and tell her to keep my name out of it. I found it easy to understand her action and realised that she must have been in an agony of mind about it. The company, however, had been very good to her. They normally telephoned her two or three times a week to make sure she lacked for nothing and even the personnel manager himself had travelled up from London to make sure she was all right. Under these circumstances, she could hardly reject their advice and so, although I would rather have been seen standing shoulder to shoulder with Arthur, I understood her motives and the pressures that had been brought to bear on her.

Three days after the BBC broadcast, we had news that four more westerners were to join us: three British and one Swiss. We reckoned the new prisoners would be dispersed throughout the four blocks and in due course Des Smith, an announcer with Radio Riyadh was admitted to our block. Des had spent thirteen years in Saudi Arabia and when he joined ARAMCO, the oil giant, had been issued with a small still, an issue made by the company to all its expatriates.

At nine o'clock the previous evening while he was preparing to broadcast, the police had raided his villa. At the time only his wife and two-year-old son were at home and the police, who had been tipped off about the still by Smith's Arab houseboy, seized the apparatus. His wife was ordered to telephone him and say the police wanted him but Des explained that he could not leave the radio station until broadcasting had finished. As a result, the police had driven out to the radio station and waited until 2 a.m. to arrest him. Des had offered to drive himself to the police station as his expensive car was parked outside the studios but the police lieutenant in charge said he would drive it instead and that Smith must travel in a police car. (The lieutenant continued to keep the car, even after vigorous protests by the British vice-consul, arguing that it constituted 'part payment' for the crime. When I left Saudi Arabia he still had the car and still resolutely refused to hand it back – typical Saudi 'justice'.) Des was an old friend of both Arthur and Bill and as they were fellow spirits, in more senses than one, they were delighted to see him. He filled us in on what was happening outside, apart from our own problems. He said the Saudis were still keeping up a big 'Hate Britain' campaign and that there were now no fewer than 28 Britons in Saudi jails as part of the backlash to the *Death of a Princess* programme. I said that did much to explain the behaviour of the senior prison officers who had interviewed us about our complaints.

Even so, we were able to console ourselves that that meeting had produced some slight improvement in our conditions. For a start, all western prisoners were now allowed to sleep together at the top of the block and were no longer required to wake up or move into a cell during *salha*. Some of the Muslims were upset about this, particularly when they had to move down the block and leave space for Des to be fitted in, but fit him in we did, despite their bleatings.

Des's arrival, paradoxically, boosted our morale. For a start, he had so many friends in Riyadh that he was inundated with food parcels, most of it of first-class quality and within a few days, indeed, we were suffering from a surfeit of good food rather than a shortage.

At three o'clock the following Wednesday, Arthur's name was called out and he was told to report to the warden's office. We thought this a bit strange for a Wednesday, as this was not a visiting day and it was also the warden's half-holiday. Anyway, away he went, only to return a few minutes later to pick up a copy of his 'complaints'. A 'Secret Service' policeman – one of the two English-speaking officers who had 'interviewed' us the previous Saturday – wanted to know exactly what his complaints were.

It was three hours before Arthur returned. Apparently the 'Secret Service' man wanted to know why Arthur's name had appeared in the press and why he had 'told lies'. Arthur had stood his ground stoutly and insisted he had not told lies and that all his complaints were genuine and shared by all the British prisoners. At the end of the interrogation, the 'Secret Service' man had climbed down and promised he would try to 'have things improved' for all the British.

'But you know what the Saudis are like,' I said.

Improved conditions or not, I was determined to press ahead with my escape which I had still pencilled in for 26 October, scarcely a fortnight away now. I had seen Tom again and he told me he had found a Briton who was prepared to drive a car for us – indeed, who would be eager to drive it. I turned this idea down, however, on the grounds that we didn't want to involve someone else who might get into serious trouble on our account. All we needed was the car. We also needed dummy papers to get out of the country.

When you go to work in Saudi Arabia you are issued with a photostated copy of your passport which you are supposed to carry around like an identification card. I asked Tom to arrange two photostats of phoney passports bearing false names and with photographs of Arthur and me, which I was able to give him. On his next visit, Tom told me all was fixed. A car would be waiting for us near the prison gate and the dummy papers would be in it. He was flying to England on 25 October and so would be safely out of the way but he would make sure that food parcels were delivered to both Arthur and me on the evening of the 26th so that we would have an excuse to go to the reception area from which we could make our dash for freedom. I could then drive straight to Jidda and from there sail across the Red Sea to Egypt.

'Just one thing, though,' said Tom. 'I don't want you to get any hopes up. But keep your fingers crossed – there's a chance that we can buy you out of prison.' I tried to get him to tell me more, but all he would say was that nothing had been decided and he would prefer to keep the details to himself until he could be more positive.

'I'm not sure I *want* bought out,' I told him. 'I've been thinking about this escape for so long that it seems my best chance.'

'Well, as I say, keep your fingers crossed,' said Tom. 'We'll take the best way.'

Back in the cell I told Arthur that there was just a chance that I might be released before the 26th; how did he feel about that?

'I wouldn't risk it in my own, that's for certain,' he said. 'But if that's what happens, I'll be glad for you.'

'I can only say Arthur, that for your sake, I hope I'm not.'

My next visitor was not Tom but Roger Lilly and I asked him straight away what all this talk about buying me out meant.

'Well, it seems Tom has found somebody who says they could have you released for twenty thousand pounds.'

'I'll take the money instead,' I joked. Yet something about Roger's face made me wonder. 'Look Roger, who is paying the money?'

'Your brother in Singapore,' he replied.

'In that case, stop it! There's no way I'm going to go into debt for my family for twenty thousand pounds. Tell Tom it's not on. I'll escape instead.' Roger, looking thoroughly uncomfortable, said nothing.

Then I asked him, 'Anyway, who is this person who can get me out for twenty thousand grand?'

'It's some Saudi princess to whom Tom was introduced through our company doctor. He's had quite a few meetings with her and everything seems to be going OK.'

'Well, it's not on!' I shouted angrily. 'Tell Tom to see me tomorrow – and in the meantime he's to return the money to Bob.'

Then I began to worry about what I'd do if Tom had already paid over the money. I shuddered. To start with I'd have to sell my home. Even then, I'd still need every penny I had in the bank – so I'd end up homeless and broke! With such a catastrophe looming before me that night I scarcely slept.

Next morning I had a visit from Ian Wylie. He had heard all about my attitude and wanted to put me straight about the whole deal. First and foremost, he said, Tom had decided against the deal. The company itself would have been prepared to pay the money if they hadn't thought the whole thing too fishy. I could be certain, however, that if they could make sure that the deal was a straight one – or, indeed, if any other opportunity offered itself – then they would be happy to pay up. In the meantime, they were not letting up in their efforts to get me released in the ordinary way.

Having talked to Wylie I felt sure that the company which I had always believed to be 100 per cent behind me, was still behind me. I was so relieved that nobody had let me down that I told Ian I was planning to escape.

'For God's sake, Ian, don't do that,' he exclaimed. 'I'll get you out, I promise you.'

'When, Ian?' I asked.

'We are trying all the time. Before Christmas – I'm sure.'

'Well, I don't think so, Ian,' I told him. 'I know you're trying but there's too much anti-British feeling in this country at the moment. They're trying to make an example of every Briton in Saudi Arabia – to strike back at us in any way they can. Anybody who could help is afraid!'

'I don't agree with that,' he said. 'But all I can do is ask you to be patient.'

Tom visited me two days later to confirm that the deal was cancelled. He had already sent back the fifteen thousand pounds which Bob had sent to get me released. To this sum, he explained, he had been prepared to add the two thousand of my own money which Anne had sent out and three thousand pounds of his own.

Arthur was very pleased when I broke the news that the plan had flopped. 'I'm sorry for you, of course, Ian – but glad for myself.'

'No need to apologise, Arthur,' I said. 'I'd have behaved the same way myself.'

We sat down to further discussions of my escape plan. 'Were the guards in the towers likely to be good shots?' asked Arthur. I said I didn't think any Saudi guards were good shots but I had to admit that a man with a machine gun didn't have to be good! If we were fired on from the towers to each side of us, then we could be in trouble – for surely they couldn't miss from both towers. I felt convinced, however, that when the guards spotted us making a break for it, they would be too surprised to shoot and so the chances were that we would have cleared the gates and got into the buildings opposite before they were really aware of what was happening. While they were still in a state of confusion we'd jump into the parked car and hare off for Jidda as fast as we could. Once there, we would either try and buy a rubber dinghy, hire a boat or pick up a passage on a ship bound for Egypt.

On Saturday morning, 20 October 1980, Arthur's name was called and he went to see the warden. When he came back, he announced the news that he was being released.

I could hardly credit my own bad luck. All my strength

suddenly drained away from me. Then I remembered that the boot had very nearly been on the other foot and I mumbled, 'I'm glad for you, Arthur.' Arthur, looking at me sadly, said, 'I'm sorry, Ian.'

'Don't worry,' I assured him. 'I'm still going to try on my own.' But I realised, of course, even as I said this, that this was an almost impossible idea. I'd have to think of some other way out or simply resign myself to what seemed an indefinite stay in one of the worst prisons it is possible to imagine.

TWELVE

That night, while the other prisoners around me slept soundly, I lay awake trying to work out new plans for what I should do now.

My mind wandered over certain possibilities. First, there were the privies; there was a window in that part of the block but it was heavily barred and I saw little chance of sawing my way through this while other prisoners kept coming in and out. Then there were the 4 a.m. prayers . . . fuck it, there seemed no way out. I thought of Arthur and how he would be home in England again within six weeks; suddenly I began to envy him as a lucky bastard.

A new prisoner called Eric Price joined us on Sunday in Arthur's stead; he worked for BAC and had apparently been a whisky dealer in a big way. He had run into Arthur in Malaz, while the latter was awaiting his final release, and Arthur had advised him to get into our block. I wasn't sure I could hit it off with Eric but I decided to do my damnedest as I didn't want the Arabs to see us westerners as other than a united group. By this time, of course, Claud had ceased to be one of us and we never talked to him; he even ate with the Arabs.

I had become more friendly with Horst. The German eventually told me how he and his chums had robbed their company of over a million pounds in Saudi riyals. Three men had been involved: Horst, a foreman electrician on the site, Dieter, a foreman steel fixer, and Rulf, the cashier. They had been helping to build a new military hospital in Riyadh, ten minutes from Humming Bird House. As the first phase of the theft, Rulf had had a duplicate key made for a safe in the site office. He then returned to Germany on Christmas leave, leaving the key with the other two who intended to drug the nightwatchman and clean out the safe. As it was Christmas, they expected to find two million pounds sterling in it.

Everything went *almost* according to plan. Horst dropped a sleeping pill into the watchman's tea jnd waited outside the office until the drug had taken effect. Then he and the giant Dieter, who was well over six feet and built like a tank, had opened the safe. They had filled two sacks with riyals but when Horst had tried to carry them, he found they were too heavy. Dieter had then grabbed the sacks and although he had managed to carry them some distance, he ruptured himself in the process. Indeed, there was so much money in the safe that they had been forced to leave half of it behind. What they did take they hid in secret panels prepared behind a fire extinguisher in another part of the site office. Then, very pleased with themselves, they went home to join their families who had come out to Saudi Arabia for the Christmas holidays.

So far, so good; but the trick then was to turn the Saudi riyals into German marks. When Rulf got word that the operation had been successful, he incautiously telephoned a friend and remarked that he was now a German mark millionaire. The German police who had already been alerted by the Saudis, had put a tap on Rulf's telephone and when they heard this, pounced on him and accused him of being involved in the robbery. Rulf stoutly denied all knowledge and to prove his 'good faith' offered to return to Riyadh, despite a warning by the German police that he would be arrested on arrival. Whatever his motives, he went through with his bluff and was, indeed, arrested as soon as he stepped off the plane. Once in Saudi custody, he revealed the whole plot and within two days both Horst and Dieter, realising that they had no hope of ever recovering the money, had revealed its whereabouts. They were shocked by their savage sentences – not so much because of the five years that each had been given, as at the threat of having their hands chopped off. Only the resolute action of the German Government in insisting that they be allowed facilities to sew the hands back on had saved them from this mediaeval fate. The most extraordinary part of the entire story to me was that neither Horst nor Dieter, whom I got to know quite well, appeared anything but ordinary guys. They seemed to me the kind of people who would even pay a parking fine.

We never even saw our new Swiss prisoner. Apparently he simply paid somebody £70,000 and was taken straight from the office in Al-Ould to an aeroplane and flown out of Saudi Arabia at 3 a.m. Money, it was clear, would open any gate in Al-Ould.

Friday, 26 October was a low day for me. While Horst, who had taken over from Arthur as chef, prepared our evening meal, I couldn't stop blurting out that Arthur and I had planned to escape that day. Bill Shunk immediately asked me to explain the whole idea and I did so and the general view was that I had been lucky. Everybody thought the whole idea a madcap one and believed that both Arthur and I would have been shot – if not while still on prison premises then on the road to Jidda.

'Maybe,' I agreed reluctantly. 'But madcap ideas sometimes succeed better than others. There's nothing wrong with being audacious, you know.'

'I agree with that,' said Eric Price. 'I do wish, Ian, you had decided to stick to your plan and had told me about it. I'd have gone along with you.'

'I'll certainly try to escape if I can,' said Horst. The consensus still, however, was that an escape would not be easy and that the risks were high. The Saudis could always claim the right to shoot an escaping prisoner.

That night, while the others slept, my brain continued to work overtime. I decided I would have a better chance to escape if I were back in Block Two where there was much less traffic to the piss-house during the hours of darkness. But how could I arrange a switch?

Saturday, 1 November, again proved a pretty low day for me. Tom was on leave and so he was not there to boost my morale. In England, my brother Bob's daughter was being married – the very wedding I had sworn to attend. The best I could do was to propose a toast to my niece and her new husband at our evening meal that day. The other fellows cordially joined with me in an effort to keep up my spirits.

On the morning of 5 November when I went to pick up my food parcel, I was delighted to welcome Tom back. He was only back that morning and had come rushing out to see me immediately with a piece of the wedding cake steeped in brandy. He had attended the wedding and said it had been a great success with Bob giving a toast in my honour. Anne and the kids were fine and Bob had returned to London with them to see if there was anything more he could do to secure my release. With Anne's permission, he had approached certain Fleet Street newspapers. He was told that the newspapers did not want to exacerbate the delicate situation with Saudi Arabia, particularly as relations now appeared to be returning to normal – there was even talk of the British Ambassador being allowed to return in Riyadh. In such circumstances, they felt that the less was said about the plight of British prisoners in Saudi, the better.

Bitterly disappointed, Tom had been ready to fly back to Riyadh the next day when Bob, determined to do something, flew to Manchester, booked in at a hotel and telephoned the Manchester offices of the national press. The *Daily Express* had at once jumped at the story and next morning the full story, plus a photograph of Anne and the kids, was blazoned all over their front page.

Once the *Express* had taken up the story, of course, every other newspaper in the country had leaped on the bangwagon and my home had been under siege. Anne was asked to appear on television and did so where she pleaded for my release on medical grounds. She also wrote to our local MP, David Tripper, who promised to take up my case with Lord Carrington, then British Foreign Secretary, who was due to fly out to Riyadh in an attempt to repair some of the fences wrecked by *Death of a Princess*. I was delighted to hear of the fuss but was sceptical that it could do any good. I thought the Saudis were unlikely to become more favourably disposed to me following the press coverage, but on the other hand, it was true that exposure had helped to get Arthur released. Ian Wylie also visited me that day to express his 'disappointment' over the press fuss.

'Well, I'm not disappointed, Ian. And I can't help how you feel.'

'I thought you and your family trusted me,' he said.

'Look, Ian – I just want out of prison. The company doesn't seem to be able to manage it, so if my family can do anything about it, then I'm willing to try it that way. So far as I'm concerned, anything that causes the Saudis embarrassment, suits me.'

It proved an unsatisfactory interview and we parted on less than our usual cordial terms. It was easy for people outside prison to counsel patience and to advise against making waves, but the whole picture looked different from inside the walls of Al-Ould. I did not feel like a criminal; indeed, nothing would ever convince me I was a criminal; and I thought it the height of injustice that a hardworking, law-abiding British construction manager, prepared to suffer the discomforts of Saudi Arabia in order to assist in bringing that country into the twentieth century should be punished in such a savage way – and for something which was really no more than a technical offence.

Three days later, my name was called out and I was told to report to the warden's office. This was a reversal of the usual procedure for it was usually me who wanted to see the warden rather than the other way around. However, when I walked into the office, my spirits sank like a stone for I could see that he looked extremely happy which, conversely, meant bad news for me.

Abdul came straight to the point. 'I have to tell you, Fraser, that your appeal has failed and that on Prince Niaf's instructions you have also lost your remission and so you will stay as our guest for three years.'

'Abdul,' I said, 'I don't wish to stay as your guest – not even for a week. I want to go home.'

For some reason he failed to appreciate my humour and lost his cool, shouting, 'You'll stay here and like it, Fraser! And don't forget, I run this prison – and not you!'

'Hold on, Abdul,' I shouted back. 'Of course you run this prison and the prisoners in it. But the only thing you're doing so far as I'm concerned is preventing me from walking out. You do not control me in any other way. However, as you are upset, I'm not going to talk to you today.' And I simply turned and walked out, trying to appear unconcerned – an act that ought to have won me an Oscar.

Two days later I had a letter from Anne in which she said that David Tripper, our MP, had arranged for my medical records to be sent on from Edinburgh in the hope that once the Saudis realised the problems I suffered from as a result of my plastic skull plate, they were bound to release me. Replying to Anne, I did not tell her about the trouble I had been giving inside Al-Ould or that in my own opinion, I had gone too far for the Saudis to take a compassionate view of my behaviour. Although I was capable of seeing that perhaps my behaviour had not been in my own best interests, I also realised that there was nothing else I could have done or would consider doing in the future. I simply did not intend to knuckle down and take my imprisonment quietly.

A week after my meeting with Abdul, I was again asked to report to his office. This time he was all smiles for a change and welcomed me most politely. Des Smith was also there as was his attractive wife.

'Sit down, Fraser. You want tea?' began Abdul affably.

'Yes,' I replied. Abdul gave the order and then turned to speak to some Arabs. While I waited for him to give me his attention again, I chatted to Des Smith and his wife. Suddenly Abdul broke in, 'Fraser,' he said, 'you know what this is?' And he held up a buff-coloured envelope. I wondered what the hell he was driving at, then noticed that the envelope bore a British stamp.

'Yes, Abdul,' I said. 'Those are my medical records.' He seemed surprised that I knew, as officially I was neither allowed to send letters nor to receive any. However, he passed on quickly to the problem.

'Do you know what they say?' he asked.

'I've a pretty good idea – but I'd like to read them anyway,' I replied. Without a word, Abdul handed over the file and I began reading it. In all, there were about ten pages and as a I went through them, I turned to Des Smith and remarked, 'Good God, Des – if they don't release me on this report, then nobody will ever be released.' While I was still reading, Abdul ordered a guard to ask the prison doctor to come and see him. When the doctor turned up Abdul asked him to read my record. When the doctor had finished, he said, 'His headaches must be very bad. These could be the cause of the trouble he has been giving us. In my opinion, this man should be released.'

'No, Fraser stays,' announced Abdul curtly and dismissed the doctor. Then he turned to me. 'Fraser, I could release you on medical grounds but I am not going to. You are bad.'

'That's OK, Abdul. I like you, too.'

At that moment, in walked the British vice-consul, Richard Northern.

'Hello, Richard, you're just in time,' I said to him and, reaching across Abdul's desk, took my medical records and handed them to him. 'Read this,' I told him.

Northern glanced quickly through the records and then I said to Abdul, 'Abdul, will you please repeat what you have just said to me?'

The warden was taken aback because both Smith and his wife had heard him, so he had no option but to repeat his remark. This time, however, he added, 'Whatever the circumstances, Fraser stays for three years.'

In some extraordinary way, this stubbornness, instead of making me feel depressed, seemed to make my adrenalin flow all the faster. The more stubborn and bloody-minded Saudis like Abdul became, the more stubborn and bloody-minded I became also. The whole thing, in a strange way, had become a battle of wills – British guts and determination, as I saw it, against Saudi deviousness and manipulation. At that moment, if Abdul had opened his door and told me I was free, I would have considered myself cheated. I was full of plans for escaping and my only goal in life was the simple desire to beat these people and beat them by outwitting them and out-manoeuvering them against the odds.

I asked Northern what he intended doing about Abdul's statement and he said there was nothing he could do. He said I was behaving badly and the Saudi Government had complained to him several times about me.

'Never mind their complaints,' I said angrily, 'what about mine?'

'Look,' he said finally, 'if you cool it down a bit and behave yourself and give as little trouble as possible, when the ambassador returns we might be able to help you.'

'Why the fuck are you and the British Government afraid of these Saudi shits?' I said. 'Why don't you tell them to stick their oil?'

Northern looked anything but amused and mumbled that it would be better all round if I behaved myself.

I went back to the block and told the other fellows what had happened and mentioned my outburst to the vice-consul. They warned me that if I continued to behave in this way and to insult and abuse the Saudis at every opportunity, I'd come to a sticky end. I considered this for a few moments and then agreed that they were probably right. But at least, I said, I now know what my options were.

I started to work again on methods of just getting out of the prison itself; all ideas of waiting cars, dummy papers, 600-mile journeys across the Red Sea and any other plans were useless until and unless I could actually get out. If I made a solo dash for the main gate, would I be shot by the guards in the towers or simply jumped on by the police and overpowered? The prison walls themselves, at 25 feet high, were obviously unscaleable, and worse, every inch was within sight of the guard-tower.

While I was still mulling over these problems, Eric Price said he thought there was a gate at the side of the prison. 'I heard a truck come in when I was in the piss-house,' he said.

'I don't think so,' I said. 'All the trucks come in the main gate. I think that's the only way out.' But I decided to ask Tom to walk round the prison perimeter and find out for certain.

Eric then asked if he might join my escape attempt, if I decided to go ahead that is. I told him he would first need two thousand pounds for expenses as there was no way I could afford to lay out that sort of money on his behalf.

'Money's no problem,' he assured me. 'I've got thirty thousand quid on the outside.'

I thought about this offer for some time, then I told him I was willing to take him along. Once I had finalised my plans, I said, I would reveal them, but not before. In the meantime, he was to say nothing and not even speak to me about an escape – the less said the better. A few days later Tom confirmed that there was indeed a side door; it was a double steel door similar to the one at the main gate and with a watch-tower just beside it. He didn't think there was any way I could get out that way without being shot.

My plan now depended entirely upon getting back to Block Two for that was the only block, I had discovered, where the piss-house window was not overlooked by any of the watch-towers. But there were no westerners left in Block Two, so how could I get in there?

Inspiration came to me one evening when we were sitting on the floor while Horst and Des handed round our evening meal of cold meats. I suddenly shouted, 'I'm on hunger strike! And so are you, Eric!'

'Why?' demanded Des, mystified.

'Because I want a proper bed. And exercise. The same as the Saudis. And until they give it to us, I'm not going to eat.' Seeing the look on their faces I added quickly, 'But don't worry, none of you will suffer. I'll collect my food parcels every day and you'll still have those.'

Des was the first to put his paper plate down. 'I'm joining you,' he said. At once, the others chimed in, also offering to strike and I thought, Christ, this has fucked everything. I saw that there was nothing for it, however, but to go ahead and so I called the block foreman and told him we were not eating and that he should put that information in his report. I knew I would be moved as a result – but there was still the question of where to.

Later that evening, we heard on the grapevine that all the blocks were to be thoroughly searched. Every block was to be hosed out and all tins of – all things – Nivea cream were to be confiscated. This bit of news thoroughly upset Des who used the cream daily on the skin grafts on his legs, the result of burn wounds he had suffered in the RAF. The tins were sold openly in the prison shop and had been a staple item for a long time. We tried to figure out why the Saudis should want to ban such an innocent article and then heard that some prisoners had been using the tops to fashion primitive knives with which to cut up their food. I told Des to give me all his tins and I promised I would look after them for him. None of the guards would try and take them from me, I said.

Next day we watched the prisoners in Block One moved out into the yard along with their bedding while the entire block was hosed down. I was told that the clean out arose from my complaints about the filthy conditions in Saudi prisons and about lice and bugs. Although the prisoners had little or no room to move about in the yard, particularly as all their bedding was spread about, at least it gave them six hours of freedom outside the block – the first time some long-term prisoners had been out for longer than an hour since their imprisonment had begun.

Roger Lilly visited me that day, bringing my food parcel. I told him I had gone on hunger strike again and he said I was being silly. There was a big meeting in London that day about me and the company's Saudi connection was going to get me out.

'Shit!, Roger,' I told him, 'I've been hearing the same thing every day since my arrest. What I want you to do is to give Tom my passport.'

'I can't do that,' he said.

I was so angry I walked away.

On the second day of our hunger strike Horst and I were called to the warden's office. Abdul greeted us by saying he was not very happy. 'Why are you not eating?' he demanded. 'Why do you lead others to do such bad things, Fraser?'

'I don't,' I told him. 'If others won't eat, that's their business.'

'Look, Fraser, this is my prison and I run it. You do not run it.'

'Of course, you run it,' I told him. And then I laughed. When I laughed, he rose to his feet angrily and bawled at me, 'You're mad, Fraser! You're mad!' Horst and I walked out.

Back in the cell we told the others that we had not been able to get any promises from Abdul about beds or exercise.

'In that case,' said one of them, 'we intend to remain on hunger strike, provided you back us.' I took this to mean that they would continue the strike so long as I was prepared to take the blame for leading them! But so what the hell – I'd get blamed by the Saudis anyway.

Block Two was also deloused that day which meant that our block, Block Three, would be cleaned on the morrow. Next morning, we were told to take our belongings outside into the courtyard. We were sitting together in a group when Horst and I were again called to Abdul's office.

This time the warden was in a much better mood and the shouts and insults of the previous day had apparently been forgotten.

'Would you like tea?' he commenced.

'Thank you.'

Tea duly arrived and we drank it slowly. Meanwhile, Abdul talked to three important-looking Saudi visitors whom, we were later told, were from Prince Niaf's office. Abdul eventually turned to us and announced that the prison authorities had decided to give all westerners beds.

'When?' I demanded immediately.

'Today,' replied Abdul, clearly delighted to be able to crack back at me so quickly. He said we would be moved into Block Two.

'What about exercise?' I asked.

'You can exercise with the Saudi prisoners every day,' he said. 'But that does not apply to the German prisoners. They are great criminals and therefore will not be allowed to exercise.'

'In that case,' I shouted, 'the hunger strike is still on – by all of us.'

I rose to leave but immediately one of the three visiting Saudis who had been listening came across and said, 'I am sure we can sort this out. But why do you worry about the Germans? That can get you into trouble as you are the ringleader.'

'Christ,' I told him, 'what can you do to me that you haven't already done? Torture me? Shoot me? Get this – I'm not going to put up with the conditions in this prison and I'm going to go on complaining until you do something about it.' And I turned to leave again.

'No, wait!' interrupted the Saudi. 'The Germans can have exercise, then. But only six westerners will be allowed daily exercise. You, however, can exercise every day, Fraser.'

I turned to Horst. 'Are you satisfied with that, Horst?'

As Horst had spent two years sleeping on a hard floor and had had hardly any exercise during all this time, this meant an important victory.

'Yes,' he said. 'It's very satisfactory.'

I refused to let up on the pressure, however. Again I turned to Abdul, 'What about the beds? When do we get them?'

'You will have beds today in Block Two,' he promised.

'OK,' I said, 'that's fine. By the way, we're sitting out in the yard at the moment while Block Three is cleaned. Is it all right for us to return to Block Two?'

'Certainly.'

'When does the exercise start?'

'Tomorrow,' he said and I knew he had only agreed to the concessions under the pressure from his superiors.

Horst and I left the office, feeling almost elated and returned to join our group in the yard, surrounded by their belongings. We were allowed to enjoy the sun for another four hours while Block Three was cleaned out. I put in most of the time working out final details of my escape in my head. The more I thought about it, the more the snags faded away and the more optimistic and more certain I became that I would be successful.

THIRTEEN

We drifted back to the blocks and as we did so I noticed that as the prisoners filed up to the gate, they were searched thoroughly and their possessions such as writing paper, pens, Nivea cream or foods like salt or hot sauces – all the little things they had bought in the prison shop for added comfort – were taken away from them. It did not take a genius to realise that all this stuff would end up in Abdul's office and would be put on sale again in the prison shop.

I was the first prisoner for Block Two to reach the gate and the first to be searched. When the guard looked in my pillow case and reached down to take out the tin of Nivea cream, I roared at him, 'Don't touch that!' The man leaped back as though scalded and then shouted to his sergeant who quickly came over.

'You cannot take these things into the block,' said the sergeant stiffly.

'Fuck off! I told him and the two men stared at me astonished until the sergeant recovered and angrily stalked off. He returned with Abdul who asked me, 'What's the trouble?'

'There's no trouble, Abdul,' I told him. 'Except that these fellows are trying to help to increase your profits at my expense.'

Abdul's expression hardly changed. 'Go in,' he said quietly. So I pushed past him into the block, then turned to see how the guards were treating the others. Those immediately behind me had all their stuff taken from them but when it came to the turn of Des and Horst I shouted at them to do as I had done. I heard them both tell the guards to fuck off and they shoved their way forward without further trouble. When the rest of the line-up saw what was happening, they, too, pushed past the guards who eventually gave up the struggle and let them through.

We had hardly got inside Block Two, however, when the *seep* foreman came up to us and officiously informed us that we had to occupy separate cells.

'No, we're not!' I answered him. 'We're staying together – like it or lump it!' I told my little group to sit down in the main block hall and wait to see what would happen. The foreman eventually decided to put the five of us into a cell which held ten beds, which immediately aroused the opposition of the Arab prisoners who protested.

Faced with uproar and protests from every side, the foreman went away and returned with the sergeant of the guard. The sergeant told the foreman to put us all into separate cells. 'No, we stay together,' I insisted. The sergeant then told the foreman to put us in one cell but the foreman tried to talk him out of that pointing out the trouble it would cause. The sergeant then began shouting at the foreman and finally he called for other guards. For a moment, I thought he intended to try to do something to me but instead, he arrested the block foreman and marched him off to the punishment cells!

We remained squatting outside cell number four. The sergeant eventually came back, walked into the cell and ordered out the Arabs who were there, announcing that the cell was needed for 'Fraser and his men'. Shouts, protests and appeals to Allah himself notwithstanding, the Muslims were ejected and we marched in. Within minutes, I was ensconced in a top bunk, my blanket neatly spread across it and then I suddenly remembered that because of my threatened hunger strike, we had no food. I went to the guard at the gate who promised to fetch the sergeant. When the latter arrived, I explained I had received no food that day and would like to telephone my company. The sergeant said he would telephone on my behalf so I went back to the cell. Two hours later, such was the obvious Saudi anxiety to please me, a food parcel arrived. That night there was almost an air of celebration in our cell. I had an additional reason for celebrating, of course – but I didn't bother to mention it.

My escape plans at this stage revolved around the problem of cutting the bars on the piss-house window. But how long would that take? The answer, it appeared, was too long. The bars were strong, criss-crossed and welded in six-inch squares. There had to be a way, however, and as I lay on my bunk working on the problem, I studied the window of our cell. The bars here were held in a steel frame which had been welded to the window area. If I could find a way of breaking the welds at the side, I would be able to pull out the window bars. Problem: how to break the welds?

That night I wrote to Tom. I told him I intended to make my break for freedom on the night he planned to fly home for his Christmas vacation. I had changed my ideas about driving to Jidda and instead, intended to drive to Dammam. I wanted him to leave a car near the main gate but not too close to it otherwise I risked coming under machine-gun fire as I climbed into it. I told Eric Price as much of my plans as I thought wise, and explained that I needed him to keep watch for me while I worked through the bars of the piss-house. I did not tell him how I planned to get out of Saudi Arabia as he might not have fancied sailing across a rough sea in a rubber dinghy.

Two days later my name was called and I was told to report for exercise. When I got into the yard, there were other westerners there but they were all from Block One. I was the only westerner from Block Two. The bulk of the other prisoners were Saudis who were dressed very professionally in track suits and gym shoes. There were also two PT instructors as well as the usual guards. The instructors took us round to where a new cookhouse had been built (though never used) and halted beside a marked-out volley pitch. We were lined up and told to do PT.

I said to the nearest guard, 'Look, I'm too old for this sort of thing. It might kill me. Instead, I'll just take a gentle stroll along the wall.'

'You wanted exercise,' insisted the man.

'Not that kind of exercise,' I replied. And with that I stepped out of the line and began walking at a gentle pace along the side of the wall. For a moment the guard looked undecided but when I kept on walking he came running after me to escort me. I had walked only a short distance when I saw a massive pair of double gates let into the wall. They were kept tightly shut by three massive bolts, one at the top, one in the middle and another at the bottom. The only one which had a padlock, however, was the middle one. For a moment, I thought that if I could release the top and bottom bolts, then the doors were bound to open but when I took a closer look I realised that it would be necessary to break off the padlock on the middle bolt. Long before I could wrench that padlock off, an enthusiastic guard would have got me.

Back in the cell again, I told Eric about the doors and about the padlock. 'But don't worry,' I said cheerfully, 'the chances are we'll be shot before we get a chance to get it off. It's still worth a try, however. What do you think?'

'It's worth the risk,' he agreed.

Normally, Sunday is the day for women visitors only so I was surprised when my name was called and I was told to go to Abdul's office. When I arrived, I found the vice-consul there along with a man called Mitchell or Marshall, or consul-general.

The consul-general's first words were, 'I am told that you are the worst prisoner in Saudi Arabia. You will have to start behaving yourself, Fraser.'

'Hold on!' I said, wondering what this was all about. 'Are you here to give me a telling off?'

'Yes,' he said. 'The Saudis say you are a drug addict and you have only yourself to blame.'

I looked at him in utter disbelief. 'What do you mean – drug addict? You must be kidding. Who's been feeding you this load of rubbish?' I glared at Northern who said nothing. The consul-general went rambling on, telling me I'd have to stay a full three years in prison on the orders of Prince Niaf and that I would have to accept that and behave myself. Otherwise, the embassy would be able to do nothing for me.

'What the fuck have you done for me so far?' I demanded. 'As for this nonsense about drugs – the only drugs I take are head-ache tablets and if that makes me a drug addict, then just about everybody in Britain, and that includes you, is a drug addict. Don't you take something for a headache when you have one?'

'I never have headaches,' replied the consul-general stiffly. I saw Abdul smiling broadly. The spectacle of such dissension in the British ranks obviously pleased him mightily.

Having kicked me up the pants, the consul then asked me why I made trouble. I told him I made trouble because of the bad conditions and I also explained that to someone like me, who suffered from severe headaches, there was a need for somewhere quieter with access to proper medical treatment. He then asked me about my family and I told him I had a little son who had recently learned to talk but whom I had never heard speak.

'I will arrange for a tape-recording to be made of him talking. And then we'll have a tape-recorder brought into the prison so that you can listen to the tape,' he said.

'Bollocks to that!' I told him. 'Do you really imagine I'm going to sit in this pigsty and listen to a tape-recording of my son? You need your head examined.'

Oddly enough, my anger and insults had the opposite effect to that which might have been expected. He ceased looking stern and serious and instead gave me a friendly and indeed, an almost warm smile.

Encouraged, I said to him confidentially, 'What would happen if I escaped from here and managed to make it to a friendly country? Would the Foreign Office help me?'

The smile left his face. 'Are you serious?' he asked.

'Certainly,' I said.

'You'll never make it, you know. And the guards here will take a great delight in shooting you.'

'Don't worry about that,' I said. 'I just want to know if I would get any help.'

'Well, I can only tell you that there was a chap in Athens and the British Embassy managed to get him home. But you shouldn't try it – I think you'll be killed. And we can't help you if you're dead.'

I thanked him for his advice and felt he had been doing his best to help me. The bawling out was probably at the instigation of Prince Niaf and the Saudi Government and he had done it only to satisfy them and show British goodwill. Back in the cell, I told the others what had happened and Des Smith, who had written his will a few days earlier, suggested I do the same. We all had a feeling that the Saudi authorities were taking too much of an interest in my 'well-being' and that they might end the impasse at any moment in a rather definitive way.

I laughed at this idea but decided all the same that I had better step up my plans to escape. Trying to keep as calm as possible – although inside I seethed with anxiety and excitement – I lay on my bed and went back to studying the bars on the window. I noticed that around the frame of the window which held the frame of the bars there were quarter-inch strips of welded steel. It seemed to me that if I had a steel bar which would slot into these, I could break some of them and thus be able to pull out the frame holding the bars. I reached for my writing paper and began drawing different types of bars (or jemmies). In the end I worked out such a simple type that I couldn't understand why it had taken me so long to think of it: a twelve-inch-long flat bar, half an inch thick, with a slot at the end of it. All I had to do was slot this end piece into some of the strips holding the frame and I could easily break them out. I redrew a proper sketch for Tom and wrote him an accompanying letter asking him to have this tool made for me and to smuggle it in.

Tom planned to leave Saudi Arabia on his Christmas leave at noon on 17 December so I decided to escape in the early hours of 18 December. If I didn't reach home in time for Christmas, at least I was bound to make it for Hogmanay.

Tom came next day with the splendid news that he had already managed to get the tool made. There was only one snag; he was being sent to Hofuf for some days but hoped to be back in time to see me and to finalise arrangements. As we were already into the month of December, his news alarmed me and I pointed out that he might be asked to stay on in Hofuf or even be expected to fly home from there.

'Don't worry, Ian, I won't allow that to happen.' I knew I could rely on him.

While I waited for 18 December, events in Al-Ould seemed to flow past without my being aware of them. All my thoughts were now on my escape and I was determined to keep my nose clean without, of course, giving up my reputation for being troublesome. I told Eric I planned to go on the 18th and confirmed his part in the escape and his role as the bloke who would keep watch.

Disaster, however, struck on the morning of 9 December. That morning, Eric's name was called and he was instructed to get dressed and told he was going 'outside the prison'. None of us could imagine what this was about unless he was going to be released. Eric himself thought release unlikely but even as he walked out of the block, that thought was very much uppermost in my mind. When he had failed to return by nightfall, I decided, 'Shit, that fucks up my escape again.' Next morning a visiting lady told us that Eric had been released and flown home to Britain the previous night. I was plunged in despair. Who was now going to keep watch for me? The only one of my fellow prisoners who might agree to risk it was Horst but I felt he might prove unreliable. After all, he had nicked a million quid. In the end, I decided there was no alternative but to risk the break on my own.

To our astonishment Eric returned to the cell at eleven o'clock on Saturday morning. He said he had been kept in a police station all the time he had been away. The police had told him that if he paid them £2000 he would be released. He had agreed to do this and the police had then hauled him off to the offices of BAC where Eric had some money in the safe. While he was there he had been seen by our visiting lady who was told that he was being sent back to Britain that night. In fact, the key to the safe could not be found so Eric had been taken back to the police station and kept there until early on Saturday morning when the police had whipped him back to the BAC offices, where the safe had been opened and Eric had handed over his £2000. To his utter disgust, the Saudi police had double-crossed him. They had taken the money and then they told him that this represented payment for customs dues on the whisky which he had had in his possession when arrested. Despite his protests they had then taken him straight back to Al-Ould.

Tom had told me he had hoped to be back in Riyadh from the east coast by Monday at the latest. But Monday was 14 December and he was scheduled to fly home on the 17th. Inside those few days he had to ensure that a car was ready and that all the money and false papers I needed were stowed in it and that a hacksaw blade, plus the special tool I had designed for myself were smuggled into the prison.

That Monday morning I was edgy and very anxious. What if Tom failed to get back from the east coast as promised? My thoughts, however, were suddenly interrupted by the announcement of my name and I walked out to reception to pick up my food box. And there was Tom. He had just returned from Hofuf that morning but he assured me, he had everything ready and I was not to worry.

'Be careful with that box, though,' he advised. 'And try to look normal.' Once again he assured me that everything had been taken care of and said he would be back with another food box next morning.

Luckily I had the guards well trained by now and the search they made of my cardboard box was perfunctory. Once in my cell I placed the box on my bunk and carefully lifted out the various smaller boxes containing food and gave these to Horst to put away.

I then felt under the flaps of the big box and found a false photostat passport and driver's licence, plus the hacksaw blade I had asked for and my special tool. There was also a letter from Tom. In it he explained that the gate through which I intended to escape gave on to a cul-de-sac. The car would be parked there on Thursday night. If it were still there on Friday morning, it would be driven away but returned again to the same place on Friday night (he didn't say who was going to do this). He had also drawn a map which I would find inked in on the inside bottom of the box.

I checked on my papers and on the implements and then hid them by wrapping them in my blanket. That night, I lay awake checking the number of men who visited the piss-house and the time most of them spent there. So far as I could judge, a man would be using one of the holes every fifteen minutes which gave me approximately ten minutes in which to break through the bars of the window. I would need Eric to stand watch and warn me if anybody was coming.

All along Tom had been dead set against the idea of using Eric. However, if I were not to be caught while levering out the bars, I desperately needed someone to keep watch and he seemed to be the only one of my fellow westerners, apart from Horst, who was prepared to risk an escape. Horst would certainly come and, so far as I knew, still expected to come but he was a big-time criminal and if he broke out, the Saudis would undoubtedly call out the National Guard, which would make an escape almost impossible. Having thus reasoned things out I decided to tell Horst he would not be going.

At ten o'clock on Thursday morning, 36 hours before Tom was due to fly home, he turned up with another food parcel, packed as usual within a moderately-sized cardboard box. Inside, he told me was £2000 in twenty-pound sterling notes plus another £2000-worth of Saudi riyals in 100-riyal denominations. There was also an airline ticket to Jidda. This was a 'blind,' of course; to get to Bahrain, I would have to drive past Riyadh airport and the idea was that if we were stopped I could produce the airline ticket as 'proof' of our reason for being on that road. Tom then told me that one of Eric's friends had turned up the previous night and had handed him £2000 to give to Eric along with Eric's briefcase containing his shaving gear. Tom had been taken aback by this and was, indeed, very angry with me because until now, although Eric's name had often been mentioned, he did not know I had definitely decided to take him. He had, as I have said, advised against it, and indeed until that moment had been sure that I intended to make the break on my own. I hated having to deceive my brother, but I felt I had had no option. For Tom, however, the knowledge that Eric Price was also in on the escape increased his anxieties; the more people who knew about the plan and about his involvement in it, the more dangerous the whole enterprise was. Indeed, for perhaps the only time since he had agreed to help me, my brother had almost quit that morning. As he told me, 'You know, Ian, I sat for a whole hour outside the prison, this morning before deciding to risk coming in – I felt certain I'd be arrested once I walked inside; I was so sure the news of your plan must have leaked out.'

His reception, in fact, was the opposite of hostile. When the guards indicated that it was time for us to part. I pleaded for just another five minutes 'with my young brother', explaining that he was going on leave to England that day and that it might be weeks before he returned – indeed, he might never return at all. When the guards heard this, they insisted on shaking Tom's hand and even kissed him on the cheek and told him how good he was and in general made quite a fuss of him. This was to their credit, of course, but I wondered how they would have behaved had they been aware of what was really happening. They allowed us another two minutes together before I saw Tom, relief written all over his face, stride away towards the main gate, looking anxious to put as much distance between himself and the prison as soon as possible. Within the hour, his plane was due to take off for London and so off he went, making straight for the airport, hoping that no heavy-handed Saudi cop would stop him at the last moment.

With Tom I had sent a letter to Anne which he was to deliver to her on the following Sunday night. In this, I wrote that by the time she received it, I would be either free, dead or in a punishment cell, but that I felt I had no option but to risk an escape and I knew she would support me in anything I did. She was not to worry about me but to have faith in me. I hoped shortly to be with her again and with the children whom I loved so much; to achieve this was worth all the risks I proposed taking.

I returned to my cell and explained to the lads that a new catering firm would be providing my daily food box but, in the meantime, my brother Tom had done the best he could with some items he had bought. So I distributed biscuits, cakes and sweets, plus some old newspapers he had brought me and then began an examination of the cardboard box. Inside I found the money made up in eight packets, four concealed in the flaps and four stuck to the bottom of the box along with the airline ticket.

I handed Eric four of the money packets, two containing sterling and two with riyals. I then advised him to hide the money in his blanket, which he did. For myself I lay on my bunk worrying about Tom and whether he had got clear of Riyadh; it was not uncommon with Saudi Airlines, unfortunately, for planes to be cancelled at the last moment and I hoped that if, for any reason, he had not succeeded in getting away, that he would get a message to me. I had no intention of making a break for it while he remained in the country.

At 5 p.m. that day, my name was again called and when I went to the reception area, I found another food parcel awaiting me. This was the food prepared by Al Flouty, the new caterers. I took a quick glance inside the box and saw that they had delivered cold scrambled eggs, some dried-up salad, a piece of bread and two slices of bread. If this was intended to be my new food ration, I was not impressed and I told this to the driver who had brought it. I thought it wise to make as much fuss as possible about the parcel in order to lull suspicion. If Fraser ceased being troublesome, then the implication was that he was up to other mischief.

Back in the cell I doled out my dire little ration to the other fellows and then broke the news to Des and Horst that I intended to make my break that night. I apologised to Des for not inviting him along but explained that as he had a wife and son in Riyadh they would be held as hostages. I had more trouble making my apologies to Horst and indeed, even after I had fumbled out my feeble excuses, I almost felt like saying, 'Oh, fuck it, Horst, come along, too.' But I resisted the impulse for although I could see he was bitterly disappointed, I knew that he knew my decision was the only one. He might have been a tower of strength outside so far as ideas and initiative were concerned, but apart from the fact that his escape would be viewed more seriously by the Saudis than my own, I wanted to run my own escape, to make all the

decisions. I wanted to have nobody else to blame if anything
went wrong. So far, Eric Price had shown no signs of wanting
to make decisions or change any of the plans I had suggested.
He seemed content to tag along – and in the circumstances, that
suited me fine.

Throughout my imprisonment, I had never bothered to mix
with my Arab fellow-prisoners, although most of the other
westerners had done so. I noticed that Eric had never done any
mixing so I now suggested to him that this would be a good time
for him to show how friendly he was and that he should go and
talk to the Arabs. So off he went while I lay on my bunk, trying
to work out everything down to the last detail, to make sure that
nothing would go wrong. Fortunately the night was cold and
getting colder all the time. It was down to 55 degrees now, which
meant that the guards were likely to huddle low in order to keep
themselves warm and would probably be less alert. It also suited
me because I was lying fully dressed under my blanket except
for my running shoes. Earlier I had washed these and had hung
them out to dry on the clothesline in the wash area, next to the
piss-house and alongside a sheet which I had hung there and
which I intended to use in the escape. I stuffed my money down
the waistband of my trousers and carefully folded my papers and
airline ticket so that they fitted neatly into my pockets – I felt as
bloated as Billy Bunter. When I decided to move, I intended to
shove the hacksaw and my special tool up my sleeves.

On Thursday nights (which are Saudi Arabia's equivalent of
our Saturday nights), TV programmes in Riyadh do not finish
before 1 a.m. As I waited, time seemed to stand still. At last,
however, I heard the TV set being switched off and then there
was that strange murmuring and rustling and shuffling of bare
feet which meant that the denizens of the block were settling
down for the night. I didn't bother to check my watch for I
already knew the time.

There was just one hour to go. Then Eric Price and I would,
at long last, make our move.

FOURTEEN

I listened to the noises – of men shuffling around the block, of others coming and going to the 'hole in the floor', of the foreman and one of his deputies carrying out their nightly headcount. When one of them poked his head inside our cell, I pretended to be asleep.

And then, Christ! I suddenly realised I *had* fallen asleep! I hurriedly glanced at my watch and saw that it was 3 a.m. Fucking hell, I thought, they will be getting ready to say prayers at 3.30 a.m. I looked across to where Eric lay and saw that he was wide awake. So I got out of the bunk, taking care not to stand on any of the three Arabs who were asleep on our floor; touching Des Smith gently on the shoulder as he had asked to be awakened when I made my move. We did not speak, but just nodded good-bye.

I shuffled my way down the main hall of the block and entered the last of the cubicles inside the piss-house having first made sure that there was no one already in it. Then I waited for Eric. He knew all about *salha* being called at 3.30 a.m., but took his time about arriving and indeed, it was a good five minutes before he put in an appearance. I gave him a gentle bollocking for not wakening me earlier but his excuse was that he thought I had decided not to go. I had no time to give him the benefit of my thoughts on this excuse but instead told him to stand in the doorway while I climbed on top of the nine-foot-high cubicle wall and got to work. I looked for what I thought would be the easiest bar to break and started. However, it was either much stronger than I had imagined or I was much weaker than I thought for soon the sweat was pouring off me and I had still failed to move it.

For some reason I stopped and looked at Eric. He was standing in the doorway peeling an orange – we had agreed that this was to be his 'cover'. Some sixth sense, however, made me climb down fast. When I reached the bottom I stood there, heart pumping rapidly and my breath coming so fast through my mouth that it sounded like the noise of a elephant. The noise was so loud that I clapped my hand across my mouth as soon as I heard Eric say 'hello' and then I heard the clip-clop of sandals as a Saudi entered the first cubicle. My breathing was coming so hard and my heart beating so loudly that I felt sure the entire block would hear me but I kept telling myself that this was a natural reaction and that I shouldn't worry about it. When the Saudi had finished his business and had gone, Eric apologised for not seeing the Saudi until it was almost too late.

'Great!' I said. 'What I've got is a watchdog that doesn't watch!'

Rather than waste time, however, I climbed back up on top of the cubicle wall and got to work again on the iron bar. Suddenly and without warning, the thing broke with a noise like a gunshot. I leaped down from the wall, heart once again pounding, breath again coming in stentorian gusts, certain that somebody must have heard it. I waited, but all was silent. No shouts, no calls of enquiry. I looked at Eric, who stood there white-faced and then at my watch. Christ! Nearly twenty past three. I climbed the wall again rapidly and began twisting at the bars. A couple of movements and they started to come apart, making just enough space for me to climb through. I got hold of the corner of the barred iron frame and, with my feet pressed against the wall, pulled at it, widening the gap. Between the bars and the empty window frame (all the glass in Al-Ould prison had long ago been broken and a fine mesh covered the bars to keep out flies and other insects) lay a sill some eighteen inches deep. I waved to Eric, indicating that he should climb up behind me and as he was slim, told him to squeeze under the iron frame. I prised this open and Eric squeezed through and then tucked himself up on the sill. Once on the other side, he pushed at the barred frame, trying to make more space for me to get through but he made little impression and, as time was running out fast, I decided to make the attempt anyway. Squeezing myself as small as possible, I finally made it.

Once on the sill, I pulled back the window frame and tied it to the iron frame with a bit of cloth torn from my shirt. I then took stock of our position. The window was a good twelve feet above the hard cement floor of the prison compound. Worse, just underneath us lay three big dustbins, similar to those I had used for brewing beer, which were filled with shit because the shit sump for the block lay directly under the window. If the worst had come to the worst I was prepared to drop right into one of these but I knew that two blokes careering around Saudi Arabia smelling of something very different from roses was bound to excite some interest, particularly if the police stopped us.

I had taken the shit-bins into account in my plans. The clothes-line on which I had hung my sheet and my running shoes, fortunately, ran right up to the window and so all I had to do was to draw in the line, grab the sheet and then attach one end of it to the iron bars and lower the rest to the ground. It took only a moment for Price and I to climb down our 'rope', just missing the shit-bins as we dropped and to then run directly across the compound to the cookhouse block. This building, as I have already mentioned, was never used (nor, so far as I know, ever will be). As we ran, we veered slightly to the left for our ultimate destination was the side gate which lay almost immediately under one of the control-towers manned by two guards with machine guns. Our next move was to creep along the side of the cookhouse and then along the side of the adjoining block, an unused laundry. From the corner of the laundry wall we would be forced to race across open ground in full view of the guards in two of the towers.

The Saudis have no problem with energy resources and Al-Ould was kept brilliantly floodlit at night so that the compound was as bright as day. Standing at the corner of the laundry block, I looked round to see what the guards in the corner towers were up to. I could see no sign of them, however, nor when I glanced back at the other tower within my line of sight, could I see any there, either. I also noticed that the ladders which the guards used to climb into their perches had been drawn up. All the signs were, therefore, that because of the coldness of the night, the guards were now huddled down inside their cabins and were almost certainly fast asleep.

Despite recognising that so far we had been lucky, my heart

continued to pound like Big Ben and my body was soaked in sweat. I checked around for the roving guards who patrolled the prison compound day and night, but they appeared to have gone to ground also, presumably driven indoors by the cold. I decided that there was no point standing there any longer just gazing at the big doors and so we moved out on tiptoe. In due course we reached the big doors without being noticed. I started at once to work on the hasp of the padlock so that I could drag the two big doors open. The hasp however, proved a formidable obstacle. It was welded on to the padlock and as my tool was only twelve inches long, it was like tackling it with a toothpick. After some minutes' struggling, my hand abruptly slipped and I made a terrible noise – the noise of steel hitting and rasping on steel. As this clangourous sound rang out, we both bolted back to the comparative cover of the laundry block.

I found that my hands were raw and painful. I told Eric to wait while I ran back to the piss-house window and got my sheet. I raced back, tugging at it and managed to tear off some pieces which I wrapped around my hands, all the time wondering where the hell all the guards had got to for I had been making enough noise to be heard as far away as the King's Palace!

Al-Ould remained wrapped in slumber. We tiptoed back to the door and began work again. My hands were now feeling as though they had no skin on them and I asked Eric to have a go. He was not strong enough for this type of work, however, and I had to take over again. I was beginning to panic by now for I knew that we had to get clear by 4 a.m. Preparations for *salha* would begin at 3.30 a.m. with the prayer-callers rousting out the sleepy-heads no later than 3.45. We simply had to be out before the commencement of prayers at 4 a.m. There were only minutes left in which to break through these doors.

For a second time I made a horrendous noise as metal rasped on metal and again we had to run back to the cover of the laundry block. Hearts pounding, we waited to see if there was any movement from the guards but there was still no sign. Back again once more to the doors where, with Eric breathing down my neck, I said, 'For fuck's sake, Eric, give me a hand.' Gamely, but awkwardly, he grabbed hold of the tool and tried to lever the hasp, only to catch my hand between two pieces of metal. As an excruciating pain shot up my arm, I turned on him savagely and said, 'Christ, leave it! I'll do it myself.' But even as I restarted work on the hasp, I was also trying to figure out where we could hide if the guards caught sight of us. The short answer seemed to be that there was nowhere unless we ran back to our block and pulled ourselves inside again with the aid of the sheet. I did not bother to tell Eric, however, that I had no intention of going back; if the guard sighted us I intended to dash right around the compound and make straight for the main gate where I would jump the guard and take the consequences.

Even as my thoughts were running thus, there was a sudden crack and the hasp gave way. It made such a noise that Eric immediately bolted for the 'safety' of the laundry building and, feeling that it was a moment for discretion I followed him.

'Look, Eric,' I said, as we stood there gasping for breath, 'even if we are spotted, we should be still able to get the doors open and to make a run for the car before the guards realise what we are doing. We'll have to risk it.'

He nodded, and so, moving very carefully, we darted back to the gates. I grabbed at the massive doors and pulled – but they still obstinately refused to budge. 'Come on, Eric,' I hissed, 'give me a hand.' Together we pulled and then I realised that there was no way they were going to open. I looked at the bolts and padlock again and then realised that breaking the hasp had not been enough to release the padlock; that, too, would have to come off.

'God,' I moaned, 'this is going to be very hard.' My hands, were now bleeding badly. Worse, I no longer had enough strength. As for Eric, I felt I was carrying him. Although a motor mechanic by trade, he did not seem to be able to get any strength behind the tool when he tried to work it.

At 3.55 a.m., I again put the little tool to work. The padlock and bolt went through a big steel ring which was welded to the door. I started pushing and pulling with the tool until I felt the metal eating right into my hands. Then, and again without warning, the ring suddenly broke from the door. I pulled madly at the bolt and next second, bolt, padlock and ring were all in my hand. I passed them over to Eric but hung on to the tool which by this time was so deeply embedded in my hand that it felt like part of my arm.

I stepped back to get a better purchase and pulled at the big steel doors. They were moved on little steel wheels so, as I slowly dragged them open, they made a screeching noise that seemed enough to waken the dead. (Later Des Smith said we made so much noise it seemed as if the entire prison was attempting to break out.) We squeezed quickly through the gap, Eric going first. Then he bolted off to the left, towards the main road without waiting for me. 'Stupid bastard!' I hissed. Instead, I had to pull the big doors shut behind me all my myself to make sure that nobody would notice that they were no longer bolted. I then waited to hear if an alarm had been raised, but all I could hear was the sound of prayers coming from inside the prison and from the nearby mosque.

Calmly and unhurriedly, therefore, I walked up the road towards the place where Tom had promised to leave the car parked. It was there, all right, a brown Japanese make. I laid down my tool at the side of the prison wall, crossed the road to the car, opened the door and got into the driving seat. As promised, the keys were in the ashtray. I switched on the engine and then looked around for Eric. But there was no sign of the bugger.

I drove slowly towards the main road and then spotted him at the end of the prison wall. 'Get in!' I shouted and he ran over and jumped in beside me. 'What in hell made you run up here?' I hissed.

He looked flustered. 'I wanted to see if any of the guards had come out of the main gate.'

'And suppose they had?' I asked. 'The car was round the corner and they couldn't see it so all we had to do was to get in and drive away!' He didn't reply and I didn't pursue the matter. Instead, I drove out on the main road, going towards the 'Pink Tit' and then turned out on to Airport Road. I kept glancing behind me, but there was no sign of any police cars following. 'Keep your fingers crossed,' I told Eric.

Once on Airport Road I felt a great deal better. Even if the police stopped us now, I had papers ready and a good story off pat. Then, with horror, I realised that Eric was sitting there with the bolt, ring and padlock of the prison gates still in his hands.

'Jesus, Eric,' I roared. Immediately I pulled up and made him open the door and throw the stuff out. I drove on and quickly reached the Dammam Road. We crossed the flyover here, turned right and drove past the Saudi Royal Air Force base where Eric usually worked. Checking the time, I saw it was just 4.20 a.m.

Ahead of us lay the open road until we reached Hofuf, 150 miles away. Before Hofuf, however, there were two significant hazards; 75 miles up the road was a police checkpoint and roughly the same distance further on, the Hofuf checkpoint itself. Our escape was almost certain to have been discovered by then and the police at both checkpoints alerted.

Yet we had a good chance. Tom had advised me that driving at 80 mph, it should take me approximately an hour and three-quarters to reach Hofuf – 'But watch out for the wild camels on the road – you don't see then until you're right on top of them.' So I pushed my foot hard down and Eric was soon complaining that if I continued driving like this, I would blow up the engine. We continued to career wildly through the darkness of the early morning with Eric becoming more and more agitated about the engine.

'Why, is my driving that bad?' I asked him.

'No,' he replied diplomatically. 'It's just the engine I'm worried about.'

'Well, we'll just have to take our chances.'

Soon afterwards, while he was searching the glove compartment, he found a box of a hundred cigarettes and some matches. He lit one for himself and then one for me and as I began smoking again, I felt the tension rapidly leaving me.

'Eric,' I said, 'I don't know about Allah, but I feel certain God must be looking after us. Here we are, well away from Riyadh and the only trouble we have had so far is my hands.'

Eric clucked sympathetically.

'I feel as if I was holding a red-hot poker,' I told him.

'What do we do if we're stopped at a checkpoint?' he asked.

'What do you want me to do?' I queried back.

'I don't know,' he replied.

'Well, I'll tell you then. I'll go straight through the checkpoint and then leave the road and take to the desert. After that I'll think of the next move.' In fact, the only thing I felt sure about was that I was not going back to a Saudi prison. The very least I could hope to get would be another ten years on my present sentence while Eric, doubtlessly, would argue that I had talked him into the escapade and might get off relatively lightly. I felt I was beginning to learn a lot about Eric.

I kept checking our mileage, getting ready for the first check-

point to loom up out of the desert. We would see a large police
station on the left-hand side of the road and find that each traffic
lane had a road barrier and sentry box. And then, suddenly, I
saw the faint lights of the police station ahead and at once slowed
down to reconnoitre the situation. Incredibly, the road barriers
were still up and in the two sentry boxes the Saudi policemen
were fast asleep. I kept up a steady speed and passed gently
under the barriers so as not to raise the alarm. Once clear,
however, I stepped on the gas, rapidly picking up speed.

'Did you notice if there were radio masts?' I asked Eric.

'Yes,' he replied, 'there are.'

'That means we'll have to drive like hell, then,' I said, adding,
'Look, this is the way I figure it out. They're not likely to find
out in Al-Ould that we've skipped until at least 7 a.m. – if even
then. That means that if we can reach the checkpoint at Hofuf
before then, everything should be OK. If we can keep up this
speed, we should reach it in about an hour's time, say 6.45 a.m.
I know that only gives us about fifteen minutes to play with –
but a miss is as good as a mile.'

Eric grinned.

'We'll do it, Ian,' he encouraged. 'If anybody can do it, Ian,
it's you!'

We were only five miles from Hofuf when the sun rose over
a flat landscape. As if on a signal, I noticed that our petrol gauge
read empty.

'We're going to run out of petrol,' I said.

'Nurse it, Ian,' urged Eric. 'Nurse it.'

'Don't worry, we'll get there,' I told him fiercely. 'We haven't
come this far, just to be caught now. Tom knows exactly how
much petrol it takes to get to Hofuf and there'll be just enough
in the tank, you'll see. Keep your fingers crossed.'

With that, I stepped on the gas again and we roared down
the road. About ten minutes later, the dim shape of the Hofuf
checkpoint came into view. Even from that distance, I could see
that although the police were up and moving about, the barriers
across the road were still raised. I slackened just a little so as not
to arouse suspicion and the police paid us no attention as we
flashed under the barrier. Once through, I spotted a petrol station
on the right-hand side of the road, scarcely a hundred yards
beyond the checkpoint so I slowed down and drove into the

forecourt. When the dosy Arab attendant came out, I told him to fill the tank.

Meanwhile, Eric walked over to the soft-drinks stand and bought two bottles of mineral water and some doughnuts. I got out of the car to stretch my legs and decided to take a look in the boot. When I opened the lid, I could scarcely believe my eyes. Inside were three plastic containers – one with five gallons of petrol, the second with five gallons of drinking water and the third with five gallons of washing water. In addition, there was a large cardboard box, two blankets, two pillows and Eric's brief-case. I lifted out the briefcase, paid the petrol attendant, jumped into the car and shouted at Eric to get in. I looked at my watch – it was just 7 a.m. and the telephone wires and radio waves by now must be red-hot, for nobody, so far as I knew, had ever before escaped from Al-Ould, Saudi Arabia's top-security prison. Eric obediently jumped in and I roared off again. I told him what I had found in the boot and pointed to his briefcase on the rear seat. When he opened it, there was his washing gear and a spare set of spectacles.

Ten miles the other side of Hofuf, I stopped the car, got out and opening the boot, checked on the contents of the cardboard box. There were two more blankets inside this and a complete change of clothing for me, plus washing gear. I felt so dirty that I sprinkled water on a towel and wiped my face and hands and then changed into fresh clothes. As Eric had not sweated nearly as much as I had, he looked comparatively clean. It took me about five minutes to change and finish my ablutions and then we were off again. It was vital, of course, that we reached Dammam as quickly as possible. Once there, we could mingle with hundreds of other westerners and in that way lessen the risks of being caught. At one stage Eric offered me a drink and a doughnut but I was too wound up to take them and so he ate them instead.

At long last we arrived at the outskirts of Dammam where at the junction of the Dammam and Dhahran crossroads, I spotted a set of traffic lights ahead. As we drove up, I also saw a police car parked at the side of the road. The driver was at the wheel but his mate was standing beside the door.

'Christ! Let's hope the lights stay green!' I muttered to Eric and stepped on the accelerator. But just before we approached them, the lights turned red. 'Shit!' I said. But there was nothing

I could do and I pulled up. Our situation rapidly became worse for the policeman who had been standing beside his car started walking towards us. 'Shit!' I said again, 'What shall we do?' Our options were limited, however, for there was no way I could outrun a police car on a straight road. All I could do was play it as it came. I noticed that the policeman was wearing a gun but as his hand was not on it, I took this as a good omen.

He stopped outside Eric's window and then, glancing at us curiously, asked, 'English?'

'No, American,' I said quickly.

He paused, then asked, 'You have cigs?'

'Oh, sure,' I said and I motioned Eric to open the glove compartment. Eric handed over four packets of cigarettes. Even as the cigarettes exchanged hands, the lights turned green and with a cheery good-bye, I waved to the cop and drove away. I continued to keep the man in sight in my rear mirror to see if he had rumbled us but I watched him saunter slowly back to his car, unwrapping the cigarettes. I looked at my watch; 8.30 a.m. Surely Abdul, back in Al-Ould, had by now discovered we had broken out. Yet why did those two policemen not show any interest in us? After all, there were only two roads we could have taken out of Riyadh – one to Jidda, the other to Dammam.

I quickly decided, however, that that was a problem for the Saudis and not for me.

FIFTEEN

We drove straight to the Gulf Hotel in Dammam and I parked the car outside. I was so desperate to taste freedom that I wanted to walk among crowds. Eric, on the other hand, wanted to go into the hotel for breakfast but I said that I had to wind down first and the only way I knew how to do that was by wandering about a bit. There was a local market nearby and I intended to amble through that. Eric explained that he wasn't keen to do this but I told him he could suit himself and that I was going anyhow. I was not surprised when he followed me.

It was now nine o'clock, five hours since we had walked through the prison gates. 'Not bad, eh?' I remarked to Eric, tapping the glass on my watch to emphasise how long we had been free. We entered the market area and sauntered slowly through, stopping now and then to look at any articles which caught our fancy. Eric bought a pair of scissors so that he could trim his beard. I bought nothing but was on the look out for a place that looked as if it might help us to buy a rubber boat. Once I stopped and asked two Americans if they knew where I could purchase a rubber dinghy but they, too, were strangers in town.

It was three years since I had last been in Dammam and at that time, not being a sailing man, boats had not interested me. I suddenly remembered however, that on my last visit I had spotted boats along the coast road to Al-Khubar. The idea of walking around Dammam all day trying to find somebody who would tell me where I could buy a rubber boat was obviously not on so I told Eric, 'I'm sorry, but we're off again.'

'What about breakfast?' he complained bitterly.

'Listen,' I said, 'I think I know a place where we can find a boat, out along the coast road. And I plan to be in Bahrain tonight.'

We drove out along the Al-Khubar road, travelling south from Dammam. To our left lay the waters of the Gulf (Persian or Arabian according to your nationality), to our right, the bleak and featureless desert. Every now and then a new building loomed up like an island in the ocean. We were almost halfway to Al-Khubar when I spotted another new building with several boats lying along one side. We pulled up and I saw that the place was a boat showroom. We got out and walked up to the front door, only to find it locked. Looking inside I saw two blown-up rubber boats, so tantalising close that we could have touched them had there not been a plate-glass window between us. I was about to get a jack from the car and smash the window when we spotted a man moving about inside. I banged on the window and eventually he came to the door.

'I'm sorry but we've just moved in here,' he explained, 'so we're really not open yet. But is there any way I can help you?'

'We want to buy a rubber boat,' I told him.

'Well, there are those two,' he said, indicating the two craft we had spotted through the window. 'You're welcome to look at them.'

They turned out to be two Zodic boats – a sports model in red and another, more basic, in grey.

'May I ask why you want a boat?' he inquired. 'In that way perhaps I can help you.'

'To go fishing,' I told him and he seemed to be satisfied.

In the end I decided to buy the grey boat and along with it a Volvo 4.5 outboard engine which, together, would knock me back one thousand pounds.

'No problem,' said the salesman briskly. 'Come back tomorrow and I'll have it all ready for you.'

'Couldn't we have it today?' I asked.

'Sorry, but as you see we are not really open today. I cannot sell you anything for my boss does not permit sales on a Friday. Come back tomorrow please. I am sorry.'

'Thank you. We'll do that.'

Back in the car, I told Eric we had better drop out of sight quickly. We should find it easy enough to hole up somewhere by night but our problem was hiding somewhere by day. There was no way of knowing how good the Saudi police were but they had only three towns, besides Riyadh, in w hich to conduct a search for us – Jidda, Dammam and Al-Khubar. They would find it easy to stop and check all westerners – and they had had plenty of practice running down illegal Pakistanis.

'We could drive for a bit and see if we can find a place to park the car for the night. I don't want to drive too far away from that showroom. But we can't park all night in the desert.'

'So what do you suggest?' asked Eric.

'I don't see that we have much option but to drive on to Al-Khubar. We shouldn't run into any difficulties there, provided the local police aren't too sharpish.'

There are three roads leading from Dammam to Al-Khubar. There is a coast road, a middle road and a top road, which is also the Dhahran and airport road. As this also crosses the road from Riyadh, I decided it was bound to be crawling with police and opted, therefore, for the middle road. We drove for about two miles along this before I spotted a large building on our right with a boat propped up outside. We stopped at once and I saw that it was a large store and that it was open. In the window was an outboard engine. I decided it was worth a try, so we parked the car and went into the shop which was full of westerners. The shelves were stacked with toys as it was only six days before Christmas. We had entered by the rear door from the car park so we sauntered slowly through the shop until we came to the front window where we had spotted the outboard engine. On the way we passed two rubber boats, one of them an Avon which would take an outboard motor.

I grabbed a salesman and told him I'd like to buy the Avon.

'Very good,' he said. 'No problem.'

I pointed to the outboard engine – a Mercury 7.5. 'And we'll have that, too,' I said.

The man looked at us apologetically. 'I'm sorry, but it is not possible to let you have the engine until tomorrow.'

'Why not?' I demanded.

'It has to be tested,' he explained.

'We don't need to have it tested,' I told him. 'My friend here is a trained mechanic. He knows all about outboards.'

The man looked at me doubtfully, then said he would have to see the manager. The manager turned out to be a Pakistani. We had a long argument with him as he insisted he dared not sell us the engine without first having it tested. I patiently explained to him that we did not need to have it tested and in the end he agreed to let us have it, provided we guaranteed not to come back and complain if it broke down. 'But hurry now,' he said. 'The store closes at one o'clock.' I looked at my watch. It was 12.55. Did he intend to shut down the deal bang on the dot or what? Meanwhile, the salesman and an assistant were working frantically to let down the boat and pack it into its bag. I asked also for two lifejackets which were selling at a reduced price. We then sat down at the sales desk and the manager gave us tea while he filled in the sales forms.

'There is this police certificate to be filled in, also,' he suddenly announced.

'What police certificate?' I asked.

'The one I have to take to the police station for registration. It has to do with the coastguard. When you're out in the boat, the coastguards will speed up to you in their patrol boats and ask for the police certificate. If you haven't got one, then you'll go to jail.'

'Well, I don't want to go to jail,' I told him. 'So when can I collect the certificate?'

'The shop's copy will reach the police by Sunday,' replied the manager.

'So all I have to do is to go to the police station on Sunday and pick it up there, is that right?'

'Yes, that's right.'

'OK, we'll go then. I take it that if we're too busy to go then, we can go a few days later?'

'Certainly. There is no time limit. But, of course, you must not use the boat before you register.'

'Fine,' I said. 'I understand.'

He wanted my name. So I told him, 'Ian Fraser.' I saw no point in lying about my name but I decided to lie about my address which I gave as 'care of BAC, Dhahran.' Outside, the salesman and his help were waiting to put the boat in the car, so I paid the money, thanked the manager for his attention and service and went outside.

We stuffed the deflated boat in its bag into the back seat and put the engine into the boot. Having shuffled one or two things around, we eventually managed to get everything aboard, and feeling very pleased with ourselves, drove off in a whirl of dust.

'This,' I said to Eric, with a touch of complacency, 'is a piece of cake.'

'So far, so good,' he assented.

I took stock of our assets. In the boat we had three five-gallon cans, one filled with petrol. I had decided we needed a minimum of fifteen gallons of petrol so the thing to do was to empty the water cans and fill up with ten more gallons of petrol, plus two-stroke oil. We drew up at the first petrol station, therefore, emptied the water cans and washed them out with petrol and then I asked Eric what oil I should buy. He replied 'any', so I bought a gallon of engine oil. We then filled up the other empty cans with petrol and I decided we were all set to go. But when we drove out of the petrol station I was still not certain about where would be best to launch our boat.

'It's too risky just to put off from a straight bit of coastline,' I said. 'But there's a place called Half-Moon Bay a little distance along which sounds a better place.'

'Anything you say, Ian,' agreed Eric affably.

To get to Half-Moon Bay we had first to drive along the Riyadh road before coming to some crossroads. I felt certain there would be police on patrol at the crossroads but I thought that if they were on the look-out for us – and they *had* to be by now – they would be expecting us to come *from* Riyadh, not driving towards it. I was pretty confident, therefore, as we careered up the road and finally saw the road junction hove into sight. To my astonishment, there were no signs of any police. I looked at my watch for the umpteenth time and saw it was almost 2 p.m. Where on earth where the police? Where on earth were the roadblocks? By now the prison authorities had to be aware that we had escaped. What on earth were they up to? (Later I learned from Des Smith that at some stage I had been overheard to say that I would try to escape to Jidda and from there I hoped to get away on a British ship and that the police had therefore set up all their roadblocks on the Jiddah road.)

Half-Moon Bay was agreeably crowded with westerners – but it also had a very large police station. So I decided to drive as far round the bay as possible in the hope of finding a quiet spot, well out of police sight. I followed the only road round to discover that it led straight into the Saudi Arabia Air Force Survival Training School, which was bad news, indeed. Just before I reached the survival school gates, I turned the car round and then noticed, on my right, a small valley in the sand. It was about 25 feet wide, with sand rising on either side to a height of 15 feet, and on investigation led straight down to a beach. It seemed an ideal place from which to launch our craft – or would have been if it hadn't been for that damned survival school only a hundred yards away. I decided to park the car, however, and reconnoitre the situation. I discovered it was possible to drive the car halfway down the valley, and that this would help us to get our gear to the water's edge and also hide the car. When I walked down to the water's edge, my mood became quite optimistic. Looking out across the bay there was nothing but water, stretching out into the Gulf as far as the eye could see. Although we had come up from the south, we were now actually facing south, the road having taken us around and towards the tip of a small peninsula which jutted south. The coast of Saudi Arabia, therefore, now lay to our right and to our left I could see the outline of a large island which I hoped was Bahrain.

'All we have to do now is to wait until dark,' I told Eric. Darkness was due about 6 p.m. and we had to decide what to do until then. I marked the beach by drawing a line in the sand with my foot. 'I'll use that line as my bearing when the stars come out,' I told Eric. The latter, of course, was delighted that we could actually see Bahrain from here. Or was it Bahrain? I said, 'It must be Bahrain – where else could it be? I know of no other island in this part of the Gulf and as this thing seems to be about twenty miles away, it can only be Bahrain.' Eric agreed, though he still looked doubtful.

But how to kill the next few hours and make sure we were not caught? If we drove back to Al-Khubar, we would probably run into roadblocks. We could not stay on the beach because the police checked the beaches regularly, and, in particular, all the cars that were still there after dark. I decided we should drive back to the crossroads and then go to the Mariott Hotel which was not far from there. This might be dangerous, of course, because the police would look for us in hotels. It seemed to me, though, that the only reason why there had been no police activity so far was because the authorities were sure we were still holed-up in Riyadh. If we did spot a roadblock as we neared the hotel, then we could always turn back before they noticed us.

There were no roadblocks near the crossroads – and no police. I suggested that this had to be because it was Friday and everybody was praying. I parked the car at the hotel, a little uneasy because our car looked out of place besides the various Rolls-Royces, Cadillacs and other expensive cars parked alongside and I hoped that we did not look too scruffy as we entered. I was reassured that Eric, at least, was reasonably presentable. We walked into the large front lounge where we took a seat and ordered tea and sandwiches from the waiter.

'Tea, yes,' said the waiter, 'sandwiches, no. I'm afraid the restaurant is open and the chefs are too busy.'

'That's great,' I said. 'We'd prefer a meal, actually. I just thought the restaurant wouldn't be open.'

So we went into the restaurant where we ordered soup, steak and french fries. As I don't eat steak, I gave mine to Eric. The service was efficient and we got through the meal in no time.

'Coffee in the lounge, sir?' enquired the waiter deferentially.

'That'll be fine,' I said.

The coffees were on the table within seconds and so Eric and I were able to sit there, for the first time since our break-out, almost relaxed. Although we had been together now for almost twelve hours conversation with Eric had so far been rather limited and I thought it time to try and establish a rapport with him. Had he any thoughts about the spot from which I had chosen to sail, for instance? Eric had no particular thoughts, it seemed; he was only too happy to leave everything to me. It was like trying to get ideas out of a pillow, so after a while I sank back in my chair and quietly sipped my drink. Eric, for his part, went off to have a wash.

A group of American women entered the lounge and took their seats in the group of armchairs next to me. At first I ignored them although the nearest was sitting less than two feet from me. When coffee was served, however, one of them saw she had no sugar bowl so she leaned across and asked if she could borrow mine.

'Only too happy,' I said and passed my bowl.

'Gee,' she said, 'I love your accent – you must be Irish.'

'No, miss, Scottish.'

This exchange proved to be the ice-breaker. The group, it turned out, had arrived in Saudi Arabia only seven days before to work as nurses in the Saudi Military Hospital. So far they had found the social life of Saudi Arabia conspicuous by its absence. The restrictions imposed on all Arab women also applied to them, it seemed. I wanted to be friendly but I felt I had to be careful what I said. All the same, at one stage I was almost overwhelmingly tempted to tell them that I was an escaped convict, if only to see how they reacted. But I managed to hold my tongue.

When Eric returned I introduced him to the ladies who then told us their names. The one next to me was called Helen and she simply would not stop talking. As I had been to America myself, we found we had something in common. Then I noticed that it was 5.15 p.m. so I said to Eric that it was time we were on our way. Helen broke in to plead that we stay a little bit longer. 'I'd like you to come up to my room for five minutes,' she said.

'Listen,' I said, 'if I go up to your room, we'll be there for longer than five minutes.'

'That's the idea,' she answered pertly.

I almost gasped with astonishment. I had been eight and a half months in prison and I certainly wanted a woman. I wanted freedom, however, even more than I wanted a woman.

'Any other time,' I mumbled, hoping desperately to make her understand that I was not rejecting her because she was unattractive. 'I cannot explain to you now, but my friend and I simply have to go now. I can only say that I hope you'll understand. As it is, I'll always regret the circumstances, I assure you.' She looked very disappointed but at least I believe I left her without damaging her confidence in any way.

When we got back to the bay, I was staggered to see the lights still blazing from the police station. I had been confident that the place would only be manned during the daytime. I put out the lights on the car and drove past in the dark. Once I got used to darkness, I found I could see pretty well, so I kept the lights out and drove slowly to our launching position without mishap. I drove straight on to the sand and continued halfway down the 'valley' in the hope that if a police car did happen along, it would still fail to see us.

'Right Eric,' I said, 'we'll have a look at the beach now and make sure that there's no one about. Then we'll get the boat down.'

He nodded and we walked down to the sea edge to see how the situation lay. The lights of the police station, now at least a mile away, were a blur, so we decided that there was no problem there. Hauling the gear down to the beach, however, proved to be easier said than done. Eric found that both the boat and engine were too heavy to carry so I told him to get the petrol out and to mix the oil instead. While he fiddled about with these, I dragged out the bag containing the boat and laid it down in the sand near the water's edge.

'Do you know how to put this thing together?' I asked him.

'No, I'm sorry,' said Eric.

'That's great, neither do I – but it shouldn't be all that difficult.' A pump had been supplied with the equipment so I started pumping and soon a bulbous grey shape emerged on the sand. Once I had it up, I had no problem fitting in the floor boards and I was soon able to announce to Eric that everything was ready. All we needed to do now was to fit the engine. I trudged up the little sandy valley again, lifted the engine from the car and carried it down to the water's edge. Getting the engine fitted proved an easy enough job. By this time, Eric had the mixture of oil and petrol ready and we were all set to go. I kept my fingers crossed that the engine would start.

I told Eric I now intended going back to bog the car in the sand. If the police came by, they'd probably think some stupid bastard had got himself into a mess and was away to get a breakdown truck to pull himself out again. I locked all the doors, and put the keys in the boot. Then I went down to the water's edge again and looked for my mark in the sand. It was there, all right, and I looked up at the stars to check that they were all in the right line for us.

'God, Eric,' I said, 'this is too easy. I hope we're not doing something wrong!'

Eric mumbled something I couldn't catch, so I told him to help push the boat into the sea and then get in. We did this, both jumping in and then I rowed the boat out so that we could start up the engine; about the only thing Eric or I understood about the engine was that we weren't supposed to start it until the propellers were well in the water.

Eric took a seat in the middle of the boat while I sat down in the stern. As captain, of course, I said I would steer the boat. When we judged we were out far enough, Eric leaned across and pulled the starting cord. To our relief, the motor leapt into life first time and away we went. I found the little boat extremely easy to steer and control and we headed out confidently towards Bahrain.

We had gone about 100 yards when the sea got choppy so we put on our lifejackets. I checked the time; it was just 6.15 p.m., which all in all, had to be considered good going. I had no idea of the time it might take us to get to Bahrain for I had no experience of rubber boats or, for that matter, outboard engines but Eric was supposed to be an expert and I asked him; he however, had no idea either – which was a great help. However, so long as we reached Bahrain while it was still dark, so that we could get ashore without being seen, all would be well.

I warned Eric to keep his eyes skinned for Saudi patrol boats. In the meantime I looked back to where we had come from and was surprised to see the dazzling display of lights that was created by the Air Force Training School. It was much greater than anything I had imagined and seen from the Gulf waters themselves, the lights seemed as bright and extensive as those along Blackpool's Golden Mile. Anybody watching from there, I decided, must surely see us. Worse, the moon was now up and I had the feeling that we were sitting there with a bright torch shining down on us. Could we avoid being spotted much longer, I wondered?

I noticed that the water was getting a great deal choppier which was good because it meant we must be getting into the open sea. Whenever I looked back, the lights from the training school were growing dimmer so obviously we were making good progress. Soon they disappeared altogether and I reckoned we must be in the open sea. The bows of the boat were dipping and rising sensationally and I judged that the waves, with a high wind scudding across them, were at least two feet high. Eric looked worried but I told him that if he remained calm and sat still, we should be safe. I added that, although I was a landlubber myself, I had seen a lot of this sort of thing in the movies; I was sure we'd be all right.

Like an experienced matelot, I kept an eye on the line of stars we had to follow. After a while, I spotted beams of red light ahead and said to Eric that I thought I could see Bahrain airport ahead. I told him that once we got ashore I intended to stowaway on a British ship and then when it was well at sea, give myself up and offer to pay the fare. With luck, we might find ourselves in that happy position some time tomorrow.

I asked him if he were happy with this plan and he said he

was. Had he any other suggestions to offer? No, he was quite happy to go along with whatever I put forward.

'It's your escape, after all,' he said.

As we nearer our target, the red beams turned out to be from beacons in the water. We slipped past the first beacon and I felt sure we were getting close to land. I still could not see it, however, and the waves were still high – indeed, they were crashing over the little boat soaking us.

'It's a small price to pay for freedom,' I comforted Eric.

At 11.30 p.m., a second beacon disappeared into the night behind us and I remarked, 'It won't be long now.' I still couldn't see any coastal lights but thought that that was a good sign for it meant that there would be nobody around to see us land.

The last light disappeared and then we saw Bahrain. It took us completely by surprise. One moment it was simply not there, the next we were just a hundred yards offshore.

SIXTEEN

Trying to keep our excitement under control as best we could, I steered the little craft towards the rocky coastline. Some 50 yards out, we hit rocks and discovered that we were sailing in only 12 inches of water. I was wearing my running shoes and had another pair of proper shoes in my baggage, so I was happy to jump into the water and pull the boat in as far as I could. Eric then climbed out and together we pulled the craft up to the water's edge. We grabbed hold of our belongings and dumped them on the beach and I told Eric to hide anything we didn't need, including the life jackets so that if anyone spotted the boat, they'd think we had run out of petrol.

The craft's five-gallon tank still had some fuel left in it. Besides that, we had extra supplies amounting to ten gallons in two cans in the boat. I quickly released the fuel remaining in the engine tank and then carried the two cans up to the beach where I first emptied the petrol into the sand and then buried the two cans in the dunes.

We worked as hard and as fast as we could and when we had finished, Eric cleaned himself up while I took everything out of the boat that might have been a give-away. Both the boat and the engine would have to stay behind, of course – good luck to some Bahraini who would eventually come across them.

I changed my shoes and we both had a look round. It was not a very inviting place – indeed, I had rarely come across a more desolate landscape. I knew that the main town lay on the other side of the island which was some 30 by 5 miles in extent. As I reckoned it, we had to face a cross-country walk of a few miles only which ought not to be beyond our capacities. Girding our loins, so to speak, we started off, slipping and staggering as we climbed from the sand dunes. When we reached the top, we could see the lights of a large town, apparently not much more than four miles away. I checked the time again and found it had just gone midnight. I led the way forward, remembering my days in the army and our forced route marches. I stepped out energetically calling to Eric to keep up with me. For all his apparent lack of strength he kept up without difficulty. Then, after about 30 minutes of crisp walking, we suddenly found ourselves walking on what seemed like giant potato crisps.

'What the hell's this?' I asked Eric, but he had no more idea what they were than I did.

We kept going forward, walking towards what we took to be the lights. Strangely, however, they never seemed to come any closer. After a while we stopped and took a five-minute rest. I had terrible pains in my legs and in my back and, indeed, was unable to sit down. I smoked standing up. Eric sat on his briefcase until I had finished the cigarette and it was time to go. I stepped out again at the same brisk pace but was forced to stop now and then to shout at Eric, who kept falling behind.

In a short while, I noticed that the lights seemed to be coming closer. I thought they must be coming from some high-rise flats because all were white except for some red beacon lights which I took to be the lights of the airport. It had to be the airport, of course, although we hadn't seen any planes in the sky. We decided to stop for another break and get our second wind. Suddenly Eric said, 'I think we're on the wrong island.'

'What do you mean?' I asked him, puzzled.

'It doesn't *feel* like Bahrain,' he said.

'How in hell is Bahrain supposed to *feel*?' I demanded. 'I wouldn't know how it was supposed to feel. So how do you?'

'Well, there's no movement in the town. There are no car lights travelling along any road. I can't see any house lights going on and off.'

I took another look at the place, this time giving it a much closer inspection. What Eric had said was absolutely right – and even from a distance there seemed to be something spooky about it. What was our alternative, however?

'We have to go on,' I said. 'We can't do anything else now.'

'I suppose not,' agreed Eric morosely. It was clear that he was convinced we were not on Bahrain. But if not Bahrain, where on earth were we?

By about 3.15 a.m. we were close enough to the lights to see that what we had been imagining as a town with an airport was nothing but a large chemical factory with giant tanks and a series of metal structures. We kept walking towards this and eventually stumbled on a dirt road which we decided to follow. We had gone fewer than a hundred yards, however, when I spotted a building on our left which had a big sign written up in Arabic and English. We stopped to read this; it stated clearly that all boats had to be registered with the Saudi police.

I stared at Eric in bewilderment.

'What the hell does this mean, Eric? Surely the Bahrainis don't have to register their boats with the Saudis?'

'Well, we know the Saudis are helping to build a causeway to Bahrain.'

·'Yes, and part of the price of that is that the Bahrain Government has agreed to outlaw both pork and drink in defence to the Saudis.'

Buoyed up with the idea that the sign merely indicated a Saudi-Bahraini arrangement, we followed the dirt track towards the factory. As we neared it, however, we suddenly spotted head-lights coming down on a road to our right. They turned and came towards us.

'Get down at the edge of the road,' I shouted to Eric, 'try and keep out of sight.' We dropped to the ground and rolled a little way from the dirt road trying to bury ourselves in the sand. The lights proved to be those of a police truck which swept past without apparently seeing us but squealed to a halt at the build-ing we had come across at the start of the dirt road.

'They must have seen us,' I whispered to Eric, 'but now they've lost us.'

'Perhaps they imagined us to be a mirage,' said Eric hopefully.

The truck turned at the building and this time, we were convinced, they wouldn't miss us. We were lying only six feet off the road and, under a full moon, must have stood out like jet-black shapes on the golden sand. As we lay there, scarcely breathing, the police truck revved up its engine and came roaring up the road again. We waited for the impatient screech of brakes but to our astonishment, the truck again swept by and raced back the way it had come. We stared at each other in amazement, unable to credit our luck.

We waited for ten minutes or so to give the truck enough time to get clear, then we got up and continued our walk along the road. On one side lay the factory itself and a little farther on what turned out to be the campsite, presumably housing workers. Keeping close to the plant fence, but still on the road, we reached the main gate about a quarter of a mile farther on, expecting trouble. Fortunately, there was no one in sight, either near the factory itself or at the campsite on the opposite side of the road. However, we spotted several police cars, though from that distance we could not tell whether there were policemen in them or not. Certainly if a policeman had spotted two men walking along that road in the middle of nowhere at four o'clock in the morning, we would have found ourselves back in prison pretty quickly. Nor could we have put up much of a fight; at that moment I could not have punched my way out of a paper bag.

Nobody spotted us, however, and we continued along the road following the plant fence and then I saw a big sign, again in both English and Arabic, announcing 'Desalination Plant'. I realised that the 'potato crisps' we had been walking on were clumps of salt.

Opposite a gate to the plant, the road forked, presenting us with a new problem; did we carry on straight ahead or fork right? I decided we should continue on the road we were already on but after we had gone a short distance, I spotted the oncoming lights of a motor vehicle. It had to be the police again, of course, but this time, luckily, we had plenty of time to hide ourselves and we got well away from the road before the truck came roaring past and went away down the road again.

'I don't like this road,' I told Eric. 'I've got a feeling that this is a dead end. And anyway, that patrol car seems to be ignoring the other road.' So we turned back and struck out across the sand towards the other road. By now, the pain in my legs and back was agonising. I felt I couldn't go on much farther and began to curse the Saudi authorities who had deprived me of exercise for so many months. Eric also began to complain about his pains but I feebly joked, 'The exercise will do you good.' Somehow or other, the mere fact that I could even *try* to be funny did miracles for our morale and we both seemed to find fresh strength.

Ahead of us we could see a red sky which could only mean a town. I thought we stood a good chance now of not being caught, for the road along which we were walking was absolutely straight and we were bound to see any car lights from a long distance away. I decided that we should stop for a break to ease the pain in our legs and so we walked into the sand with the intention of lying down. Our tortured bodies creaked in agony as we tried to lower ourselves to the ground and it was only after much pain that we managed to stretch out on the cold sand. I drew in several deep breaths and lay there trying to relax my overworked muscles.

After a while I said to Eric, 'We'd better get moving. We'll look around for some place to hide and then we'll try and get ourselves some kip.'

'Where on earth do you hide in a flat desert?' demanded Eric. 'It's all right now – there are clouds over the moon and we're in the dark.'

'I know, I know,' I replied impatiently. 'Anyway, we won't solve any problems by just lying here. We're bound to see something if we keep going.'

I don't know how we lifted ourselves up but somehow we managed it. We started our trudge again and then, a little later, I spotted what I took to be a clump of palm trees just off the road on our left-hand side.

'Come on,' I said to Eric. 'We'll have a look.'

We stumbled across the sand for about twenty yards or so and then I saw our 'palm trees' dissolve into the shapes of several big container trucks. As we edged around these, the door of a container opened and a Pakistani came out. I walked across to him as nonchalantly as I could and asked him if he spoke English. When he had recovered from his surprise at seeing two figures emerge from the night, he said he did.

'What is your trouble?' he asked.

My mind was racing now. 'Our car broke down last night,' I explained. 'It happened on the salt flats and we've been wandering around ever since looking for a lift into town. Any chance of one?'

'Yes,' he replied. 'Come in.'

We followed him into the container and to our amazement saw

that the floor was covered with sleeping bodies. All I could think of was that this was like being back in Al-Ould and wondered if that were a bad omen.

'Would you like tea?' asked the Pakistani.

'Please,' I replied.

He invited Eric and I to sit in the only two chairs in the container. By this time, some of the sleeping figures had begun to stir and soon nearly all had got up. Some of them spoke good English and were quite concerned about our problem. By this time, I had begun to believe in my own lies about our broken-down car and was even concocting elaborate descriptions. We were interrupted by the return of the first Pakistani carrying tea, bread and cheese, plus excellent news. His foreman would be driving into Abqaiq shortly and would be happy to give us a lift. I glanced at Eric – Abqaiq was a Saudi Arabian oil terminal which meant that, far from being safe in Bahrain, we were still in Arabia! My heart sank and I saw that Eric, too, was shattered.

'Ian,' he whispered, 'shall we give ourselves up?'

'Shut up!' I hissed under my breath.

'What will we do then?' he asked.

'There's nothing for it but to get back to the car somehow and then try to buy another boat.'

'But that will cost a lot of money,' he objected.

I could hardly credit it – what did money matter in these circumstances? 'I'll pay for it, don't worry,' I told him furiously. I was really angry with him now but there was nothing much I could do or say as we had to speak in whispers, not knowing which Pakistanis spoke English and which did not. We were then told that the foreman was ready and would we please join him in his car. We didn't waste any time and jumped in, thankfully noting that the foreman did not speak English which meant that at least we would be spared difficult explanations.

We rode for some 30 miles towards Abqaiq, with the foreman driving through security gates without any trouble. The foreman, it seemed, was bound for the oil terminal itself, so he dropped us off on the Dammam road indicating in a mixture of sign language and pidgin English that we would be able to hail a taxi from there. We thanked him as profusely as we could, annoyed that we couldn't express our appreciation well enough but the man seemed to understand and we waved him good-bye.

We came to a corner and turned it to find three police cars

right in front of us, parked at the side of the road. The first thing that enters one's head in such circumstances is to believe it is a trap but I rapidly reasoned that it could not be so and boldly continued walking.

'Morning,' I nodded to one of the two policemen who were standing beside the cars. These were parked outside a building which I quickly noticed was a police station. The cop nodded pleasantly but paid no particular attention to us, so I whispered to Eric, 'Just follow me.'

I had seen a taxi on the opposite side of the road, parked just beside a Pepsi stand. I crossed over, followed by an anxious Eric, but couldn't find the taxi-driver; however, the Pepsi man told us the driver would be along in a few minutes and that we should wait. So we stayed there, in full view of the police station and the two chatting officers. So far our luck had held but how much longer could two westerners, obvious strangers to the town, hope to get away with it? Surely every police station in Saudi Arabia had been alerted by now and were looking out for us? There is a phrase for how we felt at that moment, but it is not one usually used in polite society.

Five minutes later the taxi-driver turned up at last. I told him our car had broken down at Half-Moon Bay and asked him if he could take us there. Eric added that he was carrying the spare parts in his briefcase and asked how much it would be.

'One hundred riyals,' answered the driver.

'OK,' I snapped, 'let's get in.'

'That's too dear,' objected Eric. 'Sixty riyals.'

'What in hell!' I exploded at him. 'We'll pay the money. We're only fifty yards from a police station and here you are worrying about a few bob.'

I wasn't prepared to stand any further nonsense from him, so I took out 100 riyals and handed them to the driver.

After a short distance, the driver stopped outside a house. We had some trouble understanding him but finally gathered that this was where he lived and that he wanted to pick up his two daughters and bring them to school. Two youngsters quickly emerged wearing heavy veils and we judged them to be somewhere between twelve and fourteen years old. We knew, of course, that we were not supposed to speak to them for according to the Qur'an this would mean that we were entertaining dirty thoughts.

'God!' I said to Eric, 'what a country! We can't even talk to kids!'

We dropped the girls off at the school and then turned and drove towards Half-Moon Bay some 50 miles away. I slumped down in the back seat, my mind filled with foreboding as I thought of everything that must by now have gone wrong. In particular, surely the police had noticed the car in the sand and pulled it out?

It took us almost an hour to reach the bay area and then we were brought up short at a T-junction.

'Which way?' enquired the driver. 'Right?'

'No, left,' I told him.

The driver objected, explaining that he wasn't allowed to go that way because of the Air Force school.

'All right,' I said, anxious not to waste time arguing, 'we'll walk the rest of the way.' Although all my muscles still ached I got out and yelled at Eric to follow. I was still feeling annoyed with him for his stupid behaviour over the taxi fare so I forced the pace which was not to his liking.

'We've got a hell of a lot to do,' I shouted at him, 'so you'd better move your arse!' And without further ado, he quickened his pace.

We finally reached our little 'valley' and as we stumbled off the road and walked down towards the beach I saw that the car was still bogged down just as I had left it.

'Look at that!' I shouted to Eric. 'Our luck's still in.'

I almost ran the last couple of yards. I yanked up the boot, found the keys, opened the offside door and jumped in behind the wheel. The engine purred immediately when I turned on the ignition. But that was as far as I got. For the life of me, I couldn't get that damned vehicle to move. I had bogged it down only too well.

We were still pondering what to do when I heard the noise of a heavy machine engine apparently coming from the Air Force Survival School.

'Wait here,' I instructed Eric. 'I'm going to see if we can get help.'

I left him there and clambered back up on to the road and then walked towards the school. As I neared it, I noticed a building contractor at work inside. Without any hesitation I walked up to the main gate and spoke to the guard. Could I speak to the boss?

I enquired. The man nodded and beckoned to a big westerner who seemed to be in charge of the men working nearby. The man came across and turned out to be an American.

'Have you a Cat 951? by any chance?' I asked him and I told him about the car.

He was a big, exuberant, good-humoured man. 'I saw your car down in the sand this morning when I was driving in,' he told me. 'I was expecting somebody to come along and ask for a tow. I can have one along for you in ten minutes – is that OK?'

'Great,' I said. 'How much do I owe you?'

'Nothing, Scottie,' he said. 'Only too glad to lend a hand.'

I returned to the car and informed Eric, who seemed to be about to give birth to kittens, that help was on the way. We got into the car and sat down. I could see he was really edgy.

'What are we going to do, Ian?' he asked finally.

'Buy another boat – this time from that showroom that was closed yesterday. Then we'll sail tonight. But instead of going that way – and I indicated the way we had gone last night, 'we'll go straight out and across that way,' and I pointed in a new direction.

'OK,' he said, 'that sounds all right.' Then he paused and asked me, rather pathetically, 'Can we eat today, do you think?'

I laughed, which at least had the effect of easing some of the tension. 'Sure, Eric, we'll buy some food today.' Food was the last thing I had on my mind but perhaps this was because, despite my spell of prison, I had more flesh on me than Eric.

The machine, driven by a Filipino, soon arrived and with the assistance of a helper and some chains we were quickly dragged out on to the road. I thanked the two men and handed them 100 riyals each but they declined it and I finally had to insist that they took it. As they drove away in their clanking machine we climbed back into the car which was in perfect shape despite its night in the sand, and we purred off making for Dammam. It was eleven o'clock in the morning and I said to Eric, 'My, how the time flies when you're having a good time.' This raised a laugh with him and he appeared to forget all about his nerves.

As soon as we hit the outskirts of Al-Khubar Eric said, 'Look, Ian, I must have something to eat.' I was still anxious to avoid large public places but recognised that his request was a legitimate one. In fact I needed to eat myself, if only to keep up my strength and mental alertness. Fatigue had begun to bite into me for I'd had only six hours sleep in five days. I reckoned, therefore, that a rest and a bit of food would help to keep us both going.

'OK,' I said. 'There's a Kentucky Fried Chicken place here, so we'll go there.'

To get there, I had to take the top road and as we passed the airport, I spotted a police car parked at the side of the road. Flashing past it, I saw the driver start up and he was soon following right behind us. I checked my speed and then remembered that there are no speed restrictions in Al-Khubar. So what did the guy want, for heaven's sake? And what was I going to do when we reached the Kentucky Chicken? Then suddenly, we had hit the town proper and the eating place was looming up on the right. Taking my courage into both hands, I pulled off into the side of the road and stopped. To my relief, the police car flashed past, paying no attention to us and we both gave sighs of relief.

'I'm not taking any more chances like this just for food,' I told Eric, 'so you'd better make the most of what you get here. We're not going to eat again until we get to Bahrain.'

Eric didn't argue. We entered the premises, went upstairs to the restaurant and ordered a fairly large meal. When it arrived, however, I found I couldn't eat anything so I settled for a cup of tea and a bottle of Pepsi and left Eric to scoff the grub. I went into the washroom for a quick clean up. When I looked in the mirror I could not recognise myself. I looked like some fellow who had been lost in the jungle for years. For a start, my beard was long and unkempt. I was surprised that it looked so bad for although Eric had also grown a beard, his had remained trim and neat.

An idea had been ticking away in the back of my mind and now it surfaced again. I remember that Tom had mentioned, almost idly, that there was a firm in Al-Khubar whose boss, an American, was a decent sort who had told him that if there was ever anything he could do to help me escape from Saudi Arabia, then he'd be only too happy to assist. I still wasn't sure of the right direction to Bahrain; perhaps the guy could help? When I returned to the restaurant, I spotted a water tower nearby and remembered that Tom had said the man's office was somewhere near by.

'I've got to go and see someone in an office,' I told Eric. 'You'd better wait in the car in the meantime.'

We left the restaurant and went downstairs where Eric got into the car and then I tried to remember the name of the company the American worked for and also his name.

'Look, we'd better drive around for a bit,' I said and we started out on a short tour of the centre. The quest proved hopeless and eventually I had to admit defeat. I then pulled up several times to ask people who looked as if they could speak English if they could give me any help. All I had to go on was the kind of business the firm was engaged in. The fourth person I spoke to, a Saudi, who was getting into his car when I spoke to him, said yes, he knew the company well and if I cared to follow him, he'd lead me there. We did this and we drove around the town until he pointed at a building and I slowed down. I waved him my thanks before pulling up and thought, thanks mate, but I wonder what you'd say if you knew we were the convicts your magnificent police force is looking for?

I entered the offices, the name of the boss having by now come back to me and asked for him. Reception said they knew of no one working there by that name.

'He's an American,' I explained. 'He runs the company, for heaven's sake.'

There was no American working there any longer, it seemed, and even if he had been, he would no longer be running the company which had been taken over by the Saudi Ministry of Electrics and was staffed, so far as westerners were concerned, by British only. I debated with myself whether to ask a Briton the way to Bahrain but decided that that would be taking an unnecessary risk. The men might well wonder why on earth a wild-eyed-looking Scot, sporting an unkempt beard, wanted to know how to get to Bahrain when there were obviously dozens of legitimate enquiry outlets where he could have picked up such information. If, for any reason, he also recognised that I was one of the two escaped convicts, would he consider it his duty to turn us in? All in all, I decided, it would be a silly risk to take and so I walked out without speaking to anyone.

'It's no good,' I told Eric. 'The guy I wanted to see isn't there any more.'

'What do we do now, then?' he asked.

'Back to the showroom,' I replied and headed towards the coast road.

The boat showroom, of course, had been expecting us to return and pick up their craft. The salesman had the boat all ready for use and the engine had been tested and was satisfactory. The Saudi owner invited us to have tea and I decided that the showroom was as good a place as any to wait until the local shops opened at 4 p.m. when we could purchase all the cans we needed to carry petrol.

The Saudi proved to be a nice chap who knew England well. He had a house in Bournemouth and visited it once a year but he had begun to feel that England was too expensive.

'You get ripped off in the south of England, that's why,' I told him. 'Now the north – ' and then, allowing my patriotic instincts to surface, I added – 'or Scotland! Up there you would get value for money!'

At 3.45 p.m. I paid over the money for the boat and engine and the Saudi carefully wrote out a sales receipt and provided us with a copy of the Police Registration Certificate, warning us, however, not to use the boat until we had been to see the police and had had the certificate countersigned. I thanked him for his help and with the boat and engine already loaded aboard the car, said good-bye.

I drove straight back to Al-Khubar and decided once more to park the car outside the police station. I told Eric to wait and said I intended going into the market to see if I could pick up what I needed. Once in the *souk*, I found a shop selling sports equipment, so I went in and bought two lifejackets, a small compass and three five-gallon containers for petrol. When I returned to the car, Eric was sitting there biting his fingernails as the whole place was crawling with policemen.

'For God's sake, Eric, work it out for yourself,' I told him in exasperation. 'The last place anybody would expect to find us is outside a nick.' All the same, he must have gone through several nerve-racking moments.

We stopped to collect petrol and oil and a bottle of drinking water, Eric seizing the opportunity to buy a packet of crisps and some cans of mineral water. Then we headed straight for Half-Moon Bay and after about an hour's driving, pulled into the same little sand valley as before. I parked in almost exactly the same spot as previously but took care not to bog the car down again. I then got out and walked down to the water's edge. The wind had come up since yesterday and the sea looked rough – too rough, anyway, for me to risk trying out the boat. Anyway,

I was completely exhausted and in no condition to sail to Bahrain. So I went back and told Eric that I planned to leave at midnight and as he had not slept for two nights, suggested he ought to get some kip. I took two blankets out of the car and gave one to him. I then climbed into the back seat, pulled the blanket round me and fell asleep.

I awoke shortly before midnight to find Eric already awake but with the wind now howling at gale force. I still felt like death, drained from fatigue and tension. The Gulf was white with choppy waves and I could see that a heavy sea was running.

'I'm too bushed,' I told Eric and he looked relieved. 'It wouldn't be safe for me to go now, feeling as I do – I'd only drown the two of us. I suggest we get more sleep and try for it again tomorrow night when I'm feeling better.'

'Suits me,' said Eric. 'I'm fairly whacked too – and that sea doesn't look all that inviting.'

We were both so tuckered out that it was nine o'clock next morning before we both rolled, literally, out of our blankets. As soon as I could think again, I decided that we should lay the blankets on the sand and pretend we were sunbathing, thus allying the suspicions of anybody who happened to pass by on the road. I took off my shirt and trousers and lay down on a blanket in my underpants. Eric decided to sleep in the car and I could see no harm in this provided I made myself reasonably conspicuous. Besides, the pain in my back legs was still pretty grim and I decided that a spell of sunbathing would do me good. We hadn't been bedded down very long, however, before Eric began worrying about his stomach again. 'What about getting something to eat?' he demanded.

'You've got plenty of water,' I told him. 'And you've got the crisps and the mineral water. You'll have to make do with that. It's too dangerous to go farting about looking for food now. Even in this area, the Saudi police must be looking for us now.'

Eric never disagreed with me when I announced a decision as firmly as this. In one way it was helpful; in another it made me wish to God that he could come up with some useful suggestions for a change. We were supposed to be a team pooling our resources; instead, he seemed content to tag along, alllowing me to think things out and make the decisions. Even before I had taken him along I had spotted that he did not have my determination or my willpower. On the other hand I didn't want to be the boss all the time. Yet I had no intention of losing my liberty, either, so I was left with no choice but to make the decisions for the two of us.

At four o'clock that afternoon, with nightfall not far away, I decided it was time to get the boat down to the water's edge and to prepare it for the sea. For once, Eric pulled his weight and helped me carry both the boat and the engine down to the water. My back was still giving me hell and I found it difficult to bend; unfortunately, Eric was scarcely in much better shape. Between us, however, we managed somehow to get everything into position and I started to pump up the boat. Eric left me to it, and went back to the car to see to the mixing of the oil and petrol for the outboard engine. I had just finished my pumping when I heard a strange voice ask, 'Oh, hello, what are you doing here?'

I swivelled round as though bitten by a snake and I saw a Saudi Air Force police sergeant standing there, looking at me in a puzzled way. I noticed that he had a revolver in the holster at his side.

SEVENTEEN

'Oh, hello sergeant,' I said and I could hardly believe I had succeeded in making the remark sound so casual. 'We're going fishing tomorrow and we're just getting things ready for an early start in the morning.' Christ, I thought, I hope he doesn't ask to see our fishing rods.

'Will you be here tomorrow afternoon?' he enquired.

I had the wind thoroughly up by now. For even if, by some miracle, I could butt this guy in the face and knock him cold, what good would it do us? As I saw it, indeed, it would only make matters worse. So I said the first thing that came tripping to my tongue.

'Yes. In fact, we intend camping here for three days at least. That is,' I added, 'if the police allow us to.'

'Don't worry about the police,' said the sergeant. 'The police never come here – this is Air Force land. I'm in charge here and if I say you can stay, you can stay.'

I thanked him and as he seemed very interested in our rubber boat I let him have a good look at it, mentioning one or two of its good points – lore which I had picked up from the showroom owner.

'Very interesting,' he said. 'It seems a nice boat.' I nodded idiotically. 'Well, I'll come back and see you tomorrow – around about two o'clock say? Will that be all right?'

'Fine,' I said, wondering how many heart failures I could stand. 'Goodbye and thanks for allowing us to stay here.'

He waved nonchalantly and went off. When he had disappeared, I walked up to the car, my step almost springy and told Eric what had happened.

'That was a close one,' said Eric. 'I've been sitting here wondering which of you two was going to come out of it alive. I was sure one of you was going to get himself killed.'

'Someone up there must like me,' I replied.

My knees, strangely enough, had turned to water and I suddenly found myself needing to sit down and recover. The strain, it seemed, was becoming almost unbearable. When I was in the actual presence of danger itself I was all right but when the danger had passed, I seemed to feel worse and worse. How long, I thought, before I crack? There was a lot to do, however, and perhaps it was the very need to keep going which came to my rescue. We carried the petrol down to the boat and then, working together, fitted the engine into place.

It was then just 5.30 p.m. which meant that we had just another 30 minutes to wait for darkness.

'Christ,' said Eric suddenly, 'the cunt is coming back!'

I had been waiting for our luck to run out and now it seemed that the moment had arrived. Striding towards us along the beach came the Air Force sergeant. What to do? Well, the car was too far away to run for it and anyway, neither of us were capable of working up a gallop, so there was nothing for it, it seemed, but to look as welcoming as possible. I put on one of my best smiles, therefore, as the sergeant approached us.

'Just one thing,' enquired the sergeant very casually. 'Would it be all right if I brought a friend along tomorrow, too?'

'Certainly,' I said, hardly able to speak. 'Glad of the company. The boat will take four all right, so that's no problem at all. See you tomorrow, then.'

'Thank you,' he said. 'Two o'clock, then!'

I walked back to the car and told Eric, 'At this rate, we'll have the whole Saudi Air Force here tomorrow wanting to go fishing.' Eric grinned, 'Pity there'll be only the car,' he said.

'Well, if they can sail that, then they're welcome to it,' I joked.

When darkness fell Eric threw the blankets into the boat and I again bogged the car down in the sand. As before, I put the keys in the boot, with the intention, once clear of Saudi Arabia, of sending Roger Lilly a postcard telling him where I had left the car and how it could be recovered. Then we pushed the boat out and we were on our way again.

Studying the compass, I found that we had gone south on our first attempt when we should have gone directly east. Our boat, too, seemed rather better than our first one and the engine was sound, starting at the first touch. This time, I felt, nothing could stop us. The waves were rough and much higher than I would have liked, but the little craft rode them well and although we were not able to work up any great turn of speed, our progress was at least proving steady.

The lights of the Air Force school itself soon vanished but to my left I spotted the approach lights to the school's airport and wondered just how big Half-Moon Bay really was; we had cast off shortly after 6 p.m. and it was already eight o'clock and yet we were still obviously not yet clear of the Saudi coast. And then suddenly the engine jumped! We appeared to have hit a rock in the middle of the sea.

'This is impossible!' I yelled at Eric. 'How in hell could this happen?'

On investigation I found to my horror that there were fewer than six inches of water below our propeller. Meanwhile waves were pushing hard against the little boat and shoving it further and further up on to what was either a sandbank or a rock. I jumped over the side and round myself standing in a foot of water.

'I'll pull her off!' I shouted.

I had to drag her clear against the push of the waves and tide and was soon standing in the water up to my armpits. I gave the boat a final shove, then shouted to Eric to start the engine and clambered aboard again.

Once again the engine fouled.

'She's stuck,' remarked Eric helpfully.

'Christ!' I said, jumped back in the water and began dragging the craft clear. By the time I climbed aboard again, however, the heavy sea had pushed the boat back on the rocks – or whatever it was that we had grounded on.

For the third time, I dragged the craft clear and climbed in, only to find that we had been driven back once more and were again aground.

I got out again and shouted at Eric, 'Now, this time, for Christ's sake, steer for deep water!' It was no use. Almost as soon as I had let go and prepared to get back in, the little boat was swung back by the waves.

'I'm going to have to stay here and keep pushing,' I yelled.

'You steer into deep water and when I give the signal, start up the engine. Then I'll climb in.'

I dragged, pulled and pushed and suddenly we were in deep water once more.

'Start the engine!' I yelled and began to climb aboard. Eric pulled the cord and the engine blasted into life. But even as I lifted myself up, I felt my feet touching the propeller. Christ, I thought, I've lost a foot!

I dragged myself into the boat and found, somewhat to my amazement, that I still possessed both feet. 'There's something wrong,' I shouted. 'The damned propeller isn't working. Take the engine off. I'll steer the boat.'

After some fiddling and fumbling, Eric managed to get the engine off. Then he turned to me and asked, 'What'll I do with it?'

'Sort it out! You're the mechanic, aren't you?'

He finally found our breakdown kit and extracted a screwdriver and a pair of pliers.

'Ah, the holding pin has broken,' he finally announced. He had hardly said this when I noticed something extraordinary. 'Hold it, Eric!' I bawled at him, 'Get down!'

I could hardly believe my own eyes. There was a pick-up truck sailing along in the middle of the sea.

'Christ! What is it?'

And then light dawned. 'It's a bloody causeway, that's what! That's why we've run aground.' As I watched, the pick-up truck stopped and turned about so that its headlights were shining out in our direction.

'You know, that bastard's actually looking for us,' I said. As the moon was full it was obvious he must have spotted us. The sea was rough, however, with waves running at least two feet high so I realised he must have lost us again. Again, luck was with us. Several times, as we bobbed about, we almost ran into the beams of the headlights but each time another wave bounced us clear. For almost fifteen minutes the bastard sat there, trying to pick us out and then, obviously fed up, started up the truck again and resumed his journey towards the land.

'Can you sort the bloody engine out, Eric?' I demanded.

'To some extent – yes.'

'Now what in hell does a remark like that mean?'

'It means I'll be able to put the broken pin back in but that it won't last long and that we'll have to go slow.'

I sat there for a moment, trying to decide what to do. 'OK,' I said finally, 'I'll get as near the causeway as possible and pull the boat along until we come to the open sea. Meanwhile, you can try and sort out the engine.'

'That won't work,' he said. 'The sea's too rough. We'll never be able to hold the boat right.'

For once he was correct about something and I told him so. 'OK, put the engine back on and start her anyway.' I jumped into the water and Eric started up the engine. Although the engine itself was full of life, the propeller still refused to work.

'Fuck it!' I said, exasperated. 'We'll have to row out!'

I remained in the water and at the same time, helped to fix the oars. I was still trying to fix them – and it isn't easy when you are treading water or walking on rocks – when Eric suddenly announced, 'I don't want to row out to the open sea.'

'Like it or not, that's what we're going to do,' I told him, ignoring his protest as I had ignored all his others. I began to row. Again it was useless. Within seconds of clearing the rocks or stones or whatever the causeway was made of, we were beaten back by the sea.

'Bugger it!' I said. 'This isn't going to work, either.'

I climbed out of the boat and somehow or other scrambled myself up on the outlying foundations of the causeway and then, using the rope which normally tethered the little craft, I began hauling it after me. I soon discovered I was walking in two or three feet of water, sometimes stumbling and falling or cracking my shins as I ran into a particularly nasty rock. It was a nightmare and even to this day, I cannot explain where I found the determination and energy to keep going. It was simply a question of deciding not to go back to that awful prison, I suppose, and that was all there was to it. Certainly, the harder I was forced to strive, the more murderous and determined my mood became. For a whole hour, by my watch, I stumbled and fought my way along the edge of the causeway, battling with both the buffeting sea and the sharp edges of the rocks or stones, and dragging the rubber dinghy behind me. At the end of that time, I decided that there was no opening to the sea – or if there were, that I was never going to find it. So I told Eric that I would have to climb up on to the causeway itself and *carry* both the engine and the boat. The impossibility of such an idea was apparent almost as soon as I tried it. In my exhausted condition, there was no way I could carry them more than a yard or so.

'OK,' I shouted to Eric, 'I'll try and pull it out into deep water and we'll simply have to row back to where we started.' It was a miserable thought but what else could we do? After that, we'd simply have to see if there was a way of working out a clear passage from the beach to Bahrain, even if it meant asking for outside help.

I got the boat out into deep water and along with my other troubles and anxieties I was now suffering bitter discomfort. The cold water rose to my armpits. The idea was that I should try to tread water and hold the boat steady while Eric attempted to fix the propeller. 'Hurry up, for Christ's sake,' I told him, 'I'm freezing in here.' I watched the sweat break out on his face as he struggled with the heavy machinery.

'There,' he said, finally, 'that's fixed it, I think.'

'And about bloody time, too,' I said and climbed back into the boat.

Eric reached over and whipped the cord and the engine again burst into life. But to our amazement the boat still wouldn't move – the propeller still wouldn't work.

'I'll have another go,' said Eric but I knew he was a blind man feeling his way forward.

'OK,' I said, 'but if it doesn't work this time, I'm going to sink this bloody boat and then we're going to climb up on the causeway and walk back to land. We can buy a new boat tomorrow and try again.'

I got back into the water once again and once more Eric pulled the starter. At least the engine was up to scratch, I thought bitterly, and would certainly have done us proud if we hadn't run aground. Then, to my astonishment, for I had reached that stage where I believed that the damned propeller would never work, the boat suddenly began to move.

'She's working!' yelled Eric delightedly. 'Though I've no idea for how long.'

I crawled back into the boat and sat down in the bows feeling cold, dejected and angry with myself; I ought to have made absolutely sure it was possible to sail out of the bay and to reach Bahrain. The sight of Eric looking tidy, dry and warm heightened my resentment and I had to remind myself that the only way to get out of this predicament was to remain cool and dispassionate.

We headed back slowly, again passing the red beacon lights which we now recognised as airport land lights built in the sea. Eric, however, was proving to be a lousy navigator and I shouted to him that he was off course. He swung the little craft to port and even as he did so, I heard the thunderous roar of an approaching aircraft coming straight towards us as it swung in to land. The roar became earsplitting as the plane swept over us, lighting up our position like day; it was so low that we could make out the faces of the passengers at the window. Although there was only a remote chance that either pilot or passengers would report our position, I felt we were in peril; when you are down below, bobbing about, trying to escape from a country and knowing that there is a nationwide alert out for you, you believe every man is watching out for you, determined to help recapture you.

The plane vanished with another tremendous roar as the pilot cut his engines back. We were still unable to see the coastal lights but I kept advising Eric which way to steer and eventually we saw the first glimmer in the distance.

'Straight on!' I said. 'Can you see where you're going now?'

I was sitting in the bows, half-screwed around to see if I could glimpse the coast. Now I turned around properly and sat with my back to the coast and facing Eric in the stern. I was wet, cold and starting to shiver. Worse, I felt defeated. I had tried so hard, pitting my brains and strength against the challenges involved. I had got this far and yet here I was, as far away from freedom as ever.

This was just the moment chosen by Eric to start moaning. This time, however, it wasn't one of his ordinary beefs; this time he was talking for real.

'We'll never get out,' he said hollowly. 'There's nothing we can do except give ourselves up.'

His words angered me – and with anger came a renewed determination to survive.

'Don't be a cunt!' I told him. 'We'll sail from the open sea and this time we'll make sure nothing goes wrong! We're both miserable and dejected now but if we get some kip and get ourselves warm and dry again, we'll feel different. I'm not going back to prison, anyhow, that's for sure.'

Eric did not reply but I saw his head droop in dejection. I turned again in my seat and glanced at the coast.

'Jesus, you're off course, Eric,' I bawled at him.

'No, I'm not,' he replied apathetically.

I felt so cold and miserable that I decided not to argue. Besides, if he were heading the wrong way, he'd soon find out. For the next hour I let him alone, slumping back in the seat, doing my best to keep warm, while at the same time desperately trying to think things out. After a while, I looked round again to see where we were.

'You are an absolute cunt, you know, Eric. That's the bloody police station you're heading for.'

'No, it's not,' he challenged me.

'For Christ's sake, don't argue about it. Change course.'

He said nothing but looked stubborn.

'Eric,' I said slowly, 'if you don't change course this minute, I'll throw you overboard! And I mean it! I'm cold and miserable but I haven't lost my sense of direction and I'm not likely to confuse the lights of the training school with those of the police station. So for Christ's sake, steer for the school, as I tell you.'

When he saw that I meant what I said, he swung the boat a degree or two to the left. For a moment, I had the suspicion that he was up to some game but I then decided it was just his general inexperience; the very first time I had left him to perform a simple task like steering for the right part of the coast, he had made a mess of it. It was bad enough trying to escape from Saudi Arabia with everything in your favour but saddled with a companion who for most of the time seemed more of a hindrance than a help, it was beginning to make my job seem impossible.

As we sailed closer to the training school, I told Eric how to come in so as to avoid the school's lights. We needed to hit the coastline well to the left of the school. The instruction seemed simple to me but not to Eric. 'You're wrong!' he shouted. 'We've got to come in the other way!'

'What in hell, Eric!' I bawled back at him, exasperated. 'You almost took us into the police station. Now, you're going to land us in the school. Do as I say and no more nonsense.'

This time he did not argue and we were soon running alongside the coast; and then I spotted our beach again.

'There it is,' I shouted to him, 'Do you see it, all right?'

'OK, Ian,' he said. 'I see it now.'

Seconds later, the bow of our little boat had bitten into the sand. I jumped over the side immediately and plunged into the water. I felt myself sinking pleasantly and then my feet found the bottom. To my surprise, however, I no longer seemed to have the strength to stand up properly and I promptly collapsed in the water, going right under, gasping for air. Fortunately, I still had the boat's rope in my hand and with a supreme effort, tugged my head back up out of the water.

'I'll get out, too,' shouted Eric.

'I'll manage somehow,' I yelled.

It turned out that we were not actually on the beach at all, but on a shelf of projecting rock so that, instead of finding the water lapping pleasantly around my ankles, I was up to my shoulders once more in at least five feet of water. In my exhausted condition it was a terrible struggle but I somehow managed to reach the edge of the beach and pull the boat in. Eric, showing commendable initiative for once, jumped out and helped me drag the boat clear of the water.

'I'll see to the rest,' he said. 'You go up to the car and dry yourself down.'

'Thanks,' I mumbled through chattering teeth. I walked up to the car, took off all my soaking clothes and spread them out over the car. I continued to shiver, however, even when I got into the car and wrapped myself in a blanket. I don't think I had ever been so cold in all my life.

Eric came up to the car and informed me that the boat was OK. 'But,' he asked, 'what are we going to do now?'

'If you wait until I stop shivering, I'll think about it,' I replied.

It was 6 a.m. which meant that we had spent nearly twelve hours on a fruitless journey, ending up right back where we had started. But I still couldn't think out our next move for my whole body was wracked, as if by ague. Eric, meanwhile, curled up and went to sleep while I sat there shivering with the cold, desperately waiting for the sun to come up. Indeed, as the minutes spun out, I wondered what in hell had happened to the famed Middle Eastern climate and finally decided that if I didn't get out of the car and wait for the direct rays of the sun to work on me, I was certain to come down with pneumonia. So I got out and lay down in the sand, with the blanket wrapped around me and waited for the sun to come up and do its heating work. By nine o'clock, I had ceased shivering and although I was not yet warm, I no longer felt cold. I was well enough, anyhow, to start talking to Eric again and to begin formulating plans. I told him we'd put the boat in the car and take the engine for repair. That night, we would have another go at making Bahrain, but this time we would leave from the open beach near Al-Khubar.

'We'll take a look today and see if we can spot a good place to go off from. But this time I'm not coming back to Saudi, even if it means sailing the entire way down the Gulf to the Indian Ocean.'

By 10 a.m., my clothes were sufficiently dry for me to put them on again. Soon afterwards we walked down to the edge of the beach and having deflated the boat, I packed it away in the rear seat of the car and stuffed the engine in the boot.

'Now, Eric,' I said, 'it's time for you to use your charm. Up you go and get that machine in the school to pull us out of the sand again.' Eric walked off without even a protest. When I heard him returning, I also heard the sound of a heavy engine and soon afterwards the big machine came lumbering down the road, just behind him. The driver and helper were the same chaps as before and as I watched them approach our bogged-down car, I knew that they must think us a real pair of idiots, bogging ourselves down in the same place twice. The opinion wasn't important, however; the only thing that mattered was that they pulled us clear.

Eric was at his very best that morning. He offered a willing hand with the chains needed to tug us out and as I jumped into the driver's seat and started up the engine, I gradually felt the car move out of its trap. Something, however, did not seem to be right with the steering. I tried to tell myself that it had to do with the car being hauled across the sand. Then, when I found myself once again firmly on the road I decided to check the steering again. This time I was left in no doubt; something was definitely wrong!

I jumped out of the car and took a quick look at the front wheels. One of them was sticking out at an angle. 'Christ, Eric,' I roared at him, 'you've gone and put the chains round the track rod!'

Eric looked at the wheel which was badly askew. He didn't seem too upset, however. 'Sorry,' he apologised, 'I can repair that. All I need is a few tools. I can probably borrow some from the lads on the site.

If some of the Olympian gods were against us others, obviously, were for us because Eric returned shortly carrying the things he needed and soon got to work on the bent rods. Just looking at them, it seemed to me a hopeless job, but somehow, between us, we managed to straighten them out and Eric, his mechanical genius finally surfacing, managed to do the rest. He then returned the tools and we again thanked our helpers and we were back in business once more. All the struggles, disappointments, and despairs of the night were forgotten and I felt very confident. Our first stop, obviously was the boat dealer where we could get the engine repaired. It was now twelve noon, however, and the Saudi's workshop, we knew, would be closed until 1 p.m.

'OK, Eric,' I said. 'We'll go to the Kentucky Chicken in the meantime and have something to eat. Let's hope nobody spots the salt we picked up last night and starts to wonder.' Eric seemed a little alarmed at this thought and began a careful check of his clothing.

His appetite in no way diminished by our misfortunes, he ordered steak and chips in the restaurant. I was still not hungry. (I know now that this was because of all the tension and excitement, for I could hardly contain myself worrying about the workshop and waiting for it to open.) By the time Eric's steak and chips were on the table, it was almost one o'clock so I told him to hurry up. I don't think he got very much enjoyment out of his steak for we were out of the restaurant within the next ten minutes and on our way to the boat showroom.

The Saudi owner looked delighted to see us – not, alas, because of our pretty faces but because, or so he claimed, he had undercharged us £15. I didn't argue with him but handed over the money. I told him about the engine and he said that was no problem, his mechanic would look at it.

'Unfortunately – ' He paused and my heart sank, 'the mechanic is still at lunch and will not be back until two o'clock.'

Following on all the disasters we had experienced, an hour's wait didn't seem too bad. 'We'll wait,' I said.

The mechanic appeared on the dot and hurriedly put the engine in a test tank – which was nothing more elaborate than a 45-gallon drum. He spent some time examining it and then pronounced on his findings.

'First,' he said, 'you have used the wrong engine oil.' I glared at Eric.

'Second,' he said, 'the broken pin is not a problem. The pin is *meant* to break whenever the propeller hits anything.' He lifted the engine cover and showed us three pins and three split-pins. 'These are the spares supplied with every engine,' he explained.

I could have kicked Eric.

The man inserted a new pin in the propeller, cleaned up the spark plug and ran a further test on the engine before declaring himself satisfied. We then bought some more engine oil from him and listened carefully to his instructions.

It was three o'clock by the time we got back to Al-Khubar which gave us roughly two hours to reconnoitre the coast and find a safe place from which to shove off. I took the coast road and drove until we came to a promising bit of coastline. The beach here turned out to be very small, with hardly any sand, being mainly a dirty shingle. Nevertheless we turned into the beach road and after a short distance, I spotted a Saudi coastguard station to our right. It was a large station with an impressive cluster of radio and radar masts. I knew, of course, that the Saudi coastguards along this stretch of water had at least 50 high-speed powerboats at their disposal. The big problem, however, was their radar – would it be good enough to pick up a small object like our rubber dinghy?

I got out of the car and walked down to the beach and there I spotted a small mound about 50 yards away from the coastguard station. This, it seemed to me, was bound to interfere with their radar. I therefore decided to risk it from there. There were too many street lights and buildings along the beach anywhere else nearer the town and anyway, I had to be certain that we had a straight crossing to Bahrain. I got back into the car, turned it round towards Al-Khubar and told Eric that I intended to make the attempt from that beach that night.

He looked very uneasy and said he thought it was impossible. 'We are bound to be seen from here,' he insisted.

'That's a chance we'll have to take,' I replied curtly.

In Al-Khubar I again parked the car outside the police station. I needed a change of clothing and telling Eric to stay at least twenty yards behind me so that we would not appear to be together, I went into a shop and bought a pair of jeans, socks, a T-shirt and a pair of underpants. When I came out, I happened to pass an international bookshop so I went in and took a quick look at a road map and also at a map of the Gulf which revealed the whole geographic set up, including the position of Bahrain. You are daft, Fraser, I told myself, why didn't you think of a map before?

Eric came into the shop behind me and decided to change some pounds sterling for Bahraini dinars and then we got back into the car and drove along the coast again until we reached our chosen spot. I turned in at the beach road and parked the car as near to the edge of the beach as possible. Then we waited. By my watch, it would be dark within fifteen minutes; 30 minutes after that, unfortunately, the full moon would be out, so it was vital that we were well out to sea before that.

At 5.15 p.m. I asked Eric to mix the oil but to hunch down beside the car and to keep out of sight as far as possible. In the meantime I would inflate the dinghy. So we got out, pulled the boat down to the sea's edge, unpacked it and began pumping it up. In order not to be seen I lay on the beach while I pumped. Eric, obeying my instructions to the letter, crawled down on his belly with the petrol cans while I also crawled back to fetch the engine. It was almost dark before we had got it fixed on to the dinghy and checking the time, I saw it had taken us just fifteen minutes to unpack and assemble the craft – which had to be some sort of record. I then went back and locked the car but decided not to bog it down in the sand this time, reckoning that it would have to take its chances. A few minutes later, we pushed the boat out, then jumped in and with our compass reading due east, started to row away. This time, it seemed the gods were with us. The sea was calm and there was not even the slightest ripple of wave or anything more than a gentle wind.

EIGHTEEN

I started the engine and we moved slowly out, the bow high in the water. I didn't want to go too fast, however, as the wash might show up against the shore. I headed straight out to sea, following our compass bearing. And then I spotted some damned lights ahead.

It had to be an oil rig, I decided, and steered to the port so as to get round it. I gunned the engine so as to go faster, but to my astonishment, the boat did not respond and continued to chug along in a sluggish fashion.

'We need the bows down,' I yelled to Eric, 'Then maybe we can plane over the water.' Eric therefore got up and climbed into the bow to give the craft ballast but it proved useless and I finally decided there was no alternative but to make the best of it.

All the time the lights were getting closer and then I realised that it was not an oil rig but a damned boat! I shifted our craft to port again, wondering what on earth a boat was doing out here, and anchored firmly like that. Then I realised that we were much closer to it than I had thought and that with the full moon now lighting up the smooth sea we were bound to be seen by anybody aboard. I gave the engine all it had, and slowly we sailed under the ship's bows and I saw that the ship was a dredger. It seemed to take hours to pass the hulk and as we went by, I could see three people standing on the bridge and above them, rising from the bridge roof, a radar mast. They could scarcely have missed us and surely considered the sight of two men out in a rubber dinghy at eight o'clock at night pretty suspicious. Would they radio the coastguard?

By now the lights of Al-Khubar had almost vanished astern

and I wondered if the cruel luck that had kept us from gaining our freedom over the past two nights was now about to play another trick. I leaned forward, intending to push away the petrol tank beside my feet so that I could stretch my legs. And then suddenly I slipped. The boat had jumped up in the water and the bow had gone down and we were simply planing across the open sea at full speed. It was like being kicked in the pants and for a moment I almost lost control. But I grabbed hard for the tiller and somehow kept the craft on her course.

'I don't know what in hell I did,' I yelled at Eric, 'but it's certainly done the job all right.' We skimmed across the surface in exhilarating fashion and looking back a little later I saw that the lights of Al-Khubar had completely disappeared and even the lights of the dredger which we had passed so recently were now fading into the distance. At this speed, I reckoned, we should make landfall within the hour. But landfall where, I asked myself – Bahrain or Iran? For if we had once again got our course wrong, we could easily end up with the Ayatollah. And that could mean only one thing – death. For the Iranians, we had been led to believe were at that time shooting everybody as spies.

'I see lights,' I shouted suddenly. There ahead, only a few miles off, lay a scatter of bright pinheads which indicated land. I slowed the craft down deciding to take it easy so that we could reconnoitre the coast. As the lights rapidly grew brighter, we could make out the silhouettes of towns along the coast.

'We want Mammam, the main town,' I told Eric, 'and that ought to be to our left.'

Soon afterwards we spotted road lights and I decided to make for the dark spot between the lights of two towns. Sailing in, I saw two small lumps of land and I decided we ought to stop first and carefully study the coastline before attempting to land. We were now no more than three miles out from the coast and having found the spot I wanted, I stopped the engine and pulled in. I told Eric to throw the petrol cans over the side as we would no longer need them; indeed, the engine tank was still half-full, lack of experience having caused me to over-estimate our needs. We did this and then tried to read our map by the light of the moon. Satisfied that we knew where we were I started up the engine again and cruised gently towards the coast. I once tried to increase our speed but the boat had reverted to its old habits.

The bow had shot up and no matter what I did, the craft stubbornly refused to plane.

'Ah, well,' I said to Eric, 'with the kind of luck we've been having, it's clear we're not meant to speed here. I feel sure somebody is looking after us – we were not meant to leave Saudi on our last two attempts but to succeed this time.' Eric agreed that somebody, indeed, was looking after us, and the whole idea cheered us up immensely.

Cruising gently towards the shore, I saw us sailing over the oyster beds, the water here being so clear and sparkling that it was easy to see the bottom. There were some lights to our right with a finger of land sticking out but, so far as I could see, there were no people about. I headed straight for the beach and then the engine suddenly jumped. The propeller had once again hit rocks but as we were now less than a hundred yards from the shore it no longer mattered. I put out the oars and we started to row the rest of the way. As we came in to land, I saw a large house with lights glittering from the walls of its grounds just to our left. It was no more than five hundred yards away and I devoutly hoped that nobody had seen us. We pulled the boat up on the beach and, checking the time, I saw it was just past 9.45 p.m.

I rapidly changed out of my dirty clothes and put on the fresh things I had bought in Al-Khubar. That made me feel a lot better and we were both cheerful as we set off to look for the main road. To get to it, however, I found that we would have to walk one and a half miles through a grove of date palms. I forced the pace impatiently with Eric struggling desperately to keep up. But once more the gods appeared to be taking a hand in the game for several times we fell into holes or had our way blocked by fallen trees which we had to work our way round. Stumbling about in the dark, I feared I would break a leg, or even my neck. And then, out of the night, a dog suddenly barked fiercely.

'Christ!' I groaned loudly, 'we're in somebody's garden!'

We hastily retreated, putting as much distance between ourselves and the barking dog as rapidly as possible. Then suddenly, we were out of the palm grove and near a dirt road which I guessed must lead up to the main road. There were several houses around here but we walked boldly on until I saw four trucks parked just off the road.

'See what the index plates say,' I said to Eric. 'If there's English on them, then we're in trouble. If it's in Arabic only, then that means we're in Bahrain all right.' Eric went and looked and returned to report that the plates were Bahraini so we marched boldly ahead until we came to the main road. My idea was that we should walk along this until we could hitch a lift to Mammam or find a taxi. During the next hour or so, no fewer than nine cars approached us from the direction of Mammam but none stopped for us. The tenth car, a Mercedes, first went past us, but then stopped and turned round. I spotted two Arabs in it and when the car halted, the one sitting in the passenger seat asked me, in English, where we wanted to go.

'The airport,' I told him. 'Would you, perhaps, take us? We can pay.'

The man said something to the driver and then replied, 'Yes, certainly. That will be six dinars. Is that OK?'

I nodded and we got into the car which drove us back along the road from which it had come and towards the airport. After a while, the man in the passenger seat turned to me and said, 'You drink beer?' When I nodded he handed Eric and me a can of lager each.

'Thanks,' I said, and then feeling that I owed him an explanation, I added, 'Our problem is that our car has broken down.' He showed no interest in this, however, so I shut up and waited to hear what he had to say. He turned out to be a very talkative chap and told us that the driver was a policeman who, unfortunately, couldn't speak English. When we came to a group of houses, the driver pulled up and our talkative friend got out and went round to the back of the car and opened the boot.

I looked at Eric in alarm. What the hell was happening now? I wondered. Had we got this far only to run into trouble now?

There was no trouble, however. The chap banged down the lid and then walked round the car carrying several cans of beer cradled in his arms. When he got back in, we had another drink and then I lay back in the car and tried to relax. About fifteen minutes later we arrived at the airport and we got out. Eric immediately complained that he had only a twenty-dinar note.

'Hand it over anyway,' I told him.

'I won't,' he replied stubbornly, 'What about change?'

I was not prepared to put up with this sort of nonsense at such a moment and so I grabbed the note and gave it to the Arab who politely thanked me. Once inside the airport I walked across to a Bureau de Change where I changed £100 sterling into local dinars.

Then I led the way outside again and we jumped into a taxi.

'Holiday Inn,' I ordered the driver and sank back in the comfort of the rear seat to try to work out our next moves.

I knew that it would be possible to drink all night at the Inn so I decided that Eric and I would pretend to be on a bender although, obviously it would be sensible to make sure we did not really get drunk; there was nothing, clearly, we could do about arranging to get a ship before tomorrow. When we arrived at the hotel I paid the driver twenty dinars and said to Eric, 'Well, that clears us now. And cheap at twice the price!'

We ordered drinks in the hotel bar. I then went to the telephone booth and booked a call to my wife Anne. It took only a few minutes to connect me with Britain.

'It's me, Ian,' I announced into the receiver.

Anne took a second or so to reply. 'Where on earth are you? Are you safe?'

'I'm in Bahrain,' I told her. 'I'm all right.'

We talked at times almost incoherently in the emotion of the moment. Then she said that David wanted to speak to me.

'When are you coming home, Daddy?' asked David. It was the first time I had ever heard him speak and tears came into my eyes as I listened. I was still fighting back the tears when Anne came back on the phone. She told me I was to call my brother Bob in Singapore as he had the telephone numbers of British intelligence agents in Riyadh and Bahrain who would give me any help I needed. I told her I was too excited to telephone and asked her to make the call for me. I then promised to telephone her the next day and hung up. My eyes were still moist as I rejoined Eric in the bar.

I told him I thought I had managed to make a contact who would help us get out of Bahrain safely but it all depended on a telephone call. Then the barman called my name.

'Hello, Ian,' shouted Bob down the phone, 'good for you, you old rascal. Now, take down this number.'

'Hold on,' I said, 'I haven't got a pen.'

I left the receiver on the hook and got a pen from reception. Bob then gave me a number and told me to ask for a 'Mr Stevens'. I would be told that there was no 'Mr Stevens' but I was to insist on speaking to him and when I got my instructions, I was to do exactly what I was told and no arguments. 'Your running is over, Ian,' said Bob. 'There'll be no need for you to stow away on a ship. These people will look after you.'

After a quick drink in the bar, I went back to the booth and dialled the number I had been given.

'There is no Mr Stevens here,' said a male voice at the other end.

'I was told to ask for Mr Stevens and to insist on speaking to him,' I replied.

'Who gave you this number?' asked the voice.

'My brother, Robert Fraser in Singapore. He has just telephoned me,' I explained.

There was a pause, then the voice said, 'Please be at the embassy at seven-thirty in the morning,' and the line went dead.

I returned to Eric and explained the situation. In the meantime he also had telephoned his wife and she was absolutely delighted we had got clear.

'So what do we do now?' asked Eric.

'The bar closes at eleven-thirty,' I said, 'but the coffee shop stays open all night – and it also serves booze. All we have to do is to find some way of emptying the stuff on the floor or somewhere.'

'It'll be a hell of a waste of money,' objected Eric.

'What other way can we stay up all night drinking unless we buy drinks?' I asked him. 'Anyway, I'll pay for the drinks if you insist. Though it's a crazy way to save money.' I was so happy, indeed, that I'd have bought the whole of Bahrain drinks that night.

We slipped into the coffee shop once the bar had closed and were fortunate to get a table beside a large indoor plant. As well as drinks, we had a pot of coffee. We stayed there all night, ordering fresh drinks from time to time and then pouring them into the plant pot when the waiter wasn't looking. God knows, that poor plant must have drunk a pint of brandy that night and no doubt died from alcoholic poisoning which must have mystified the hotel staff.

At 6 a.m. I asked the reception desk if we could have a bath and they handed me the key to an empty room. I took the first bath, filling the tub almost to the brim.

The luxury of such a moment is quite beyond description. I had not bathed properly for months now and all the accretions of Al-Ould and of the grime and dirt picked up on our break-out had to be washed away. There was only one packet of shampoo, unfortunately, which I realised I ought to share with Eric. But as I wallowed in the warm luxury, I said 'To hell with Eric,' and feeling I had shared enough with him, I emptied the entire packet over my head. When I had finished, the bath was almost black and scummy with salt. But when I stepped out of the tub it was as though ten years had dropped from me.

When Eric in turn, got in, almost the first thing he did was to complain that there was no shampoo!

I lay on a vast comfortable bed and allowed the tensions to drain from me. 'God, this is the life,' I thought and promised myself a long holiday when I finally got home. I then shouted to Eric to get out of the bath as it was time for breakfast and I had decided we would leave for the embassy at 7.15.

I paid fifteen dinars (about £22) for the baths which were worth every penny and then went into the coffee shop where they were serving early breakfast. At 7.15 we jumped into a taxi and asked to be taken to the British Embassy. The driver looked a bit surprised at this and the reason became clear when he drove us about a hundred yards before dropping us at the gates of a large white, two-storeyed building surrounded by a large garden and a high wall. The embassy was guarded by half a dozen armed members of the Bahrain army who stopped us at the gate and insisted on inspecting Eric's briefcase. Eventually we were allowed through and directed to the business visa section.

Inside we found two British women sitting behind a small counter screened off by a glass grill as in a bank. I explained I had an appointment with Mr Stevens and was told sharply that there was no Mr Stevens in the embassy. I repeated that I had an appointment at 7.30 that morning and the girl said, 'Please take a seat and wait while I enquire.' Eric and I sat down and studied the layout. I saw that the door leading from the room we were in to the main part of the building was locked – and by a combination lock at that.

'They don't take many chances around here do they?' I remarked to Eric.

After a while, a chap walked in from outside the building and having briefly studied us, walked towards the door leading to the main building. As he fumbled with the lock, he turned and said, 'Who is Fraser?' Then, without waiting to find out, he added, 'They'll send you back, you know,' and opening the door, he walked through and closed it again.

While we were still wondering what all this could forebode, a second man entered the room from outside, glanced briefly at us and then he, too, disappeared through the door.

'One of these guys must be Mr Stevens – the fellow I spoke to on the phone last night,' I explained to Eric.

Some minutes later the door opened again and out walked the two men. They crossed over to us and the first one, who had said I would be sent back, said to me, 'Mr Stevens has asked us if there is any way he can help you?'

'Yes,' I said, 'I am looking for a Mr Stevens.'

'I'm sorry, but there is no one of that name here. Who gave you that name?'

'My brother Robert. Robert Fraser. In Singapore,' I explained.

'What is your problem?' he then asked.

Anyhow, I decided to play the game, whatever it was and I told him our names and how we had managed to escape from a Saudi Arabian prison.

'That is bad,' he said. 'What do you think the embassy can do?'

'Nothing,' I said, controlling my anger. 'I was simply given a name and a telephone number and it's led me here – but if you can't help me don't worry about it. Thank you for your trouble.'

'Let's be on our way,' interrupted Eric, scared about that remark about being sent back.

I got up from my chair and made to leave the building but the man I took to be Mr Stevens suddenly stopped me. 'Just one minute,' he said. 'Please come with us.' He gestured us towards the door with the combination lock and after opening it, ushered us into a large office where we were told to sit down as, 'Mr Stevens will have to take a brief statement from you.'

I told them why I had been imprisoned and how we had escaped and exactly how and when we had arrived in Bahrain. He then asked me to show him on a map where we had landed. He produced an enormous map which had every tree in Bahrain marked on it, or so it seemed. When I had been searching about on it for a moment, I stabbed my finger at the palm grove.

'You saw a big house on your left with lots of lights?' he asked.

'Yes,' I said.

'You were pretty lucky there,' he said. 'That's the Emir's

private beach house and if any of the guards had spotted you they'd have shot you, you know.'

Our statement was taken away by the other man, whom I discovered was the vice-consul, to be typed up; then, when it was ready, it would be presented to the ambassador. As we waited, Mr Stevens asked me what I would do if no one was able to help us.

'Get back in our boat and sail down the Gulf,' I told him. 'Whatever happens – I'm not going back to Saudi Arabia. Nor is Eric here.'

I did not believe for one moment that any British Embassy would hand two Britons back to the Saudis, whatever the circumstances. Soon our statement was brought back, properly typed up and we were asked to sign it and then both Stevens and the vice-consul left us alone while they went to talk to the ambassador.

'What do you think's going to happen now?' asked Eric anxiously.

'What do you think?' I almost snarled at him (I was sufficiently anxious myself by now). 'They've got to get us home. What else can they do?'

Soon afterwards, the two men returned and this time I thought I detected traces of a smile on their otherwise poker-stiff faces. The man I believed to be Mr Stevens (at no time did anyone ever admit him to being Mr Stevens) said, 'We have decided to give you new passports and put you on the first plane home.'

At that moment, I felt certain that we had done it and that this was the finish.

The embassy's Bahrain fixer was then called in and in confidence told that we were escaped prisoners from Saudi. It was agreed that he would escort us to have new passport pictures taken.

'Have you any money?' 'Stevens' asked me.

'Sure,' I said.

'Good. Then you can pay your own fares home?'

'Certainly,' I replied and we each gave the fixer £500 to arrange for passport photographs and tickets. We left the embassy and went to a nearby shop where we had our photographs taken. Then the fixer told us to take them back to the embassy while he went to fetch the airline tickets.

Back in the embassy we were given passport forms to sign and had coffee while we waited, 'Stevens' said to me, 'You know, your escape sounds a good story. Are you going to write a book?'

'I hadn't thought of that. But if I do, I'll certainly keep your name out of it.'

'Oh, that doesn't matter,' he said. 'Who would believe the Secret Service was involved? Anyway, we'd do this for any Brit in similar circumstances.'

'Thanks, anyway,' I told him.

Our plane was due to leave Bahrain at four in the morning but we were told to report to the airport around 2 a.m. When our tickets and passports had been handed to us, 'Stevens' (or whoever he really was) said, 'Now, here's a phone number. If you have any trouble at the airport, please ring this number and they'll try to help. Go to your hotel now, book a room, but don't tell anybody about your flight.'

It was almost one o'clock in the afternoon by then. So we went back to the hotel where we booked a room and handed over our new passports to reception. I then telephoned Anne to tell her when we were leaving and said I hoped to see her and the kids, Paula and David, tomorrow on Christmas Eve. She told me we were all going to spend Christmas at Blackpool.

We did our best to sleep throughout the rest of the day but found it extremely difficult, we were so wound up with excitement. By midnight we were all set to go. I paid the hotel bill and ordered a taxi.

We were much too early at the airport, of course, so we killed the time drinking cups of tea. At 1 a.m. I walked over to the check-in desk and handed over my passport and ticket to the clerk.

'Please wait while I see to the other passengers,' he said.

What the hell now, I thought, as I stepped aside for the others. When he had dealt with these, the clerk said, 'Where is your friend?'

'Having tea,' I replied, wondering how on earth he knew I had a companion.

'When you go upstairs to the emigration desk, see the sergeant,' said the clerk cheerfully and then added, 'Merry Christmas.'

'Merry Christmas to you,' I replied and turned away.

The chaps on Mount Olympus had obviously still not finished. When I got to the emigration desk, there was no sergeant, just a constable who looked at my passport and then asked, 'Where is your entry stamp?'

'It's a new passport,' I explained. 'The other one was lost.'

'You must have an entry stamp,' said the policeman. 'You must go to the ministry in the morning.'

In other circumstances I might have been tempted to argue. However, I didn't want to rock the boat at this juncture and so, collecting Eric on the way, I went to a booth and called up 'Mr Stevens'.

'Stay there,' he said crisply and hung up.

We decided to wait for him at the main door. But we were only there a short while when, suddenly, we turned round and found him walking towards us. I have no idea where he came from.

'The vice-consul is upstairs,' he said. 'Please follow me.'

When we reached the emigration desk, the vice-consul was talking to the policeman. Even as we arrived, a police sergeant materialised from nowhere and invited us to accompany him to an office in Airport Security. There, he carefully examined our passports.

'You must have entry stamps,' he said finally.

'These are new passports, just issued,' explained the vice-consul.

'You still need entry stamps,' said the sergeant. 'But I will telephone my office.'

He dialled a number and I heard him explaining that he had two British passengers with no entry stamps, but that they had new passports in the name of Fraser and Price. I couldn't hear the reply but he suddenly put down the phone and shouted to the constable and told him to photostat our passports.

'You are going home for Christmas?' he asked me affably.

'Yes,' I replied.

'Have you any children?'

'Two,' I replied, wondering why he wasn't asking me more searching questions such as how long I had been in Bahrain.

The telephone rang and he picked up the receiver. I heard the name 'Fraser' mentioned and then the sergeant looked at me. He listened for a moment, then replaced the receiver and spoke to the vice-consul.

'They can go provided you write a letter saying that Mr Fraser and Mr Price have been in Bahrain for ten days and during that time have broken none of the laws of Bahrain.'

'I'll be happy to do that,' said the vice-consul.

Following a short delay, the vice-consul produced a letter in his own handwriting and handed it to the sergeant who, when he had glanced at it, turned to us, handed us our passports, then wished us a Merry Christmas and added, 'You'd better hurry up if you want to buy any duty-free goods.'

With relief, we left the Airport Security office and went into the departure lounge where Mr Stevens was waiting for us at a table with four pints of beer. We sat down and raised our glasses to each other and said 'Merry Christmas!' Then Eric and I went off to the duty-free shop and when we had bought what we needed, we walked back to the table where the vice-consul and 'Mr Stevens' were still waiting. It was now 3.15 a.m., so I thanked them both for all the help they had given us.

'If we hadn't,' said 'Stevens' wryly, 'we'd both have been looking for new jobs.'

At that moment our plane was called and we shook hands and again wished them both a Merry Christmas before making our way to the boarding desk. Even then our troubles were not over, however. We were told to stand aside while transit passengers (Bahrain is a stop-off for the Sydney-London flight) got back on but next minute 'Mr Stevens' had come across to ask what the trouble was. 'Stevens' then spoke to the boarding clerk saying he would like us on the plane right away and pulled a card from his wallet and showed it.

'Certainly,' said the clerk briskly and halted the transit passengers so as to allow us to proceed. 'Stevens' himself came aboard the plane to make sure that we were properly installed and stayed with us until a few seconds before take-off. Before he left, I thanked him once again.

'Don't bother,' he said, smiling broadly. 'We've been instructed from the top to get Fraser out of Bahrain and home.' And with a cheery wave he left us.

Our seats were in the club class of a Jumbo jet, just opposite the take-off and landing-seats used by the stewardesses. As the plane prepared for take-off, two stewardesses sat down opposite us. They said they had just joined the flight at Bahrain and asked us where we had come from. I looked out the window, saw we had not yet left the ground and replied, 'I'll tell you when we're up there.' And I pointed to the sky.

The girls had to leave us to attend to other passengers. When they returned, they asked us again where we had come from and I told them briefly that we had escaped from a prison in Saudi Arabia. At first, they wouldn't believe us but when we assured them that it was true, they got up and left us only to return soon afterwards with two glasses of champagne – 'compliments of the air crew.'

While we sipped our champagne, I heard the captain announce over the address system that our flight path would take us over part of Saudi Arabia.

'That's bad news for us,' I remarked to the stewardess. 'If we came down here, Eric and I would find ourselves in a right pickle.'

A few minutes later, the captain approached us and said, 'Good morning, gentlemen. Under no circumstances, I can assure you, will we land in Saudi Arabia. Well done.' And he then turned and walked away again.

Soon afterwards, I rose from my seat and moved up the plane. A movie was just starting and I sat down next to one of the other passengers whom I discovered was a Scot returning to Glasgow after eleven years in Australia. I wanted to be away from Eric for a spell. Our escape was over now and he was on his own again and we would each be going our separate ways.

I remained beside my fellow Scot for the rest of the journey but before we landed at Heathrow, I returned to my own seat and sat down beside Eric again. Just before touchdown, a stewardess approached and handed us each a bottle of champagne 'with the best wishes of the crew'.

I looked out of the window, saw we were about to land at Heathrow and realised that that night, Christmas Eve, I would be able, incredible as it had seemed only a week ago, actually to play Santa Claus.